The Geographies of Digital Sexuality

Catherine J. Nash
Andrew Gorman-Murray
Editors

The Geographies of Digital Sexuality

palgrave
macmillan

Editors
Catherine J. Nash
Brock University
St. Catharines, ON, Canada

Andrew Gorman-Murray
Western Sydney University
Penrith, NSW, Australia

ISBN 978-981-13-6875-2 ISBN 978-981-13-6876-9 (eBook)
https://doi.org/10.1007/978-981-13-6876-9

Cover illustration: Andrew Gorman-Murray, 2015, Connections, Inkjet print on Galerie Pearl

This Palgrave Macmillan imprint is published by the registered company Springer Nature Singapore Pte Ltd.
The registered company address is: 152 Beach Road, #21-01/04 Gateway East, Singapore 189721, Singapore

Acknowledgements

An edited volume is always a joint effort between so many players. A heartfelt 'thank you' to the authors who wrote such wonderful chapters, who took our suggestions seriously and did so 'on deadline.' Palgrave Macmillan has been wonderful to work with from inception to final text. I (Catherine) am deeply indebted to Andrew Gorman-Murray who initiated our working together and is such a stalwart colleague and friend. Heather Maguire, as always, made sure we stayed on track and provided such brilliant support. And finally, to Cindy who puts up with all that comes with being married to an academic.

I (Andrew) would like to acknowledge the productive environment created by colleagues at Western Sydney University. I am grateful for long-standing personal support from Rohan Tate and Barbara Murray. Thanks also to the staff at Palgrave Macmillan who saw potential in our proposal and marshalled it into production. Many thanks to Heather Maguire for unfailing editorial support. And most of all, I am both grateful and honoured to work with friend and colleague Catherine J. Nash. Your sharp intellect and intrepid curiosity push me to think more carefully about contemporary geographical change.

Contents

Notes on Contributors

Carl Bonner-Thompson is a postdoctoral researcher at the University of Oxford. He completed his PhD at Newcastle University in 2018. He has previously served as editorial assistant for *Gender, Place and Culture.*

Daniel Cockayne is Assistant Professor of Economic Geography at the University of Waterloo. His empirical research focuses on the reproduction of working norms and practices amongst entrepreneurs and others working for early-stage start-up firms. Theoretically, he is interested in the relationship between digital spaces and sexuality, as well as in the philosopher Gilles Deleuze and his influence on geographic thought. His work (with Lizzie Richardson) on the topic "Queering Code/Space" has been published in a themed section of *Gender, Place and Culture.*

Jenna Condie is Lecturer in Digital Research and Online Social Analysis at Western Sydney University. With psychology as a base, she researches cyber-urban living and what people and places are becoming with new technologies. At Western, Condie co-leads Travel in the Digital Age (TinDA), an interdisciplinary group of researchers working on the impacts of travel, transport, technology, and mobile lives for equitable mobilities and accessible cities. In 2018, Condie co-edited *Doing Research* *in and on the Digital: Research Methods Across Fields of Inquiry*. Her work on new materialist and scholar-activist approaches to researching with responsibility has been published.

Stefanie Duguay is an assistant professor in the Department of Communication Studies at Concordia University in Montreal, Canada. Her research focuses on the influence of digital media technologies in everyday life, with particular attention to sexual identity, gender, and social media. This has included studies of lesbian, gay, bisexual, trans, and queer (LGBTQ) people's use of social media, dating apps, and platforms for everyday activism. Duguay's research has been published in *New Media & Society*, *Information, Communication & Society*, and other international, peer-reviewed journals.

Andrew Gorman-Murray is Professor of Geography at Western Sydney University. His research encompasses urban and regional transformations, household dynamics and work/home interchange, and inclusive disaster planning. Across these areas, his research has attended to gender, sexuality, and space. Four of his edited collections have been published: *Material Geographies of Household Sustainability* (2011, with Ruth Lane), *Sexuality, Rurality and Geography* (2013, with Barbara Pini and Lia Bryant), *Masculinities and Place* (2014, with Peter Hopkins), and *Queering the Interior* (2018, with Matt Cook). He is co-editor of *Emotion, Space and Society*.

Benjamin Hanckel is a research fellow at King's College London. He is also a university associate at the University of Tasmania where he researches youth health and well-being, with a particular focus on the experiences of gender- and sexuality-diverse youth.

Donna James is a master of research candidate and research assistant with the School of Social Sciences and Psychology at Western Sydney University. In 2016, James completed her bachelor of arts, majoring in English and sub-majoring in social and cultural analysis, and education studies. Her research interests centre on the technological reproduction of social inequalities, particularly in tourism arenas where social relations are uneven in terms of gendered and racialised power. Her work looks at women's experiences with navigating safety while using location-aware social apps during travel and with using location-aware social apps to meet tourists who are passing through their places of residence.

Garth Lean is Senior Lecturer in Tourism and Heritage Studies in the School of Social Sciences and Psychology at Western Sydney University. He researches travel, tourism, and new technologies. He is the lead researcher of the Transformative Travel Research Project (www.transformativetravel.com), and co-lead of Travel in the Digital Age (TinDA—www.tindaproject.com), an interdisciplinary group of researchers working at the intersections of mobile lives and technology. A variety of papers by Lean on travel, tourism, and mobilities have been published, along with the monograph *Transformative Travel in a Mobile World* (2016), and the edited volumes *Travel and Imagination* (2014), *Travel and Transformation* (2014), and *Travel and Representation* (2017). He is a vice president of the Geographical Society of New South Wales.

Jason Luger is a human geographer with research interests focusing on the production and practice of urban space, urban social movements, and digital urban politics. He is currently lecturing in City Planning and the Global Urban Humanities at the University of California, Berkeley.

Sophia Maalsen is Lecturer in Urbanism at the School of Architecture, Design and Planning, University of Sydney. Prior to this post, Maalsen was a postdoctoral researcher on the EU-funded Programmable City Project where she investigated the digital transformation of cities and urban governance. Her expertise is in understanding the intersection of gender, the material, digital, and the human, and how this affects lived experience.

Emiel Maliepaard holds a PhD in Human Geography from Radboud University, the Netherlands, and works as a researcher at Atria. His doctoral study focused on the sexual identity negotiations and expressions of bisexual people in everyday spaces and practices. His work on bisexuality and space has been published in several peer-reviewed journals including *Social & Cultural Geography*, *Sexualities*, and *Journal of Bisexuality*.

Jessica McLean is a geographer in the Department of Geography and Planning at Macquarie University. Her research focuses on two areas: digital geographies and water cultures. Both research areas call for critical, engaged, and situated research praxis, building on partnership approaches with community groups and individuals who are working in Indigenous, feminist, and digital rights contexts.

Sam Miles is a postdoctoral research fellow in social science at the London School of Hygiene and Tropical Medicine (LSHTM). His work focuses on adolescent sexual health and behaviour. His PhD in human geography at Queen Mary University of London explored the impact of location-based dating apps including Grindr and Tinder on men seeking other men in London, UK, for intimate social and sexual encounters. You can read Miles' work on queer lives, technology, and digital-physical hybridisation in *AREA*, *Geography Compass*, and *Gender, Place and Culture*.

Catherine J. Nash is a professor in the Department of Geography and Tourism Studies at Brock University, Canada. Her research focus is on sexuality, gender, and urban places. Her current research interests include changing urban sexual and gendered landscapes in Toronto; international resistances to LGBT equalities in Canada, UK, and Australia; digital technologies and sexuality in everyday life; and new LGBT mobilities. Her books include *Queer Methods and Methodologies* (2010, with K. Browne) and *Human Geography: People, Place and Culture* (Canadian edition) (2015, with E. Fouberg, A. Murphy, and H. de Blij).

Lizzie Richardson is a research fellow in the Department of Geography at Durham University. Her research focuses on geographies of urban life and liveliness, specifically on work and representation, shared spaces, and embodiment and urban technologies. Her work (with Daniel Cockayne) on the topic "Queering Code/Space" has been published in a themed section of *Gender, Place and Culture*.

Beverly Yuen Thompson is Associate Professor and Chair of Sociology at Siena College, in Albany, New York, USA. She is the author of *Covered in Ink: Tattoos, Women and the Politics of the Body*. Her research focuses on subcultures, gender, and deviant behaviour.

Jantine van Lisdonk is a researcher at Rutgers, Centre of Expertise on Sexual and Reproductive Health and Rights, based in the Netherlands. Her expertise is in sexual and gender diversity with special interest in inclusivity and normativities. She has conducted studies on same-sex-oriented youth and elder people, marriage migrants, teenage pregnancies, intersex, and bisexuality. She is the Dutch coordinator of the Flemish-Dutch Network for LGBTI research.

Martin Zebracki is Associate Professor of Critical Human Geography at the University of Leeds, UK. His work about the intersecting geographies of public-art practice, sexuality, citizenship, digital culture, and social inclusivity has been published in journals such as *Progress in Human Geography*, *Urban Studies*, and *Social & Cultural Geography*. He is the editor of *Public Art Encounters* (2017, with Joni M. Palmer) and *The Everyday Practice of Public Art* (2016, with Cameron Cartiere). Zebracki is a member of the Editorial Board of *Public Art Dialogue* and the Chair of the Royal Geographical Society-Institute of British Geographers' (RGS-IBG) Space, Sexualities and Queer Research Group.

List of Figures

1

Introduction

Catherine J. Nash and Andrew Gorman-Murray

Contemporary life is increasingly experienced through the 'screen'—a life lived within a complex agglomeration of digital and material worlds. Our engagements online can no longer be understood as discrete from 'real life' and our real life is increasingly ordered through online behaviours, habits and practices. This digital/material intertwining reflects "both [the] expression and emergence of new spatial practices" marking how we are increasingly experiencing a "complex interplay between real and digital geographies" (Cohen, 2007, pp. 212–213). Geography has arguably taken a 'digital turn' as geographers pursue the "digital as both object and subject of geographical enquiry" (Ash, Kitchin, & Leszczynski, 2018, p. 25).

C. J. Nash (✉)
Brock University, St. Catharines, ON, Canada
e-mail: cnash@brocku.ca

A. Gorman-Murray
Western Sydney University, Penrith, NSW, Australia
e-mail: A.Gorman-Murray@westernsydney.edu.au

C. Nash, A. Gorman-Murray (eds.), *The Geographies of Digital Sexuality*,
https://doi.org/10.1007/978-981-13-6876-9_1

In this book, we use the term 'new technologies' to encompass a vast array of hardware and software assembled into the artefacts and practices now shaping our lives. These technologies include information and communication technologies (ICTs) such as the internet, Web 2.0, digital media, location-based services (LBS), social networking applications and locative and mobile social networks (LMSN) (Nash & Gorman-Murray, 2016a). And while these new technologies are increasingly ubiquitous in everyday life, our central focus here is the transformations we are experiencing in the realm of intimacy, romance and sexual and gendered life. Engagements with the digital are reshaping bodies and embodied practices, domestic intimacies, our habits and routines, what we consider erotic and who we understand can be the object of our desire and perhaps even the meaning of 'desire' itself. As we have argued elsewhere, new technologies are shaping "a new 'sexual revolution', one that is rewriting how we understand what our bodies can 'do' and how we comprehend ourselves as sexual beings" (Nash & Gorman-Murray, 2016a). Garlick (2011, p. 223) goes so far as to argue that we are experiencing "a technologically-mediated reorganization of the social relations of sexuality" and as geographers, we would assert the reorganization of the geographies of sexualities and queer geographies.

These new geospatial relations of sexuality are not universally welcomed or revered. While some scholars celebrate life online as a place of liberation and celebration, others worry about the seemingly unconstrained access to all things sexual including the dangerous, the perverse and the pornographic (e.g. Cooper, McLoughlin, & Campbell, 2000; Griffiths, 2001). And yet, life online is spawning new communities of interest around sexual/social relations and supporting intimate relationships over great distances (e.g. Sandow, 2014; Whalen & Schmidt, 2016). Intimacy, largely understood as including a physical closeness, is being reshaped as people develop genuine connections with others who they may never meet in real life. The rapid development of mobile technologies and locative media has strengthened the merging of digital and material spaces, helping to forge new sociabilities, mobilities and environments—enveloping social worlds where body, screen and space are continuously being transformed.

Geographers of sexuality and queer geographers argue that these developments have profound implications for how we understand both material and 'cyber' spaces. Online life is increasingly portable, mobile and connected and we need to understand how such engagements rework material, social relations and places with as of yet less well-understood dimensions of how we experience our everyday lives. And despite initial claims that virtual spaces offer a degree of liberating anonymity, it cannot be denied that "articulations of gender, sexuality and embodiment are intricately interwoven with people's physical embedding in everyday life as well as the new technologies they employ to extend daily experiences into digital locales" (van Doorn, 2011, p. 532). Further, our absorption into layered digital and material worlds is palpably evident in the social practices relating to sexualities, such as online spaces (both websites and mobile applications) for a variety of sexual practices (e.g. long-term dating and casual sex) and for constituting specific sexuality-based (and gendered) communities (e.g. LGBTI and queer networks; heterosexual Bondage/Discipline, Dominance/Submission, and Sadism/Masochism (BDSM) communities and crossdressers).

The aim of this collection is to explore the complexities of these newly constituted, technically mediated and interwoven sexual and gender landscapes through empirical, theoretical and conceptual engagements. The geographies of everyday life are where embodied sexual identities, communities and practices unfold at the interface of digital lives and material encounters and are profoundly transforming spatial experiences and knowledges (Nash & Gorman-Murray, 2016b). As Wilken (2009) argues, conventional sense of place is now inadequate for understanding digitally mediated mobile life.

We have organized the chapters into three parts reflecting three overall themes. In Part I, entitled 'Making Worlds: Conceptualizing the Digital/Material Divide', the chapters provide a broad range of theoretical and conceptual frameworks for thinking about how new technologies are implicated in the making of new digital worlds and how emergent online communities are intertwined within and implicated in the (re)constitution of material places. Part II is concerned with 'Dating and Intimacy at the Interface' and the four chapters explore how dating life and the practices, protocols and experiences of intimacy and community are being reshaped through various digital engagements. Finally, Part III examines the connections between 'Activism, Politics and Communities' as these are experienced through sexual and gendered individuals and groups across diverse landscapes.

In Part I, 'Making Worlds: Conceptualizing the Digital/Material Divide', Daniel Cockayne and Lizzie Richardson's chapter takes a theoretical or conceptual approach to consider the queer temporalities of the internet. They assert that geographers need to come to grips with the temporal as well as the spatial structure of internet systems. They draw on queer theoretical musings to counter the heteronormative understandings of temporality that underpin understandings of the nuclear family and the life course. Temporal internet systems, they argue, are very much embedded within concrete histories that are linked to the "heteronormative-reproductive times of state-capitalism" which also characterizes "imaginaries of the digital".

Catherine J. Nash and Andrew Gorman-Murray explore three distinctive and not necessarily commensurate approaches to conceptualizing the intersections between queer place-making and technology. First, they draw on scholarship in feminist digital geographies to sketch out the starting points for understanding the nature and constitution of subjectivities and identities developing through and within the use of new technologies. Second, they draw on Elwood and Leszczynski's (2018) research on new spatial media to consider how user-generated geographical information can have the effect of constituting new geovisualizations that raise the possibilities of seeing material spaces queerly. Finally, they consider Kitchin and Dodge's (2011) notion of code/space to think about the disciplining and normalizing processes always-already in play in code/spaces which continue to constitute places as heteronormative. Taken together, Cockayne and Richardson and Nash and Gorman-Murray suggest cogent theoretical interventions into how we might conceptualize queer digital and material experiences that include the constitution of sexual and gendered subjects through new technologies that incorporate both temporal and material factors.

Donna James, Jenna Condie and Garth Lean's chapter theorizes world-building and community-making at the level of the individual and the intimate through an empirical study of how heterosexual tourists, through the use of apps, facilitate sexual encounters while travelling 'abroad'. In particular, they consider the so-called *Tinder* tourist and how *Tinder*, as a 'hook-up' app, facilitates sexual experiences that intersect with travel and colonial encounters. These digitally mediated experiences underpin or contribute to some tourists' perceptions about the 'authenticity' of their geographically bounded local experiences.

Beverly Yuen Thompson's chapter on digital nomads (Makimoto & Manners, 2008) also examines a form of world-building grounded in the use of technology to facilitate intimacy and romantic connections for lives lived on the move. Increasingly, technologies are facilitating the formation of so-called mobile workers who can create location-independent careers while building romantic and intimate lives linked to and constituting specific geographies. Through a series of in-depth interviews, Yuen Thompson examines how technologies orient romance, geographic travel and location.

Part II, 'Dating and Intimacy at the Interface', begins with the work of Stefanie Duguay on queer women's use of the dating app *Tinder* and how their everyday practices shape their sense of proximity to other queer women and a queer women's community. Her research draws on interviews with participants located in Australia, Canada and other "passport strong" countries, living in relatively large urban centres. In using the app, her respondents reported a sense that queer women were 'scarce', a feeling often exacerbated by constraints on search criteria, the need for anonymity and the need to evade the advances of men, heterosexual women and couples. Her research demonstrates how claims that dating apps unproblematically link people and places are called into question and undermine the sense that technologies have somehow overcome geographical constraints.

In his chapter, Sam Miles proposes we consider how apps such as *Grindr* and *Tinder* are reshaping the geographies of sexualities conceptualized as a form of "digital-physical hybridisation". His work on the experiences of non-heterosexual men in London, UK, highlights how users are negotiating a hybridized set of experiences that reflect reconfigurations of notions of community, technology and public and private spaces. This is brought into sharp relief through a consideration of how common and established codes of conduct continue to mediate digital encounters, although not seamlessly and often in ways that require reworkings of established practices and habits.

Emiel Maliepaard and Jantine van Lisdonk's chapter continues this exploration of the concept of hybridization in their consideration of the use of online dating apps by Dutch men who have sex with men (MSM). The authors are interested in users' shared interpretations of various scripts that are facilitated through both social learning and intimate interaction. Their research demonstrates that despite contestations (and potential misunderstandings), scripts (and their interpretations) are grounded in both online and offline social worlds although attention needs to be paid to both embodied experiences and communications that may differ in various contexts.

Finally, Carl Bonner-Thompson's chapter refocuses our attention on the visceral geographies of sense and sound for men who meet in public spaces after connecting through online apps such as *Grindr*. Drawing on interviews with men in Newcastle-upon-Tyne, UK, he explores how various identities emerge as users shift between digital and material spaces. In using *Grindr*, with its multiple visualizations and communications, expectations about users develop that may not be realized in a 'real life' encounter, thereby highlighting how digital encounters do not necessarily materialize in public spaces as well as reflecting how "bodies, gender and sexuality" are constantly being made meaningful in unexpected ways.

We conclude in Part III with scholarship on 'Activism, Politics and Communities'. These chapters focus on sexuality, online activism and their related material geographies. Activists have found new technologies exceedingly useful for pursuing any number of political and social causes, and issues related to sexualities and gender are no exception.

Jessica McLean and Sophia Maalsen's chapter begins with a focus on how digital spaces are being used to support social movements dedicated to anti-sexism and pro-diversity goals. Drawing on the Australian Marriage Law Postal Survey as a case study, the authors examine how the online feminist group *Destroy the Joint* targeted sexism and misogyny, and they trace how emotions and affect are reflected in the geographies of disruption and digital feminism.

In his chapter on queer youth in East and South East Asia, Benjamin Hanckel considers how, given the daily marginalization experienced by queer people in heteronormative spaces, digital media spaces and practices allow youth to engage in forms of identity formation and queer world-making. Hanckel draws on in-depth interviews to understand how digital media spaces are incorporated into their digital practices. These online practices reflect how queer youth engage with multiple international, regional and local web spaces where they are able to explore various aspects of sexuality, sex and gender identity. Their online/offline work is symbiotic, providing the tools to both respond to and shape their intimate lives.

Jason Luger, in his chapter on queer encounter in Singapore, considers how legal, political and social restrictions on LGBTQ urban spaces affect the formation of both digital and material places. He notes that the relationship between digital and material urban spaces is both complicated and relational. Using interviews, site observations and digital ethnography, Luger explores how, in illiberal contexts such as Singapore, LGBTQ identities, networks and spaces of sociality operate in the liminal places available at the digital/material interface. Such activities reflect an activism that constitutes a tactical performance of identity and reappropriation of space for survival and community formation.

Martin Zebracki's chapter examines how public artwork can constitute forms of social engagement in digitally networked places. Zebracki uses Paul McCarthy's *Tree*, a temporary installation in Paris, to examine how digital technologies provide new tools for engaging with public art as well as reconfigured spaces for such engagement in ways that highlight how public art can increasingly be understood through the "dialectic between the physical and the virtual" (p. 247).

In this edited collection, using a diverse range of methodologies, the authors explore digital/material sexualities through the lens of spatiality—of space, place, location, scale and geography. The scholarship included here is innovative, wide-ranging and original research in a new but rapidly expanding field of study. As a collection, the chapters here reflect a diverse set of geographies including France, Australia, the UK, Canada, Singapore, Netherlands (Holland) and South Asia more broadly and engage two broad communities of scholars: geographers working on online/offline sexualities and scholars drawn from across the social sciences and humanities who are also bringing spatial theory to bear on intersections between technology and sexuality. In bringing forward new forms of theorizing and conceptualizations of sexualities, technologies and the spatial with empirical research, we trust this scholarship fills an important gap around technology, place, sexuality, intimacy and social relations.

References

Ash, J., Kitchin, R., & Leszczynski, A. (2018). Digital turn, digital geographies? *Progress in Human Geography, 42*(1), 25–43.

Cohen, J. E. (2007). Cyberspace as/and space. *Columbia Law Review, 107*, 210–256.

Cooper, A., McLoughlin, I. P., & Campbell, K. M. (2000). Sexuality in cyberspace: Update for the 21st century. *CyberPsychology and Behavior, 3*(4), 521–536.

Elwood, S., & Leszczynski, A. (2018). Feminist digital geographies. *Gender, Place and Culture, 25*(5), 629–644.

Garlick, S. (2011). A new sexual revolution? Critical theory, pornography, and the Internet. *Canadian Review of Sociology/Revue canadienne de sociologie, 48*(3), 221–239.

Griffiths, M. (2001). Sex on the Internet: Observations and implications for internet sex addiction. *Journal of Sex Research, 38*(4), 333–342.

Kitchin, R., & Dodge, M. (2011). *Code/space*. Cambridge: MIT Press.

Makimoto, T., & Manners, D. (2008). *Digital nomad* (Kindle ed.). New York, NY: Wiley.

Nash, C. J., & Gorman-Murray, A. (2016a). Digital sexualities: Section introduction. In K. Browne & G. Brown (Eds.), *Routledge research companion to geographies of sex and sexualities* (pp. 353–358). London: Routledge.

Nash, C. J., & Gorman-Murray, A. (2016b). Digital technologies and sexualities in urban space. In K. Browne & G. Brown (Eds.), *Routledge research companion to geographies of sex and sexualities* (pp. 399–405). London: Routledge.

Sandow, E. (2014). Til work do us part: The social fallacy of long-distance commuting. *Urban Studies, 51*(3), 526–543.

van Doorn, N. (2011). Digital spaces, material traces: How matter comes to matter in online performances of gender, sexuality and embodiment. *Media, Culture and Society, 33*(4), 531–547.

Whalen, H., & Schmidt, G. (2016). The women who remain behind: Challenges in the LDC lifestyle. *Rural Society, 25*(1), 1–14.

Wilken, R. (2009). Mobilizing place: Mobile media, peripatetics and the renegotiation of urban places. *Journal of Urban Technology, 15*(3), 39–55.

Part I

Making Worlds: Conceptualizing the Digital/Material Divide

2

The Queer Times of Internet Infrastructure and Digital Systems

Daniel Cockayne and Lizzie Richardson

Introduction

This chapter challenges some of the dominant ways of thinking about the temporal structure of the internet. Geographers and other scholars have been quick to redress the dominant spatial imaginaries associated with internet infrastructures (Dodge & Kitchin, 2005; Graham, 1998, 2011, 2013; Kirsch, 1995, 1998; Zook, 2000), though fewer scholars have examined the temporal imaginaries that underwrite internet systems and the effects of these imaginaries. As Doreen Massey (2005, p. 47) has influentially argued, there is an "interconnectedness of conceptualisations of space and conceptualisations of time," which merits thinking through space and time together, moving from a separation of these concepts to "space-time" as one simultaneous idea. Our attempt to think through the

D. Cockayne (✉)
University of Waterloo, Waterloo, ON, Canada
e-mail: daniel.cockayne@uwaterloo.ca

L. Richardson
Durham University, Durham, UK
e-mail: elizabeth.c.richardson@durham.ac.uk

C. Nash, A. Gorman-Murray (eds.), *The Geographies of Digital Sexuality*,
https://doi.org/10.1007/978-981-13-6876-9_2

temporality of internet infrastructures follows too from interventions in queer theory that have sought to counter heteronormative understandings of temporality. Queer critics have challenged the temporal logics that underpin the reproduction of the nuclear family (Edelman, 2004), and understandings of queer pasts as abject and queer presents or futures as necessarily progressive (Love, 2007).

Queer theory may be particularly suitable to the task of thinking through the temporal imaginaries of digital infrastructures because of the relative contemporaneity of queer theory and the birth of the commercial web browser—both often narrated as phenomena of the early 1990s. Writings on queer futurity emphasise asynchronous temporalities, time out of joint, non-linear time, and time out of sync with the reproduction of capital or of the nation state (Freeman, 2010; Muñoz, 2009). These perspectives allow space and time for feeling backwards, disoriented, and out of alignment with the normative organisation of society. However, these possibilities for temporal disjuncture and malfunction are contrary to dominant imaginaries of the internet that tend to narrate it as a system of instantaneous presence in a 'network of networks' in which space and time collapse to render distance meaningless so that time becomes perfectly coordinated. Geographers have done much to counter these assumptions (see Cockayne & Richardson, 2017; Gieseking, 2017) by illustrating the continuing unevenness of access to the web and the differential geography of internet infrastructure. The internet in critical geographers' framing is a system that has a distinct and material, though often hidden, geography that reproduces the unevenness and inequality of state and capitalist violence.

This geographical perspective provides a starting point for our queer temporality by connecting modern digital systems with an imperialist past in ways that challenge the idea of the internet as having a time without history. Nicole Starosielski (2015) details these themes, examining the historical development of contemporary internet infrastructures through undersea cables that have been laid along trenches dug out for nineteenth-century systems of telegraphy. The modern internet is a system built upon legacies of British colonialism, implicating its contemporary material geography in today's prevailing patterns of global inequality. In emphasising the history of the internet, Starosielski and others like Janet Abbate (1999) demonstrate the militaristic and academic beginnings of early internet technologies and defy common imaginaries of the internet as essentially of the present or the future—and by implication, lacking some of its fundamental spatial and temporal dimensions.

The spaces most essential to the continued working of the internet are those least-often associated with its functioning in the popular imaginary—undersea networks, beaches, islands and rural spaces for infrastructure like data centres that function as key nodes and connections. These kinds of spaces are berthing points without which the essential function of maintaining key internet infrastructures would be far more difficult or fundamentally different. So connecting the modern internet with its imperialist past, as well as rendering it in its 'proper' place of islands, rural areas, and the deep ocean, is a necessary first step in queering our attitude towards the internet as a system commonly thought of as without time and place. Attention to this material geography enables the appearance of an internet that is strangely outmoded by a past of which it attempts to divest itself. Far from the zenith of modernity to which its popular imaginaries attempt to lay claim, the internet becomes anachronistic, anchored on past and continuing inequalities that heteronormative futurity would prefer to forget.

From this beginning, our aim in this chapter is to draw on different ideas of temporality from contemporary queer theory, and to think through alternative ways of conceptualising the internet and its infrastructures, outside of the dominant tempo of biopolitical state-capitalism (Zalnieriute, 2018). Our intention is not to frame the internet as less pernicious and dangerous for queer lives than it indeed is but to seek value in multiple conceptualisations that can be held together ambivalently. This is based on the conviction that "everyday theory qualitatively affects everyday knowledge and experience" (Sedgwick, 2003, pp. 144–145). In order not to reproduce the internet with a capital 'I' as a totalising force in alignment with the state-capitalist agenda, it is necessary to find ways to conceptualise it differently, as a complex and ambivalent multiplicity (see also Gibson-Graham, 2014). While recognising the threat of highly discretionary and only-sometimes-convivial state-capitalism associated with internet systems, for many LGBTQ people digital systems are also necessary for everyday survival (Jenzen, 2017).

The queer theorisation of the internet we present here attempts to hold these two asymmetrical realities together—the threats and the opportunities—without attempting to resolve them, so as to conceptualise the internet queerly as a problematic object out of sync with its own representations of itself. In this sense, we attempt a "suturing of two times but leaving both times visible as such" (Freeman, 2010, p. 69). In the next section, we draw on Elizabeth Freeman's (2010) concept of temporal drag to outline the beginnings of this suturing. We then develop these points by building upon Lauren Berlant's (2016) framings of glitches in infrastructures of presence. We conclude with the merits of conceptualising a complex object like the internet through multiple spatio-temporalities that allow for the flourishing of a perspective that privileges difference and ambivalence.

Internet Infrastructure as Temporal Drag

Freeman (2010, p. 93) develops the concept of temporal drag to describe how identity is "constituted and haunted by the failed love-projects that precedes it" in which, as a critique of temporalities, one aim is "to feel the tug backward as a potentially transformative part of movement itself." Freeman persistently links temporal drag to her concept of time binds, which describes both a problem and an attachment—for example, to identity categories—that has a temporal structure that often remains hidden. Through these ideas, she examines the supposedly foreclosed promises of past liberation movements to see what gets stuck; becomes anachronistic; *does not* progress but instead moves sideways, or not at all; and how the demands of the past may seem incongruous to the demands of the present. Temporal drag is deployed as a temporal reappraisal of Judith Butler's (1990) notion of performativity. Freeman's (2010, p. 62) critique of performativity is that the concept unfolds an understanding of temporality in which "time is basically progressive, insofar as repetitions with differences hold the most promises." She explains further:

> Repetitions with any backward-looking force are "citational," but Butler tends to read these as consolidating the authority of a fantasised original,

> even if citationality itself unsettles the idea of an original: in *Gender Trouble*'s "repetition with a difference," the crucial difference seems to be novelty, not anachronism. Ordinary masculine and feminine performativity are retroactive, of course, but not in a way that intersects with any actual past, for the "original" sexed body that seems to guarantee the gendered subject's authenticity is in fact a back-formation, a kind of hologram projected onto earlier moments. (Freeman, 2010, p. 63)

Freeman's critique is that Butler ignores the lived reality of the past, substituting for actually experienced-temporalities a citational simulacrum against which the representational fiction of gendered performances reproduces itself. Butler therefore ends up, perhaps inadvertently, privileging the novel queer futures of non-normative performances in ways that Freeman (2010, p. 63) argues "are symptomatic of late-finance capitalism before the crashes of the early twenty-first century." In doing so, performativity dismisses earlier feminist and lesbian models of thought such as the supposed anachronisms of, for example, femininity and butch/femme as available models for change, rallying points, or opportunities for solidarity.

Similarly, Freeman claims that in Butler's model of normative masculinity and femininity—heterosexual melancholia—the lost but unknowledgeable object of homosexual desire that forms the condition for heterosexuality is evacuated of its historical specificity. This is because for Freeman (2010, p. 70) identification is not an Oedipal repudiation but instead a more complex "story of disjunctive, sticky entanglements, and associations." For Freeman then, these figures of, first, the radical feminist for the queer subject, and second, the same-sex parent for the normative straight subject, are superseded by the reality of the repeated simulacrum in a way that problematically disavows the past and places the potential for radical change in an only future-oriented performativity. The actual past cannot *really* be felt since it becomes only a symbolic backdrop to be repeated or transgressed in the present. The figure of the drag queen thus becomes the privileged subject of a progressive gender politics and transformative difference. In this light, Freeman asks what looking back to radical feminism might afford to contemporary queer theory.

How might we fold these notions of temporal drag and time binds that are based on questions of subjectivity into a temporal re-theorisation of internet infrastructures and digital systems? These systems appear to always and only point towards "new" technologies, developmental frontiers and narratives of liberal progress and progressive change. Technologies, and specifically internet-driven technologies, are so often communicated in terms of the supposed 'transformative difference' of libertarian-liberal digital utopianism (i.e., innovation, iteration, pivoting and disruption; see Turner, 2006) that forms the key to Freeman's critique of the temporal structure of performativity. What now-seeming-anachronous histories and aphorisms of the past might trouble the contemporary temporal imaginary of digital technology? Emphasising the histories of the internet and digital technologies, and how their present function is dependent on and constituted by these oft-forgotten pasts, may be one way to do this. Freeman (2010, p. 64, original emphasis) describes temporal drag as "a *productive* obstacle to progress, a usefully distorting pull backward and a necessary pressure on the present tense." In giving the internet a history, its temporal imaginary may be one that is no longer oriented only towards the future. To theorise internet infrastructures and digital systems as a form of temporal drag in the manner that Freeman intends, it is important to examine how forgotten, repressed, and lost pasts *come back*, are folded into the present and persist, in spite of attempts to defend against them. In casting the internet through histories of empire—most obviously in the context of nineteenth-century British colonialism and the cold-war politics of the mid-twentieth century United States—we can connect past moments of constitutive minority politics to see how they continue to structure the contemporary.

Situating a critical history of internet infrastructures as destabilising their future-oriented temporalities is a much longer task than we have space for here. However, it is worth highlighting some key historical moments in order to complicate the synonymy that 'modernity' and 'internet' seem to easily achieve. Freeman suggests that a queer historiography should be conceptualised in terms of *feeling*, rather than being conceptualised in terms of *understanding*, in which the historian situates herself in a position of relative mastery over her object—history—that is then organised as a more or less continuous and linear narrative. In this vein then, we might feel our way into histories of the internet through the laying of undersea cables, mentioned above, that open up a host of events illustrating the incoherent development of digital systems.

Early- to mid-twentieth century developments in mathematics that implicate both the modern personal computer and the atomic bomb were deeply embedded in militaristic and public spending (Dyson, 2012). Other key events include Grace Hopper's 1952 invention of the compiler and the parallel development in the United States and United Kingdom of packet-switching technologies in the 1960s (Abbate, 1999). The first ARPANET (Advanced Research Projects Agency Network—the first network that utilised modern internet protocols) connection was made in 1969 between the University of California at Los Angeles and Stanford University. Concern with these developments, with an archetypically post-Second World War Cold-War inflection, was for systems of security and redundancy with a military focus that are features of paramount importance in both the network and packet-switching. As many scholars and writers argue, the internet is central in a logistics network that facilitates the organisation of a highly financialised global capitalism (Cowen, 2014), as well as a dense system of predominantly US-governed state surveillance (Paglen, 2010). Despite these complex and overlapping histories, the first web browsers—made available during the 1990—characterise most popular modern internet narratives and imaginaries, and temporally sediments dial-up internet and web usage as an archetype of 1990s popular culture. The 1990s also saw the privatisation of internet technology, which undermines common theorisations of the internet as holding a radical democratic potential (Zalnieriute, 2018). As geographers remind us, internet infrastructures and digital systems continue to underwrite the modern politics of international warfare and the highly sophisticated methods of killing that have accompanied them (Smith, 1992). To view the spatio-temporal structure of the internet in these terms—as a complex historical mix of public and private interests, academic and military concerns, and implicating histories from the high points of nineteenth-century British colonialism and twentieth-century US imperialism, that stretch back 150 years even in a narrow historiography—is one way to feel the temporal drag of the modern internet and its usage. In doing so, we can view the internet less as proleptic and more as anachronistic.

Continuing along these lines, Freeman (2010, p. 68) describes how temporal drag might involve "resuscitating obsolete cultural signs," "embarrassing pre-histories," "the love of failure,"[1] and "the rescue of ephemera." Here we might point to the quotidian sensation that accompanies the circulation of aphorism online in which the late 2010s' experience of internet use is folded back into the 1990s. This might include being directed through a Google search to now rarely used websites like MapQuest, coming across a static-HTML Web 1.0 read-only site,[2] or the sonic warping that occurs when the sound of dial-up internet (e.g., when watching an old television show or used as a novelty ringtone) meets the twenty-first century era. Meme culture and the circulation of viral content often self-consciously draws attention to the 1990s fashion and music (or, in the common 'rick-rolling' meme, 1987, which might still *feel* like the 1990s), designating the web as an 'originally' Gen Y space that may confound newer Gen Z users. Imagining the internet as an obsessively archival, referential, and inter-textual space also complicates and contorts chrononormative imaginaries, given the archive's common association with material spaces and physical boxes that contain documents solidly located in the past. In this sense, the digitisation of archival materials presents an osmotic membrane between past and present. Similarly, many facets of the internet are in a rapid process of becoming-archive even as we use them. What seeming-staples of today's internet usage might join the ranks of Napster, Myspace, ICQ, AltaVista in the near-future? With these examples, the hubris of the planned obsolesce of commodity-time (Freeman, 2010, p. 89) that characterises the production of many historical and modern technologies (e.g., the automobile and the smartphone) may collapse awkwardly into the market failure of an *unplanned* obsolescence. If temporal drag is about preserving the improper object of the past as a way to disorientate the hegemonies of the present and future, asserting these perhaps more cultural and playful aspects of temporal folding and collapse may be one way to juxtapose this improper object against the present moment.

[1] We understand this failure in the sense that Jack Halberstam (2011) intends it, not in the language of digital media firms to "fail forward" in which failure is a kind of startup hazing strategy, but in the sense of a failure to adhere to the modes of subjectivity that characterise heteronormativity.

[2] It is interesting to observe that the term 'Web 1.0' is itself a retronym.

These latter examples point to the disjunction—that we suggest is a temporal as well as a spatial one—between, on the one side, the geopolitical and capitalist realities of internet infrastructures and, on the other, their usage. This is something like "a way of forcing the present to touch its own disavowed past or seemingly outlandish possible future" (Freeman, 2010, p. 78). This doubling and juxtaposition of an object (e.g., internet infrastructure or digital systems) that is-not-itself characterises the concept of temporal drag, which seeks to take seriously how histories remain stubbornly contemporaneous with presents, despite attempts at disavowal and performative turns towards novel iteration. It is the second of these twin temporalities to which we now turn, moving from (in this section) a discussion of the internet infrastructures and digital systems as a kind of anachronism, to thinking (in the next) through queer presence online.

Queer Presence Online: Network Time and the Glitch

What is queer presence online? Any answer to this question must begin by addressing presence as a problem of both queer theory and studies of mediation. Regarding the former, there is a general ambivalence surrounding presence in the constitution of queer experience. This can be traced in the concern with histories and futures denoted by the turn to temporality in queer theory (Dinshaw et al., 2007). Such a desire to retrieve lost histories or (im)possible futures that are named queer responds to an uncertain politics of the "post-recognition" present in Western LGBTQ experience. Recognition of LGBTQ individuals, most notably through the extension of marriage to same-sex couples in many countries, has meant that what were non-normative sexual practices lose some of their distinctiveness as a defining marker of queer identity (Halley & Parker, 2011). One result of this has been the dissipation of senses of oppositional struggle that propel political movement, producing a lack of direction that mirrors the questioning of anti-normativity as the signature critical move of queer theory (Wiegman & Wilson, 2015). It is unclear what exactly is queer about the present moment, and how queer presence can be known as such. Even before thinking about mediation then, queer presence has an ambiguous constitution. Mediation itself also alerts us to the insufficiencies of any account of absolute presence. It evokes the necessary role of transmission between a live presence and its reception. In this way, media construct a sense of presence that is qualified through the clarity and accuracy of the transmission process. The quality of mediation can be judged through the proximity of the space and time of the transmitted experience to the present event. Thus, if the problem of presence in queer theory is one of definition and constitution, through mediation it becomes one of transmission and proximity.

From this more general problem of presence, we might look to particular features of the present of contemporary media that could constitute queer experience online. To understand this, first it is necessary to consider how the conditions of online presence reconfigure relationships between representation and temporality. One way of defining online presence is through the representations that take the form of the update, the uploading of content, and may entail a self-narration through the curation of one's personal profile. In these cases, representation moves from being a more cognitive reference to past events to a formal and action-oriented process directed towards the future. Rather than functioning in a descriptive mode, producing what Roland Barthes (1968) termed "reality effects" through an historical time, representation becomes an operation of probability, producing a predictive, communicative temporality (Halpern, 2014, p. 50). Thus, that which previously fixed the present through reference to the past instead becomes constructive of potential presence through transmission into the future. Containing no grammar by which to problematise their abstraction from space and time (Halpern, 2014), these are representations that do not speak of experience but rather seem to produce the immediacy of the now. This condition of contemporary mediation has been termed 'liveness' to denote the "new coordinated forms of social reality manifest in the contemporary social world" (Back & Puwar, 2012, p. 7). Extending the transformations rendered by previous new media, like television (Williams, 1974), the sensation of liveness moves closer to the processes for knowing such experience so that the representations of 'being live' are even more entangled in its occurrence.

Secondly, this live performance constructed through the generation of representations means that online presence occurs through network time (Hassan, 2007). This is a time that is reliant on multi-directional processes of transmission created and inhabited by people and information and communication technologies (ICTs) together. Network time generates asynchronous spaces in which connection and direction occur through the flows and rhythms of communication with others, rather than organised by the disembedded linear time of the clock. The desire to continuously update or narrate the present can be understood within this context, fulfilling the demand for content generation that through its transmission produces a live presence that is realised asynchronously through connections with multiple nodes in the network. As has been well documented, this time of the network can be construed as alienating. Manuel Castells (1996), for example, saw network time as a non-time of an extended present of flows that is sealed off from localities. Likewise, Paul Virilio (1998) envisaged the "real-time" of the network as moving outside of human experience, a non-lived machine time. In this sense, the demands of the network for constant transmission of observation and participation extend processes of modern subject formation wrought through engagement in spectacular culture (Crary, 1999). The construction of the spectacle is "not founded on the necessity of making a subject see, but rather on strategies in which individuals are isolated, separated and inhabit time as disempowered" (Crary, 1999, p. 3). Jonathan Crary (2013, p. 29) later deepens this depressing analysis in his depiction of a contemporary 24/7 temporality as "a time without time" that "celebrates a hallucination of presence, of an unalterable permanence composed of incessant, frictionless operations." Drawing on Hannah Arendt, Crary (2013, p. 21) sees the command of this 24/7 temporality as an assault on sleep, and thus on domesticity and the "twilight that suffuses our private and intimate life."

It is possible then to paint a picture of online presence as that which creates a condition of liveness, but one that tends towards alienation rather than shared experience. However, considering what might be queer about online presence can provide an alternative account. One aspect of this is a critique of the claim that networked time is necessarily alienating. As in the previous section, this could follow the queer temporalities literature that challenges the logic of a homogeneous, linear time of reproduction (see also Edelman, 2004). Equally though, a closer attention to the experience of network time indicates the potential for all online presence to *become queer*. There are two issues here. The first is that accounts of online presence as uniform tend to either underplay the body or rely on a simplistic model of embodiment. As Mike Crang (2007, p. 69) argues, the interest in and valorisation of speed of transmission in these accounts of the network sketch a general picture of a temporal order in which "the everyday and the bodily gets coded as the authentic and slow." In other words, they fail to address the nuanced ways in which bodies already experience time differently, variations in rhythm that do not necessarily individualise but rather require nuanced forms of cooperation. This means that intimacy then, contra Crary (2013), does not pre-exist the forms of spatial and temporal organisation through which it occurs; with a morphology that manifests not through "some abstract frame of reference but producing shared time-space relevancies and shared coordinates" (Crary, 2013, p. 76). Network time thus extends syncopated or aleatory rhythms, which have long been necessary for queer intimacies, to diversify practices of intimate life.

Without a sufficiently nuanced approach to embodiment, the second issue is that the potential for heterogeneous experiences of time and space is undermined. The multiple shifting morphologies of intimacy that may emerge through the network result from the "fragmentation of episodes into smaller and smaller 'units' thereby increasing the challenge of co-ordinating what become separate events" (Shove, 2002, cited in Crang, 2007, p. 69). Whilst this certainly creates problems of squeezed time, and temporal overflow (Jarvis & Pratt, 2006; Southerton, 2003), Robert Hassan (2007, p. 52) argues that there is a form of freedom in the network as "temporal experience becomes disconnected from the local clock time of the users." This means control over time is experienced "once more through our own contextual self-creation of it" (Hassan, 2007, p. 45). Individuals begin to have a feeling for time through the relations of the network, though they may no longer have a standardised measure for its understanding. The example Hassan (2007, p. 45) gives to evoke this sense, rather than metre, of time is communication with others, where one can "get to the point where the clock does not matter, so deeply have we shared the flow and rhythm of the constructed time" of the conversation. The implication of this is a social experience of time that is not dictated by an external temporal order but rather allows for more unfamiliar, more unexpected temporalities. Thus, the time of the network is in no way simply one of alienated and individualised presence but rather a queer one that affords opportunities for a reworking of experiences of shared temporality, including the reconfiguration of intimacies.

Queer presence online might have another form too, one that disturbs the apparently alienating temporality of the network in a more material manner. This form is a presence that disrupts communicative operations, a *glitch* that stops them working the way they should. The glitch is "a troubled transmission" (Berlant, 2016, p. 393), a disturbance in the seamless communication that constructs the liveness of the network. For Berlant (2016, p. 393), the glitch is an interruption in "the conditions of the reproduction of life," and thus one that might challenge familial models of generation and transmission. More than this though, the glitch is an aesthetic that denotes a certain state of continuity amidst a shift, but one that is incoherent and uncongealed (Berlant, 2011, p. 198). In this context, the glitch has some purpose but one that cannot be comprehended within an existing system of meaning or order (Nunes, 2012). Technical failure echoes a broader hermeneutic and interpretive failure (Kane, 2016, p. 130). In this way, the glitch aesthetic produces the sort of anti-social relation that has appeared in contemporary queer theory (Caserio, Edelman, Halberstam, Muñoz, & Dean, 2006). Through a rhetoric of "anti-communication" (Kane, 2016, p. 129), it causes complexity and obfuscation by emphasising the background noise that is normally filtered out (Cascone, 2000). The indeterminacy of (queer) presence is confronted by retaining and indeed focusing on, incommunicability that is constitutive of any networked transmission. Thus, the glitch operates as both material and aesthetic failure in the communication network, an online presence, which like the ambivalence of contemporary queer experience, breaks up its own conditions of appearance.

Conclusion

This chapter has conceptualised the internet through writing on temporalities that derives from queer experience. In doing so, our aim has not been to diminish the real dangers that the internet poses as a system of global surveillance aligned with the chrononormativity of state-capitalism that is so often antagonistic towards queer lives, bodies, and to expressions of difference in general. The urgency of these dangers can be witnessed, for example, in revelations regarding Facebook's role in the circulation and dissemination of propaganda, and the role of such propaganda in electoral politics in the United States. Yet, it is important to be able to hold multiple imaginaries of spatio-temporality in mind to recognise that objects are rarely only one thing; they are rarely totalising, monolithic, and intransigent in all circumstances.

With these thoughts in mind, we presented the internet in terms of temporal drag to show how oft-forgotten pasts are related to present-day internet infrastructures. Here we drew attention to how the internet is already out-of-sync with its dominant representations. As a nineteenth- and twentieth-century technology, the internet is the result of British and American imperialisms, with material geographies and histories that tend to be underplayed. Conceptualising digital systems as *archives* evokes them as a retainer and mobiliser of the past, as intertextual, citational, and self-referential. We then turned to embodied experiences of the present of internet usage to show how the body tends to resist normative temporalities. This is a tendency that continues through the glitches in transmission that often break up appearances of (embodied) presence with digital systems. Together these observations point to an already-queer conceptualisation of the internet characterised by indeterminacy, forgotten pasts that nevertheless fold itinerancy, and undecidability into the present.

Our suggestion is not to resolve the tension between these two conceptualisations—between the internet as an aspect of homophobic state-capitalist hegemony and a necessary opportunity for resistance to that hegemony. Such a tension cannot, and arguable should not, be resolved. Instead, it is productive to imagine internet infrastructures and digital systems through the incommensurability of these two conceptualisations, to magnify the tension rather than to (re)solve it. Imaging the internet in terms of its ambivalence allows for a diversity of queer, contradictory experiences that both shape and are shaped by, this spatial-temporal system. Though this chapter has not been exhaustive in terms of this theorising, it makes a start in understanding this ambivalence.

References

Abbate, J. (1999). *Inventing the Internet.* Cambridge: MIT Press.

Back, L., & Puwar, N. (2012). A manifesto for live methods: Provocations and capacities. *The Sociological Review, 60*(1_suppl), 6–17.

Barthes, R. (1968). *The rustle of language.* Berkeley: University of California Press.

Berlant, L. (2011). *Cruel optimism.* Durham: Duke University Press.

Berlant, L. (2016). The commons: Infrastructure for troubling times. *Environment and Planning D: Society and Space, 34*(3), 393–419.

Butler, J. (1990). *Gender trouble.* London: Routledge.

Cascone, K. (2000). The aesthetics of failure: 'Post-digital' tendencies in contemporary computer music. *Computer Music Journal, 24*(4), 12–18.

Caserio, R., Edelman, L., Halberstam, J., Muñoz, J. E., & Dean, T. (2006). The antisocial thesis in queer theory. *PMLA, 121*(2), 819–828.

Castells, M. (1996). *The rise of the Network Society.* Oxford: Blackwell Publishers.

Cockayne, D., & Richardson, L. (2017). Queering code/space: The co-production of socio-spatial codes and technology. *Gender, Place and Culture, 24*(11), 1642–1658.

Cowen, D. (2014). *The deadly life of logistics: Mapping violence in global trade.* Minneapolis: University of Minnesota Press.

Crang, M. (2007). Speed = distance / time: Chronotopographies of action. In R. Hassan & R. E. Purser (Eds.), *24/7: Time and temporality in the network society* (pp. 62–88). Stanford: Stanford Business Books.

Crary, J. (1999). *Suspensions of perception: Attention, spectacle, and modern culture.* Cambridge: MIT Press.

Crary, J. (2013). *24/7: Late capitalism and the end of sleep.* London: Verso.

Dinshaw, C., Edelman, L., Ferguson, R., Freccero, C., Freeman, E., Halberstam, J., et al. (2007). Theorizing queer temporalities: A roundtable discussion. *GLQ: A Journal of Lesbian and Gay Studies, 13*(2–3), 177–195.

Dodge, M., & Kitchin, R. (2005). Code and the transduction of space. *Annals of the Association of American Geographers, 95*(1), 162–180.

Dyson, G. (2012). *Turing's cathedral: The origins of the digital universe*. New York: Vintage.

Edelman, L. (2004). *No future: Queer theory and the death drive*. Durham: Duke University Press.

Freeman, E. (2010). *Time binds: Queer temporalities, queer histories*. Durham: Duke University Press.

Gibson-Graham, J. K. (2014). Rethinking the economy with thick description and weak theory. *Cultural Anthropology, 55*(S9), S147–S153.

Gieseking, J. (2017). Messing with the attractiveness algorithm: A response to queering code/space. *Gender, Place and Culture, 24*(11), 1659–1665.

Graham, S. (1998). The end of geography or the explosion of place? Conceptualizing space, place and information technology. *Progress in Human Geography, 22*(2), 165–185.

Graham, M. (2011). Time machines and virtual portals: The spatialities of the digital divide. *Progress in Development Studies, 11*(3), 211–227.

Graham, M. (2013). Geography/internet: Ethereal alternative dimensions of cyberspace or grounded augmented realities? *The Geographical Journal, 179*(2), 177–182.

Halberstam, J. (2011). *The queer art of failure*. Durham: Duke University Press.

Halley, J. E., & Parker, A. (2011). *After sex?: On writing since queer theory*. Durham: Duke University Press.

Halpern, O. (2014). *Beautiful data: A history of vision and reason since 1945*. Durham: Duke University Press.

Hassan, R. (2007). Network time. In R. Hassan & R. E. Purser (Eds.), *24/7: Time and temporality in the network society* (pp. 37–61). Stanford: Stanford Business Books.

Jarvis, H., & Pratt, A. (2006). Bringing it all back home: The extensification and 'overflowing' of work. *Geoforum, 37*(3), 331–339.

Jenzen, O. (2017). Trans youth and social media: Moving between counterpublics and the wider web. *Gender, Place and Culture, 24*(11), 1626–1641.

Kane, C. L. (2016). Photo noise. *History of Photography, 40*(2), 129–145.

Kirsch, S. (1995). The incredible shrinking world? Technology and the production of space. *Environment and Planning D: Society and Space, 13*(5), 529–555.

Kitchin, R. (1998). Towards geographies of cyberspace. *Progress in Human Geography, 22*(3), 385–406.

Love, H. (2007). *Feeling backwards: Loss and the politics of queer history*. Chicago: University of Chicago Press.

Massey, D. (2005). *For space*. London: Sage.

Muñoz, J. E. (2009). *Cruising utopia: The then and there of queer futurity*. New York City: New York University Press.
Nunes, M. (2012). Seductive errors: A poetics of noise. In X. Burrough (Ed.), *Net work: Case studies in web art and design* (pp. 100–103). London: Routledge.
Paglen, T. (2010). Goatsucker: Toward a spatial theory of state secrecy. *Environment and Planning D: Society and Space, 28*(5), 759–771.
Sedgwick, E. (2003). *Touching feeling: Affect, pedagogy, performativity*. Durham: Duke University Press.
Smith, N. (1992). History and philosophy of geography: Real wars, theory wars. *Progress in Human Geography, 16*(2), 257–271.
Southerton, D. (2003). 'Squeezing time': Allocating practices, coordinating networks and scheduling society. *Time and Society, 12*(1), 5–25.
Starosielski, N. (2015). *The undersea network: Sign, storage, transmission*. Durham: Duke University Press.
Turner, F. (2006). *From counterculture to cyberculture: Stewart Brand, the whole earth network, and the rise of digital utopianism*. Stanford: Stanford University Press.
Virilio, P. (1998). Architecture in the age of its virtual disappearance. In J. Beckman (Ed.), *The virtual dimension: Architecture, representation, and crash culture* (pp. 178–187). New York: Princeton Architectural Press.
Wiegman, R., & Wilson, E. (2015). Antinormativity's queer conventions. *Differences, 26*(1), 1–25.
Williams, R. (1974). *Television: Technology and cultural form*. London: Routledge Classics.
Zalnieriute, M. (2018). The anatomy of neoliberal internet governance: A queer critical political economy perspective. In D. Otto (Ed.), *Queering international law: Possibilities, alliances, and risks* (pp. 53–74). London: Routledge.
Zook, M. (2000). The web of production: The economic geography of commercial internet content production in the United States. *Environment and Planning A: Economy and Space, 32*(3), 411–426.

3

Queer Mobilities and New Spatial Media

Catherine J. Nash and Andrew Gorman-Murray

Introduction

Queer urban spaces are being transformed in no small measure due to the evolution of new technologies, including Web 2.0, digital media, location-based services and locative, mobile social networks. These new technologies are fundamentally reworking sexual practices and sexual lives. As Garlick (2011, p. 223) argues, we are "in the midst of a technologically-mediated reorganization of the social relations of sexuality"—a reorganization that is having incalculable effects on the geographies of everyday life. Queer people, as early adopters of new technologies, have arguably been freed from the 'tyranny of geography' given that life online potentially offers new opportunities for self-expression

C. J. Nash (✉)
Brock University, St. Catharines, ON, Canada
e-mail: cnash@brocku.ca

A. Gorman-Murray
Western Sydney University, Penrith, NSW, Australia
e-mail: A.Gorman-Murray@westernsydney.edu.au

C. Nash, A. Gorman-Murray (eds.), *The Geographies of Digital Sexuality*,
https://doi.org/10.1007/978-981-13-6876-9_3

and community formation (Aslinger, 2010, p. 113; Cassidy, 2013; Nash & Gorman-Murray, 2016). Scholars assert that new technologies have undermined the historical, social and political need for material queer locations, such as traditional gay villages, as location-based mobile technologies enable users to operate across a range of spaces, all the while constituting new digital practices with material locations (Kuntsman, 2007; Mowlabocus, 2010; Nash & Gorman-Murray, 2016; Pullen & Cooper, 2010).

In our ongoing research on the transformations of gay villages in Toronto and Sydney, we utilized mobilities scholarship to argue that the significant legal, political and social changes for queer people in both Canada and Australia have supported a new queer politics of mobility, one that allows for the freer and more visible movement of queer people across inner-city neighbourhoods. In both Toronto and Sydney, we have detailed how these new mobilities underpin emerging (and fluid) relational geographies that constitute complex interconnections between newly queered alternative locations and each city's traditional gay village, albeit in distinctive ways (Gorman-Murray & Nash, 2014; Nash & Gorman-Murray, 2014, 2015b, 2016). However, our research to date has not incorporated a consideration of the impact or use of new technologies in the development of these queer relational geographies.

In this chapter, we attempt to address Wilken's (2009, p. 39) call to develop conceptualizations of place that can "illuminate the complexities of human-technology-environment interactions" (see also Felgenhauer, 2017). We explore how we might conceptualize the interconnections between new technologies, new queer mobilities and queer place-making. We are primarily focused here on the particularities of the nexus between queer subjects, technologies and place, that is, how queer subjects, through their use of new technologies, are being themselves remade within newly mobile, unstable and fragmented relational geographies. In taking up this discussion, we want to contribute to the ongoing scholarship seeking to conceptualize how new technologies are transforming our everyday lives and experiences in material spaces.

We explore three distinctive theoretical or conceptual interventions that provide preliminary frameworks for how we might frame research at this queer nexus. To begin, we provide a brief overview of queer mobilities research with a focus on questions of sexualities, genders and place and their potential links to the utilization of new technologies. Then, our first intervention focuses on the interlinkages between the formation of new queer subjects in and through the use of new technologies. This work considers how particular and diverse online engagements are implicated in the development of particular sets of relationships and meanings about physical locations offline and offers a rich conceptual frame to explore the implications of online/offline engagements and the constitution of new queer spaces. We want to consider how the everyday use of new social media, dating apps and location-based services are implicated (or integrated) in the formulation and emergence of admittedly unstable queer identities, subjectivities and place. In this context, we draw on existing geographical concepts to ground the discussion.

Second, we consider the application of the concept of 'new spatial media' as developed in the work of Elwood and Leszczynski (2013), particularly the impacts of 'new spatial media' on place-based meanings and material places, and we consider how new spatial media might be implicated in the constitution of queer spaces given these new technological practices. Thirdly, we consider Kitchin and Dodge's (2011) notion of code/space as another potential analytic to conceptualize the interactions between locations that are constituted in and through new technologies and the implications this has for the constitution of new subjects, practices and spatial formation (see also Dodge & Kitchin, 2005). Each framework provides an admittedly partial (and sometimes incommensurate) approach but we are suggesting that each engages with important aspects of the questions we have about the intersections between new queer mobilities and place. Finally, we conclude with a summary of our thinking and some suggestions for how these ideas might direct future research.

New Mobilities, Technologies and Queer Subjects

Our research on the changing sexual and gendered landscapes in Toronto and Sydney was concerned with where and why queer people were transforming inner-city neighbourhoods (Gorman-Murray & Nash, 2014, 2016; Nash & Gorman-Murray, 2014, 2015a, 2015b). Drawing on mobilities approaches, we argued that because of social, legal and political transformations, LGBT people enjoyed new queer mobilities that constituted new queer place-making and that such processes are implicated in the formation of the new queer subjects (e.g. Uteng & Cresswell, 2008).

Mobilities scholarship conceptualizes place-making and the subjects engaged in such place-making within a framework that stresses the significance of mobilities in both the constitution of place and of the subject. Scholarship argues that place-making is about the movement and intersection of flows of people, ideas, objects and capital. Certain places, then, arise from a specific coalescence or agglomeration of material and social flows—a 'mooring' where "mobile people, things and ideas impact each other, obtain a relative embeddedness and consequently gain political and social meaning" and constitute 'place', however unstable, temporary and fleeting (Gorman-Murray & Nash, 2014, p. 626; see also Hannam, Sheller, & Urry, 2006). Given this analytic framework, our research examined locations where certain meanings accrue within networks of mobility, thereby highlighting the 'queering' of certain locations within new relational geographies.

But a mobilities approach also argues that subjects and social relations operate within relations of power such that being mobile is "both a product of and produced by social relations" (Cresswell, 2010, p. 21). These social relations reflect the potential for movement—a certain motility—that some people, objects, knowledges and capital may possess that is both uneven and inconsistent. In other words, in understanding the constitution of new places within new relations of mobility, it is important to recognize that only *some* subjects are engaged in place-making within new mobilities, marking the power relations in play in the constitution of new queer places through the hierarchical social categories of race, gender, class and age, for example (Cresswell, 2010; Uteng & Cresswell, 2008). Therefore, in thinking about the new and emergent relational geographies in both Toronto and Sydney, we noted the fragmented and uneven place-making grounded in new queer mobilities and transforming queer subjects. However, it also became clear that these new queer mobilities are increasingly mediated, constituted and reflected in and through the use of new technologies, more particularly location-based, spatial media (Leszczynski & Elwood, 2015). It is at this point that we turned our attention to how we might conceptualize these new queer subjects and relational geographies within the everyday use of new technologies.

Queer Subjects and Technology

For geographers, it is axiomatic that there is a "recursive relationship between the constitution of and meanings associated with specific places and the organization of social relations through hegemonic categories such as gender, sexuality, race and class" (Nash, 2013, p. 244). Sexualized subjects such as 'gay men', 'lesbians' or 'queers' operate within malleable social categories that are fluid, unstable and geographically and historically contingent. Social subjects then are constituted through social relations enacted in place through everyday practices and within the limitations and possibilities of the meanings of certain places (Cresswell, 2010). These social categories, unstable as they are, are contested and reinforced within certain places and can be reworked within contingent circumstance (Browne, 2007; Butler, 1990; Nash, 2006). Taking this as a foundational assumption, we seek to consider how and in what ways the introduction of new technologies (and related everyday practices) is transformative and mutually constitutive of both emergent subjects and places (e.g. Crang, Crosbie, & Graham, 2007; Graham, 2013).

Geographical scholarship, particularly feminist geographies, argues that differently gendered, sexualized, racialized and embodied individuals have distinctive experiences and practices within urban locations highlighting the interconnections between subjects and the meanings embedded in place (e.g. Bondi & Domosh, 1992; Massey, 1994; Pain, 2001; see also Leszczynski & Elwood, 2015). Given this, we can take as a starting point the argument that 'subjects' making use of new technologies are *already* constituted as gendered and sexualized beings within the meanings available in particular locations. Therefore, in thinking about queer engagements with new technologies, it is important to begin with the notion that those taking up new technologies do so as already-differentiated subjects, highlighting how the use of new technologies is always a differentiated practice from the outset.

Not only are the subjects that use technologies always-already operating within unstable and contested social categories, the places under consideration, including newly queer locations, are themselves "always-already digitally mediated" (Elwood & Leszczynski, 2018, p. 634). That is, places are already constituted through digital mediations making such locations "contingent, necessarily incomplete comings-together of technical presences, persons, and space/place" (Leszczynski, 2015, as quoted in Elwood & Leszczynski, 2018, p. 634). Understanding why some places can be queered or are considered to be more queer-friendly than others requires a recognition that places come with always-already embedded meanings and normative practices. Such locations are utilized by subjects that also are always-already constituted within social relations—relations structured through social categories including class, race, gender, age and sexualities.

Current scholarship on sexualities and technologies has begun to put these ideas into practice in terms of thinking about the always-already linked constitution of particular subjects and place. For example, queer scholarship has attended to the impact of dating apps (e.g. *Grindr*, *Scruff*, *Tinder*) on gay male cruising practices and the navigation of urban spaces beyond traditional queer locations (see, e.g., Bonner-Thompson, 2019; Cassidy, 2013; Jaspal, 2017). Sharif Mowlabocus (2010), in his research on gay male internet dating, argues that particular place-based cultural norms and practices are integrated (admittedly unevenly and often with reformulations) into online practices which then reshape and influence offline engagements. So, despite claims that online apps have replaced more traditional, place-based ways of meeting other gay men, scholars highlight how gay male cultural norms offline are often incorporated and reworked online in ways that influence and reconstitute offline engagements as well (Prestage et al., 2015; Raj, 2013). Neither places nor subjects are 'blank slates' reconstituted through the use of new technologies. On the contrary, the specificities of both place and social relations are pivotal in how both are remade through the use of new technologies.

Miles (2017), in his examination of the 'digital hybridisation' of gay places through the use of locative media, points out how users create online representations operating with the established cultural and social expectations of certain places. Nevertheless, users are also working out new or shared understandings for mediating physical encounters within new technologies that remain in flux. Given this, and despite claims that dating apps have overcome the need for expressly queer places to meet, social interactions through apps such as *Grindr* still require a "journey from virtual communication to embodied meeting [which] is key to understanding how technology users are subject to—or actively participate in—the sociotechnical relations that mediate contemporary geographies of sexualities" (Miles, 2019, p. 119).

Scholarship also argues that new technologies may be reimposing pre-existing power relations and subject categories through the spatialization of online identities within offline places and social relations. For example, several decades of research on how lesbian experiences of urban places differ from those of gay men suggests that in taking up new technologies, lesbian and gay men's subject positions already ensure that technologically mediated practices and experiences are distinctive. Research seeking to understand how lesbians/queer women take up technologies would need to be attentive to always-already existing gendered (and racialized and classed) differences in place-making (e.g. Nash & Gorman-Murray, 2015b; Podmore, 2006, 2013). Further, the differences between queer men and women, in relation to cruising culture would arguably figure into queer women's engagements with dating apps given there is little historical precedent for a cruising culture for queer women (e.g. Duguay, 2019). As women, different cultural norms suggest that technologies and usage are taken up differently (e.g. Nash & Bain, 2007, see also Gieseking, 2017; Hjorth, Pink, & Horst, 2018).

New Spatial Media: New Constitutions of Place

Elwood and Leszczynski (2013, p. 544) use the term 'new spatial media' to denote the "mediums, or channels, that enable, extend or enhance our ability to interact with and create geographic information online". In other words, we are increasingly able to use our devices to create our own geographical information through using a variety of tools including "Twitter's GeoAPI … Google Earth, location-based social networking applications … map mash-ups, application programming interfaces (API) and geotagging" (Elwood & Leszczynski, 2013, p. 544). Our devices allow us to annotate, narrate and contest online, both individual and collective meanings about particular physical locations offline. The term 'new spatial media' includes the devices we use (e.g. smartphones) and the informational artefacts about place that are created. Taken together, this constitutes the 'geospatial web' (geoweb) where this user-generated information (e.g. geotagged social media, geowikis or personalized maps) becomes widely accessible and shapes the social and political knowledges and practices about a place (Haklay, 2010; Mashhadi, Quattrone, & Capra, 2015; Quattrone, Mashhadi, Quercia, Smith-Clarke, & Capra, 2014). Such 'geovisualizations' link meanings to place through the tying of "explicitly visual representations of phenomena, contexts and problems with geographic/spatial referents" (Elwood and Leszczynski, 2013, pp. 547–548). So in thinking about the queering of space, we can consider how new spatial practices constituting new geovisualizations of place help frame its meanings and highlight the possibilities and potentialities of seeing locations queerly.

While Elwood and Leszczynski's (2013) research is focused on how political organizations and social groups use new spatial media to further their own agendas, these ideas can be utilized to consider how new spatial media are being deployed to queer places within new mobilities. For example, through new spatial media, material locations can be queered (or potentially de-queered) through users uploading materials that lay claim to locations as queer-friendly or as supporting a queer sociality. Such knowledges circulate in ways that impact how material locations are understood by potential users. This includes information about certain bars, parks, restaurants or neighbourhoods that are rendered queer through use of devices and informational artefacts. Conversely, queer locations might be 'de-queered' through information that claims locations are unsafe or not queer-friendly. These developing spatial knowledges and practices arguably constitute a form of 'insider' knowledge that may not be available (or visible) in the material locations themselves. Therefore, one can explore the constitution of new queer locations through material practices 'on the ground' as well as (or in tandem with) the user-generated geoweb and geovisualizations constituting new spatial knowledges. A recent example of such new spatial media is the 'queering the map' project which allows individuals to mark a location and annotate it with a particular queer narrative at the global scale (https://www.queeringthemap.com).

Elwood and Leszczynski's research raises intriguing ideas about how to map power relations in this online/offline environment where some people have a greater role in constituting the geoweb and geovisualization than others. Current research has demonstrated that the creation of new spatial media and related knowledges has variable geographic coverage (Jin, Kong, Wu, & Sui, 2018; Mooney, Corcoran, & Winstanley, 2010; Zielstra & Zipf, 2010). For example, countries in the global north have better geographic coverage that others, and within these countries more disadvantaged areas often have poorer coverage (Haklay, 2010; Quattrone et al., 2014). Further disparities exist between urban and rural areas where, for example, rural areas have less geotagged social media in applications such as Instagram or Flickr (Hecht & Stephens, 2014). Researchers examining new queer locations even in urban areas will have to be attentive to the uneven creation of new spatial knowledges and the potential impacts on the constitution of queer spaces.

Further, it is not surprising that some individuals and groups have a vested interest in creating new spatial knowledges (as has always been the case) which are linked to material locations with positive or adverse results. The ability to engage in new spatial media is arguably available for a select few who create, monitor and contest alternative representations and geovisualizations as they appear (Crampton et al., 2013). Geoweb information is generally verified through the interactive interface where users monitor and assess other users' uploads. Despite the potential problems with this, some argued that this verification process promotes "transparency, peer verification and witnessing" (Elwood & Leszczynski, 2013, p. 553). Nevertheless, determining the 'truth' of the informational artefacts is not done through objective notions of truth but is a shift away from a correspondence notion of truth "towards consensus and performative interpretations" (Warfighters & Sui, 2010, p. 107 in Ash, Kitchin, & Leszczynski, 2018, p. 5). In understanding the constitution of both new spatial media, new knowledges and the reworking of material spaces, researchers will need to tackle the question of who, how and in what way these "new forms of knowledge politics" are being advanced (Elwood & Leszczynski, 2013, p. 551). Only some queer people are engaged in the constitution of new queer knowledges in ways that reflect previously existing social categories and social relations (e.g. gay men on social media) and that privilege or support the creation of certain meanings over others. Online knowledges have the potential to 'colonize' offline spaces through uneven power relations.

This discussion points to the power relations in play around how new spatial media and related spatial knowledges are created as well as understanding that the spatial knowledges produced constitute locations in multiple, fragmented and unstable ways. If we are to consider how space is queered through the geoweb and related place-making practices, we need to ask whose digital knowledges are considered 'authentic' or 'truthful' or whose knowledges constituted through digital practices come to dominate. Clearly as Elwood and Leszczynski (2013, p. 5) argue, such knowledges "remain influenced and marked by hegemonic social relations" including "race, class, gender." New spatial media may make it possible for marginal groups to create alternative or contested representations of place which offer alternative annotations of streetscapes or neighbourhoods which support alternative narratives and meanings. New spatial medial can be used to "produce spatial knowledges that are situated, reflexive, non-masculinist, emotional/affected, inclusive and polyvocal, and flexible rather than foundational" (Ash et al., 2018, p. 4). Nevertheless, such activities can lead to contestations over place as representations and narratives compete for dominance which may play out on the ground in confrontations and resistance. New spatial media deploy meanings about offline spaces that are partial and contested and have the ability to appropriate or dominate offline locations (Kwan, 2002; Schuurman, 2002). As feminist critiques have argued, researchers need to examine who is producing knowledges and who benefits (e.g. Leszczynski & Elwood, 2015; Stephens, 2012, 2013; Wilson, 2011).

Queering Code/Space

Kitchin and Dodge's (2011; see also Dodge & Kitchin, 2005) notion of code/space offers yet another approach to working out how to frame or conceptualize the intersections between queer subjects, places and new technologies. We draw particularly on Cockayne and Richardson's (2017, see also Chap. 2) approach to code/space to think about newly queer urban spaces and queer mobilities. Kitchin and Dodge (2011, Dodge & Kitchin, 2005) use the term code/space to conceptualize places brought into being through the embeddedness of specific hardware and software (e.g. airports). In these locations, a 'failure' of the software (or code) means the space cannot function in the way it was intended nor continue the meanings associated with it. As Cockayne and Richardson (2017, p. 1643) note, in Kitchin and Dodge's understanding, there is a 'mutual dependency' between the software and the production of the space. However, in their work, Cockayne and Richardson (2017, p. 1643) propose a broader view of code/space, arguing that code/spaces can be produced through more "complex relationships between software and space constituted by differing degrees of dependency". This suggests a more complicated relationship in terms of how software embedded 'in place' creates that place. While airports would arguably cease to function 'as airports' if the software failed, other locations might continue to function even with a software failure but to varying degrees and with some modifications or alterations. For example, a bar whose 'brand' is digitally constituted through Facebook, Instagram and/or Twitter, could continue to function as a 'bar' even if the internet stops working. These places can still be considered code/space even when the 'mutual dependency' is partial and unstable.

Cockayne and Richardson (2017, p. 1643) argue there are intimate links between the constitution of code/space as such and geographically specific social categories. Geographers have long argued that in physical spaces, through disciplining and normalizing processes, places are constituted as heteronormative, that is, as locations where *cis*-gendered, heterosexual subjects are the norm to the exclusion of others (see, e.g., Browne, 2007; Knopp & Brown, 2003; Oswin, 2008). Subjects in those locations work to both comply with and are disciplined to reflect these norms, while also being implicated in the policing of those locations to maintain those norms. As Cockayne and Richardson (2017) argue, online or virtual spaces are not free from these disciplining processes that actively work to produce heteronormative code/spaces as well. Given this, heteronormativity continues to play a role "in the reproduction of the social, that ... is increasingly co-produced through digital and software systems" (Cockayne & Richardson, 2017, p. 1643). To understand code/space, then, is to consider the interconnections between sexuality, power relations and normativity, and how heteronormativity remains embedded in digitally mediated spaces including public spaces such as parks and sidewalks as well as cafés, bars, restaurants and community locations that may support a queer sociability (Gorman-Murray & Nash, 2016; Gorman-Murray & Waitt, 2009).

Conversely, and despite the normative proscriptions entrenched in the production of code/spaces, possibilities for transgression and resistance also exist, allowing for the 'queering' of these code/spaces through, among other things, the creation of new social media including information in the geoweb, geotagging and geovisualization. Thinking through things 'queerly' means placing a focus on the processes of differentiating and normalizing, and the potential for subversion and contestations (Elwood & Leszczynski, 2018). Cockayne and Richardson (2017, p. 1644) argue then that 'queer code/space' illustrates "the simultaneous proliferation and regulation of social life through technologies" and also prompts us to consider "how forms of intimate life can transgress, disrupt and distribute what is normal". This is a useful perspective for examining the interconnections between new spatial media and new mobilities. Some queer people, through new social and political motilities, are able to move through urban spaces, challenging or transgressing locations that are already digitally mediated. Those alternative locations, understood as 'queer' or queer-friendly, are also code/spaces constituted through varying dependencies between software/code and place. Queers are reading, understanding and potentially queering certain locations in resistance to the normativities circulating in place through both the digital and material.

This, ultimately, suggests the possibility of a liberatory 'digital' politics for remaking our technologies and ourselves as digital subjects. As Coutard and Guy (2007, p. 713) argue, all technologies offer some liberatory potential pointing to a "significant potential of contestation of, and resistance, to technology-supported forms of discrimination, and the deeply contingent nature of the process of [technological] appropriation". While we might take heart in the ability to transgress or resist the power relations within code/spaces (or to queer code/space), as we noted earlier, researchers need to also consider who actually has access to code/space and who is engaged in the production of new spatial knowledges. We have to ask which social subjects are able to (or have the motility) to engage in acts of transgression and resistance and who do not? What are the normalizing tendencies of code/space and what new subjectivities and identities are made possible or normalized in these code/spaces? How do homonormative impulses become part of the 'mutual dependency' constituting code/spaces and how are some people excluded through these processes?

In thinking about new queer locations as queered code/space, we have argued that part of our research needs to examine how queer subjects are constituted through everyday technological practices in particular locations in ways that render them queer-friendly or queered (e.g. Gorman-Murray & Waitt, 2009). Cockayne and Richardson (2017, p. 1645) also provide some preliminary conceptual thinking about how certain subjects, embedded and constituted within code/spaces (and their normalizing processes), come into being. They suggest that we understand code/space as continually being brought into being through the "productive power of technologies", we can draw on Butler's notion of performativity, and we can conceptualize how subjects can be constituted through everyday practices and repetitive actions that engage with new technologies within and through particular code/spaces. One way to conceptualize the constitution of subjects and places is to consider how the production of code/space is embodied through the performances and interactions of subjects in place, which can be normative and/or transgressive but always digitally mediated.

Conclusion

As we have argued elsewhere, given the social, legal and political changes in places such as Canada and Australia, queer people are more mobile and, through these new mobilities, are queering inner-city locations beyond the gay village, constituting new queer, relational geographies (Gorman-Murray & Nash, 2014, 2016; Nash & Gorman-Murray, 2015a). Undoubtedly, these new and emergent geographies are coming into being through the everyday use of new technologies including the internet, new social media, location-based and mobile applications and new spatial media. Given this, we argue that the queering of certain places in inner-city locations in Toronto and Sydney, through new mobilities and motilities, is mediated through the experiences and practices of new spatial media. Second, in considering what spaces are queered within new mobilities, we need to attend to how, both individually and collectively, previously constituted queer people use new technologies within pre-existing meanings and, at the same time, are reworking these meanings. This includes working out the specificities of the subjects employing new spatial media (and why). Such experiences and practices have implications for the (re)constitution of new queer subjects and places where people, knowledges, objects and practices coalesce around particular meanings, resulting in certain queered 'moorings' (however tenuous and unstable). For our own work, these points train our attention on the particularities of the subjects, places and technologies rendered mobile. Scholarship should also consider how new spatial media are reconstituting traditional gay villages. This not only includes claims about how technology contributes to the 'degaying' or demise of the village but a consideration of the implications arising from the fact that the gay village itself is now a digitally mediated space.

Thinking about urban queers' technological practices is integral to understanding not only new mobilities and motilities but also in understanding the constitution of new queer subjects, places and relational geographies. We set as our task in this chapter the consideration of three conceptual frameworks that might provide insights into the intersections between new queer subjects, new technologies and queer place-making—feminist and queer scholarship on queers and technology, Elwood and Leszczynski's (2013, 2018) work on new spatial media and Kitchin and Dodge's (2011) notion of code/space as taken up by Cockayne and Richardson (2017). Each of these contributes important foundational principles we suggest could guide research on queer mobilities and queer places.

Work in feminist and queer geographies highlights the blind spots in research that fails to address the notion that the 'subjects' taking up new technologies are already constituted as 'subjects' within social categories such as sexuality, gender, class and race that are particular to historically and geographically specific contexts. In other words, subjects are always-already gendered, racialized, classed, sexualized and embodied in ways that influence, enable and constrain their access to and use of technologies. Queer men, for example, have been early adopters of dating apps such as *Grindr* which are utilized within the larger context of gay male cruising culture and already-existent social categories of sexuality and masculinity (e.g. Mowlabocus, 2010). Conversely, lesbians, as women who occupy public urban spaces differently than gay men, have been slower to adopt such technologies and do so within distinctive social, cultural and geographical circumstances (Nash & Gorman-Murray, 2015b; Podmore, 2013). This influences how (and by whom) urban spaces are remade and implicated in the constitution of new mobilities, motilities and queer relational geographies in places such as Sydney and Toronto.

Elwood and Leszczynski's (2013) conceptualization of 'new spatial media' highlights how new spatial knowledges are constituted online with material spatial effects. New processes enable us, through our devices, to create geographical information which we upload through such tools as Google Earth or geotagging and which rework understandings of physical locations and offer the opportunity to queer offline locations. Nevertheless, researchers need to consider the power relations involved in who has the access and/or ability to utilize new spatial media and who is excluded or limited. Conversely, the malleability of new spatial media offers opportunities for subversive or resistive practices that constitute, undermine or contextualize meanings and representations of place. Queers engaged in new spatial media have opportunities to create new individual and collective knowledges which can queer or de-queer material locations and can be used to think through the emergence of new queer geographies through new mobilities.

Finally, Kitchin and Dodge's (2011, Dodge & Kitchin, 2005) notion of code/space as taken up by Cockayne and Richardson (2017) suggests a conceptualization of material spaces that takes into account technology's embeddedness in the constitution of place. Geographical scholarship has documented how physical locations are constituted as heteronormative through normalizing processes and power relations that exclude nonconforming gendered and sexualized individuals. Online locations are also shaped and normalized in certain ways that render invisible non-heteronormative subject. Code/space, constituted through software and technological practices, continues to play a role in the reproduction of social norms in digitally mediated spaces. Contrary to more utopian notions of spaces online being more 'liberatory' for sexual and gendered minorities, heteronormative power relations still work to govern online and offline locations.

References

Ash, J., Kitchin, R., & Leszczynski, A. (2018). Digital turn, digital geographies? *Progress in Human Geography, 42*(1), 25–43.

Aslinger, B. (2010). PlanetOut and the dichotomies of queer media conglomeration. In C. Pullen & E. Cooper (Eds.), *LGBT identity and online new media* (pp. 113–124). New York: Routledge.

Bondi, L., & Domosh, M. (1992). Other figures in other places: On feminism, postmodernism, and geography. *Environment and Planning D: Society and Space, 10*(2), 199–213.

Bonner-Thompson, C. (2019). I didn't think you were going to sound like that': Sensory geographies of Grindr encounters in public spaces in Newcastle-upon-Tyne, UK. In C. J. Nash & A. Gorman-Murray (Eds.), *The geographies of digital sexuality*. London: Palgrave Macmillan.

Browne, K. (2007). (Re)making the other, heterosexualising everyday space. *Environment and Planning A, 39*(4), 996–1014.

Butler, J. (1990). *Gender trouble and the subversion of identity*. New York: Routledge.

Cassidy, E. (2013). *Gay men, social media and self-representation: Managing identities in Gaydar, Facebook and Beyond*. PhD thesis, Queensland University of Technology.

Cockayne, D., & Richardson, L. (2017). Queering code/space: The co-production of socio-sexual codes and digital technologies. *Gender, Place and Culture, 24*(11), 1642–1658.

Coutard, O., & Guy, S. (2007). STS and the city: Politics and practices of hope. *Science, Technology, and Human Values, 32*(6), 713–734.

Crampton, J. W., Graham, M., Poorthuis, A., Shelton, T., Stephens, M., Wilson, M. W., et al. (2013). Beyond the geotag: Situating 'big data' and leveraging the potential of the geoweb. *Cartography and Geographic Information Science, 40*(2), 130–139.

Crang, M., Crosbie, T., & Graham, S. (2007). Technology, time–space, and the remediation of neighbourhood life. *Environment and Planning A, 39*(10), 2405–2422.

Cresswell, T. (2010). Towards a politics of mobility. *Environment and Planning D: Society and Space, 28*(1), 17–31.

Dodge, M., & Kitchin, R. (2005). Code and the transduction of space. *Annals of the Association of American Geographers, 95*(1), 162–180.

Duguay, S. (2019). "There's no one new around you": Queer women's experiences of scarcity in geospatial partner-seeking on tinder. In C. J. Nash & A. Gorman-Murray (Eds.), *The geographies of digital sexuality*. London: Palgrave Macmillan.

Elwood, S., & Leszczynski, A. (2013). New spatial media, new knowledge politics. *Transactions of the Institute of British Geographers, 38*(4), 544–559.

Elwood, S., & Leszczynski, A. (2018). Feminist digital geographies. *Gender, Place and Culture, 25*(5), 629–644.

Felgenhauer, T. (2017). The re-imagining of the geographical tradition in the digital age. *Geografiska Annaler: Series B, Human Geography, 99*(3), 256–267.

Garlick, S. (2011). A new sexual revolution? Critical theory, pornography, and the internet. *Canadian Review of Sociology/Revue canadienne de sociologie, 48*(3), 221–239.

Gieseking, J. J. (2017). Messing with the attractiveness algorithm: A response to queering code/space. *Gender, Place and Culture, 24*(11), 1659–1665.

Gorman-Murray, A., & Nash, C. J. (2014). Mobile places, relational spaces: Conceptualizing an historical geography of Sydney's LGBTQ neighbourhoods. *Environment and Planning D: Society and Space, 32*(4), 622–641.

Gorman-Murray, A., & Nash, C. J. (2016). LGBT communities, identities and the politics of mobility: Moving from visibility to recognition in contemporary urban landscapes. In K. Browne & G. Brown (Eds.), *The Routledge research companion to geographies of sex and sexualities* (pp. 247–253). London: Routledge.

Gorman-Murray, A., & Waitt, G. (2009). Queer-friendly neighbourhoods: Interrogating social cohesion across sexual difference in two Australian neighbourhoods. *Environment and Planning A, 41*, 2855–2873.

Graham, M. (2013). Commentary: Geography/Internet: Ethereal alternate dimensions of cyberspace or grounded augmented realities? *The Geographical Journal, 179*, 177–182.

Haklay, M. (2010). How good is volunteered geographical information? A comparative study of OpenStreetMap and ordnance survey datasets. *Environment and Planning B: Planning and Design, 37*(4), 682–703.

Hannam, K., Sheller, M., & Urry, J. (2006). Editorial: Mobilities, immobilities and moorings. *Mobilities, 1*, 1–22.

Hecht, B. J., & Stephens, M. (2014). A tale of cities: Urban biases in volunteered geographic information. *ICWSM, 14*, 197–205.

Hjorth, L., Pink, S., & Horst, H. A. (2018). Being at home with privacy: Privacy and mundane intimacy through same-sex locative media practices. *International Journal of Communication, 12*, 1209–1227.

Jaspal, R. (2017). Gay men's construction and management of identity on Grindr. *Sexuality and Culture, 21*(1), 187–204.

Jin, S. T., Kong, H., Wu, R., & Sui, D. Z. (2018). Ridesourcing, the sharing economy, and the future of cities. *Cities, 76*, 96–104.

Kitchin, R., & Dodge, M. (2011). *Code/space*. Cambridge: MIT Press.

Knopp, L., & Brown, M. (2003). Queer diffusions. *Environment and Planning D: Society and Space, 21*(4), 409–424.

Kuntsman, A. (2007). Belonging through violence: Flaming, erasure, and performativity in queer migrant community. In K. O'Riordan & D. J. Phillips (Eds.), *Queer online: Media technology and sexuality* (pp. 101–120). New York: Peter Lang.

Kwan, M. P. (2002). Feminist visualization: Re-envisioning GIS as a method in feminist geographic research. *Annals of the Association of American Geographers, 92*(4), 645–661.

Leszczynski, A., & Elwood, S. (2015). Feminist geographies of new spatial media. *The Canadian Geographer/Le Géographe canadien, 59*(1), 12–28.
Mashhadi, A., Quattrone, G., & Capra, L. (2015). The impact of society on volunteered geographic information: The case of OpenStreetMap. In *OpenStreetMap in GIScience* (pp. 125–141). Cham: Springer.
Massey, D. (1994). *Space, place, and gender*. Minneapolis: University of Minnesota Press.
Miles, S. (2017). Sex in the digital city: Location-based dating apps and queer urban life. *Gender, Place and Culture, 24*(11), 1595–1610.
Miles, S. (2019). Going the distance: Locative dating technology and queer male practice-based identities. In C. J. Nash & A. Gorman-Murray (Eds.), *The geographies of digital sexuality*. London: Palgrave Macmillan.
Mooney, P., Corcoran, P., & Winstanley, A. C. (2010, November). Towards quality metrics for OpenStreetMap. In *Proceedings of the 18th SIGSPATIAL international conference on advances in geographic information systems* (pp. 514–517). ACM.
Mowlabocus, S. (2010). Look at me! Images, validation, and cultural currency on Gaydar. In C. Pullen & M. Cooper (Eds.), *LGBT identity and online new media* (pp. 215–228). London: Routledge.
Nash, C. J. (2006). Toronto's gay village (1969–1982): Plotting the politics of gay identity. *Canadian Geographer/Le Géographe canadien, 50*(1), 1–16.
Nash, C. J. (2013). The age of the "post-mo"? Toronto's gay village and a new generation. *Geoforum, 49*, 243–252.
Nash, C. J., & Bain, A. (2007). 'Reclaiming raunch'? Spatializing queer identities at Toronto women's bathhouse events. *Social and Cultural Geography, 8*(1), 47–62.
Nash, C. J., & Gorman-Murray, A. (2014). LGBT neighbourhoods and 'new mobilities': Towards understanding transformations in sexual and gendered urban landscapes. *International Journal of Urban and Regional Research, 38*(3), 756–772.
Nash, C. J., & Gorman-Murray, A. (2015a). Recovering the gay village: A Toronto and Sydney case study. *Historical Geographies, 43*, 84–105.
Nash, C. J., & Gorman-Murray, A. (2015b). Lesbians in the city: Mobilities and relational geographies. *Journal of Lesbian Studies, 19*(2), 173–191.
Nash, C. J., & Gorman-Murray, A. (2016). Digital technologies and sexualities in urban space. In K. Browne & G. Brown (Eds.), *Routledge research companion to geographies of sex and sexualities* (pp. 399–405). London: Routledge.

Oswin, N. (2008). Critical geographies and the uses of sexuality: Deconstructing queer space. *Progress in Human Geography, 32*(1), 89–103.

Pain, R. (2001). Gender, race, age and fear in the city. *Urban Studies, 38*(5–6), 899–913.

Podmore, J. (2006). Gone 'underground'? Lesbian visibility and the consolidation of queer space in Montréal. *Social and Cultural Geography, 7*(6), 595–625.

Podmore, J. (2013). Lesbians as village 'queers': The transformation of Montréal's lesbian nightlife in the 1990s. *ACME: An International E-Journal for Critical Geographies, 12*(2), 220–249.

Prestage, G., Bavinton, B., Grierson, J., Down, I., Keen, P., & Bradley, J. (2015). Online dating among Australian gay and bisexual men: Romance or hookup? *AIDS and Behaviour, 19*(10), 1905–1913.

Pullen, C., & Cooper, M. (Eds.). (2010). *LGBT identity and online new media*. London: Routledge.

Quattrone, G., Mashhadi, A., Quercia, D., Smith-Clarke, C., & Capra, L. (2014, February). Modelling growth of urban crowd-sourced information. In *Proceedings of the 7th ACM international conference on web search and data mining* (pp. 563–572). ACM.

Raj, S. (2013, August 2). 'How Grindr has transformed users' experience of intimacy. *The Guardian*. Retrieved from http://www.theguardian.com/commentisfree/2013/aug/02/grindr-sex-relationship-intimacy

Schuurman, N. (2002). Women and technology in geography: A cyborg manifesto for GIS. *The Canadian Geographer/Le Géographe canadien, 46*(3), 258–265.

Stephens, M. (2012, June 15–17). *Guns, Germans, and strip clubs*. Paper presented at SheepCamp 2012, in Lexington, KY.

Stephens, M. (2013). Gender and the GeoWeb: Divisions in the production of user-generated cartographic information. *GeoJournal, 78*(6), 981–996.

Uteng, T. P., & Cresswell, T. (2008). *Gendered mobilities*. New York: Routledge.

Wilken, R. (2009). Mobilizing place: Mobile media, peripatetics and the renegotiation of urban places. *Journal of Urban Technology, 15*(3), 39–55.

Wilson, M. W. (2011). Data matter(s): Legitimacy, coding, and qualifications-of-life. *Environment and Planning D: Society and Space, 29*(5), 857–872.

Zielstra, D., & Zipf, A. (2010, May). A comparative study of proprietary geodata and volunteered geographic information for Germany. In *13th AGILE international conference on geographic information science* (Vol. 2010).

4

Travel, Tinder and Gender in Digitally Mediated Tourism Encounters

Donna James, Jenna Condie, and Garth Lean

Introduction

Popularly referred to as 'Tinder Tourism' within media commentary (Taylor, 2017), new dating technologies now permeate travel spaces and shape the sexual encounters travellers have with other travellers and people who live in the destinations they visit. Travel researchers have long acknowledged the link between sex and tourism where sex is not only accepted in contemporary tourism but is also integral to its economic structures and geopolitics (Leheny, 1995; Ryan & Hall, 2005). As dating apps such as Tinder penetrate travel and tourism landscapes, it becomes pertinent that we continue to question how their materiality makes and remakes the socio-cultural politics of gender, race, sexuality and nationality (Condie, Lean, & James, 2018), which govern who can have sex with whom, and under what circumstances, within the spheres of travel and tourism.

D. James (✉) • J. Condie • G. Lean
Western Sydney University, Penrith, NSW, Australia
e-mail: d.james@westernsydney.edu.au; J.Condie@westernsydney.edu.au; g.lean@westernsydney.edu.au

C. Nash, A. Gorman-Murray (eds.), *The Geographies of Digital Sexuality*,
https://doi.org/10.1007/978-981-13-6876-9_4

The chapter commences with a literature review on the intersections between sex and tourism to situate the phenomenon of Tinder Tourism within the wider scope of a gendered and colonial global tourism industry. Following this, we analyse the User Experience Design of Tinder and explore how Tinder's reproduction of gendered attitudes and behaviours maintains the exclusion of women from the perceptively 'masculine' practice of independent leisure travel. To explicate the digitally mediated sexualities of Tinder Tourism, we draw data from a social survey questionnaire (*n* = 112) and face-to-face interviews with self-identifying Tinder Tourists (*n* = 10). Our survey respondents come from 28 different countries to date but are predominantly Australian (39%), heterosexual (78%) and between the ages of 18 and 29 (77%). With regard to gender, 56% of participants identify as women, 43% identify as men and 1% identify as 'other'. Our interview participants (five men and five women) were born in Australia, Canada, England, Iraq and China. We also include a critical analysis of Tinder's User Interface (UI) and User Experience Design (UXD) to ensure that the technology is included in the assemblages of sexuality and research (Fox & Alldred, 2013, 2015). We focus mainly on heterosexual dating practices from the traveller perspective given the data we have collected thus far.

Sex, Tourism and Technology

Researchers within tourism studies claim that sex, one of the oldest motivations for travel, has created and sustains a heavily gendered, colonial system underpinned by three broad principles: (1) Western male tourists who have been socialised with a sense of entitlement to sex with women in a global system that positions women of colour as overtly willing and sexually available; (2) poverty-stricken countries where women do paid work in the sex industry; and (3) political and economic institutions that reinforce and encourage Western men to travel to specific destinations to purchase sexual services (Enloe, 1989; Pritchard & Morgan, 2000b; Ryan & Hall, 2005). In articulating these three principles, we do not aim to simplify all sex during tourism as 'sex tourism', nor are we arguing that all women who participate in some form of sexual activity during tourism do so involuntarily or for economic reasons. We acknowledge that the links between sex and tourism are complex and multi-dimensional (Oppermann, 1999; Ryan & Hall, 2005), and are comprised of fluid gendered, raced and economic relations that shift within and across contexts (Sanchez Taylor, 2001, 2006). What we are arguing however, is that there are stark differences between men and women who engage in both commercial and non-commercial sexual practices during tourism, and these differences are unequal in terms of power (Jeffreys, 2003).

Western women might champion the anonymity of travel for enabling them to engage in non-commercial sex away from social surveillance (Thomas, 2005), and even procure the services of male sex workers during travel (Sanchez Taylor, 2001), but they do so in a context where men are not subject to the same sexual double standards and do not exist under the same forms of embodied self-surveillance (Berdychevsky & Gibson, 2015). As feminist scholars have argued, because men 'do the penetrating' and gain social status by engaging in sexual conquests with women, they almost always maintain their dominant position in the sex class hierarchy, regardless of their racial or economic status in relation to the woman in question (Jeffreys, 2003). Furthermore, even where Western women attempt to challenge traditional notions of patriarchy by procuring the services of male sex workers during travel, there are discursive limits to the identity claims that they can make. For example, unlike men who are 'sex tourists', women are more likely to be 'romance tourists' (Pruitt & LaFont, 1995). Similarly, men who do sex work are 'beach boys', 'gigolos', 'sanky pankies' or 'romantic entrepreneurs', and are not the deeply stigmatised 'prostitute', 'hooker' or 'whore' (Jeffreys, 2003). To equate the sexual behaviour of men and women during tourism is to overlook the "relations of power, the effects, the meanings and the contexts of the behaviour" (Jeffreys, 2003, p. 236), and as such, we maintain that sex during tourism is governed by heteropatriarchal and colonial conventions that disproportionately disempower women, particularly women of colour.

The production and continuity of gender inequality have serious implications for the geopolitical relations between countries where host countries are cast as the feminine object that must be observed, consumed and mastered under a masculine gaze (Sparke, 1996). As Graburn (1983) describes, nations can be "forced into the 'female' role of servitude" where "pleasure seeking, 'penetrating' tourists of powerful nations are cast in the 'male' role" (p. 441).

The consequence is a situation where local women in host nations become part of the package, which paints the spaces and places of tourism as a man's paradise in the drive for economic profit (Graburn, 1983). Because sex sells and works to maintain and grow international mass tourism, it makes sense that local women are presented subserviently in tourism marketing material and travel packages (Morgan & Pritchard, 2012; Pritchard & Morgan, 2000a, 2000b; Sirakaya & Sonmez, 2000), even in places such as Thailand (Hobbs, Pattalung, & Chandler, 2011) where governments have tried to neutralise their 'sex tourism' reputation through promotional campaigns (Nuttavuthisit, 2007). Yet, despite worldwide efforts to address gender inequality, the continued normalisation of sex and tourism as one and the same continues to amplify colonial attitudes and sexist behaviours that greatly limit women's capacity to participate in leisure travel (Jordan & Aitchison, 2008; Wilson & Little, 2005).

New media technologies are reshaping how Western women travel, particularly those who travel alone, by offering a sense of security and community (Germann Molz & Paris, 2015). Being connected and simply having a smartphone on your person acts as a 'safety net' when off the beaten track (Paris, Berger, Rubin, & Casson, 2015). However, researchers exercise caution around the potential for technology to further burden women who choose to participate in some forms of tourism. As Germann Molz and Paris (2015) describe, "new mediums for communicating … make it easier for travellers to meet like-minded wanderers, but also require new strategies for re-establishing a sense of anonymity and distance when those relationships threaten, fade or misfire" (p. 186). Furthermore, as technologies become central to the apparatus of gender and ethnicity construction in our society (Mackenzie & Wajcman, 1999), the capacity for racialised and gendered inequalities to be embedded in, reproduced through and amplified by technology should not be ignored. As we will argue in this chapter, Tinder Tourism is a deeply colonial, heteropatriarchal practice that, constituted by the intra-action (Barad, 2003)[1] of human and non-human forces, positions women as commodities to be consumed by male tourists from powerful and wealthy countries.

[1] Karen Barad (2003) defines Intra-action as, "a profound conceptual shift" where a typical "separation between 'subject' and 'object'" are reconceptualised to ensure "relata do not preexist relations; rather, relata within-phenomena emerge through specific intra-actions" (p. 815).

Travel, Tinder and Inequality

With more than 50 million users worldwide, it should be unsurprising that many travellers download Tinder during travel to remedy the relative ineffectiveness of travel-specific social apps such as Backpackr, which travellers claim do not work well in some locations (Lean, Condie, & James, forthcoming). Tinder has a much larger revenue stream than many travel-specific apps, and a comparably larger and more geographically diverse user-base. What might be surprising, however, is that while many young people are downloading Tinder to use during travel or to connect with travellers coming in to their local area (Lean et al., forthcoming), not all are able to embrace Tinder's connective capacity in the same way. As we have described before "we do not all travel with Tinder equally" (Condie et al., 2018, p. 111).

The potential for socio-cultural constraints to limit a traveller or host's capacity to engage in Tinder Tourism is perhaps best witnessed on the basis of gender. As researchers have noted, men and women use Tinder in different ways (Tyson, Perta, Haddidi, & Seto, 2016) and are typically looking for different things (Lopes & Vogel, 2017), with women travellers claiming that men are almost always using Tinder for casual sex during travel. Because Tinder's user-base in travel and tourism landscapes comprises a melting pot of people who are all seeking different, and sometimes multiple kinds of engagements through the one platform (Lean et al., forthcoming), it would be naïve to assume that intentions, motivations and expectations will be evenly matched. While male travellers travelling through 'Western' countries described that they were "more trying to party and meet with other travellers" (Hong, 25–29, heterosexual man, China), those moving through the Global South described they were also using Tinder to seek out 'local' women. As Jeff (25–29, bisexual man, Australia) describes:

> It was easy to get matches as a foreigner. Away field advantage. I used Tinder to meet local girls—most of whom I would not have access to otherwise. It was also helpful to meet English-speaking expats who become friends.

This distinction Jeff makes between 'other travellers' who could become friends, and 'local women' who can be 'accessed' highlights Tinder Tourism's problematic production of colonial attitudes, which could lead to serious consequences for 'host' women from 'female' (Graburn, 1983) nations who are seeking platonic connections. As Lawrence's (50–54, heterosexual man, USA) response indicates, Western men who are socialised to believe women of colour are overtly willing and sexually available assume that all women found in the sexual space of Tinder are 'already interested' in casual sex:

> I have returned to [meet] friends and fuck women with these apps, began relationships and friendships since 2012. I travel to Asia 6–15 times a year and within the USA 12 times a year. I use [dating apps] to meet women because I like human companionship and this way I know the people are already interested.

This assumption however, is simply inaccurate. Many women from the Global South described how they used Tinder mainly "to meet new people and share about their travel experiences, culture, life and etc." (Indah, 25–29, heterosexual woman, Indonesia) and were making a conscientious effort to avoid Western men who assumed entitlement to their bodies. As Indah describes: "some of [the] people just wanna hook up but we can avoid them once we know their intentions". In fact, Western men's sexual advances were so frightening to some women that their capacity to engage with Tinder was greatly limited as a result. As Fitri (25–29, bisexual woman, Indonesia) describes: "Many of them kinda scared me [because] they're only asking me for sex and [something] like that so for my own protection I didn't meet them."

Tinder is also "intimately knotted with technology and its tentacles of networked connectedness" in a social media ecosystem of entangled platforms such as Facebook, Instagram, Snapchat and Spotify, which blurs the 'agential cut' we might have once more easily placed between home and away (Condie et al., 2018, p. 102). As such, women who use Tinder during travel report that they not only need to protect their reputations but also their personal safety. While male participants like Tony (25–29, heterosexual man, Australia), for example, describe that Tinder use during travel is, "much easier" because "your security blanket is really gone", his concerns about maintaining anonymity are wholly centred around protecting his reputation so as not to appear "desperate".

Contrarily, women participants describe that when using Tinder during travel, or to meet male travellers in their place of residence, they invent new tactics for 'stalking' or investigating men through other social media platforms to confirm their identity while ensuring they did not give away their own personal information, citing fears about threats to their physical safety in the future. As Aria (21–24, heterosexual woman, Canada) emphasises, "safety is always a big thing". While Anna (25–29, heterosexual woman, Australia) recounts having felt "extremely violated and genuinely concerned for [her own] safety" when a man tracked her down and stalked her on several social media platforms (Facebook, LinkedIn and Twitter), Ryan (25–29, heterosexual man, Australia) jokes instead about his encounter with a woman who was overly keen and using explicit sexual language as 'entertaining', as he draws on gender stereotypes of 'crazy' women:

> There was one girl that I was talking to and she was just fucking psycho via text, but it was really entertaining so I just kept it going ... she was alluding to a lot of sexual things and then like anal and bondage and that sort of stuff ... I can't remember the specifics, but I remember her just being really fucking crazy, and it was entertaining but I obviously didn't go and meet up with her, [laughs] fuck that, I don't want a head case on my hands.

This not only demonstrates that male travellers find women who behave in sexually inappropriate or explicit ways as humorous rather than scary but also alludes to the sexual double-standards that continue to be reinforced by men during travel, and act to govern the 'appropriate' behaviour of women. As our participants described, women in monogamous relationships were unable to participate in Tinder Tourism in the same way that attached men could. While Ivy (25–29, heterosexual woman, Australia) describes, "That whole having a boyfriend thing really hinders your Tindering", men such as William (25–29, heterosexual man, England) reported no such hindrance. As William explains, while using Tinder did necessitate having "a slightly awkward conversation" with his girlfriend prior to leaving his home country, receiving a direct sexual approach from a prostitute who was trying to "entice" him was only really difficult because there was a "language barrier". As William's experience evidences, despite common knowledge that commercial and non-commercial sex are brought into the space of Tinder during travel, men are not expected to avoid using Tinder because their dominant position in the sex class hierarchy (Jeffreys, 2003) guarantees they always remain in a position of power when they match with women. William describes:

> It was a difficult conversation and [my girlfriend] actually understood and I showed her my profile I was using and then sending her screenshots being like 'Look! This prostitute wants to sleep with me!' So it was hilarious, but the initial conversation was actually quite tricky.

Anonymity Is No Match for Masculinity

Despite it having been widely asserted that the anonymity experienced in tourist settings can enable new freedoms for women (Berdychevsky & Gibson, 2015), 'Tinder Tourism' is a practice that can never be fully available to women. In addition to feeling disrespected after frequently experiencing direct sexual approaches from men at home (Lopes & Vogel, 2017), women who travel now contend with being made to feel unsafe through digitally mediated interactions during travel also. Participant responses such as Avery's (21–24, heterosexual woman, USA) below, illustrate how the normalisation of direct sexual approaches from men, and their role in perpetuating the predator-unsafety prey dynamic that women experience on Tinder (Lopes & Vogel, 2017) can amplify the vulnerability that women already feel when travelling alone in an unfamiliar place (Wilson & Little, 2005):

> I was traveling alone in Siem Reap, Cambodia and was looking for some friends to grab a drink with. Backpackr wasn't giving me much luck so I downloaded Bumble and Tinder. Obviously I know these apps aren't exactly looking for friends but I was hopeful! While I chatted with some

> pretty nice guys it just didn't feel super safe meeting up with them when I'm alone and there's no one checking in on me. Also kind of annoying how quickly it turns from let's grab a beer to you're really pretty let's hook up. How about no.

When Tinder intra-acts (Barad, 2003) with travel, the sexual spheres of heteronormativity hamper women's mobilities and reinforce social geographies of fear (Valentine, 1989). Much of what we know about 'Tinder Tourism', therefore, can be tied back to the patriarchal historical roots of both travel and Tinder. Practices of travel are deeply located in historical narratives of risk and adventure where, despite women having participated in travel for centuries, men are typically seen as the pioneers and adventurers (Craik, 1997; Elsrud, 2001). Consequently, women who wish to participate in travel have had to adopt 'masculine' traits (Elsrud, 2001; Falconer, 2011) and deal with sociocultural constraints and criticisms that do not equally affect men (Jordan & Aitchison, 2008). The masculinity of travel creates dilemmas for women, where, in trying to embody masculine narratives, feelings of inequality and vulnerability are internalised and obscured under the guise of empowerment (Falconer, 2011). This might be why the sexual behaviour of women travellers is typically explored through the lens of situational disinhibition, anonymity or liminality (Berdychevsky & Gibson, 2015), and not the sociocultural and non-human forces that contribute to women's ongoing exclusion from public places.

It is not just men's behaviour which excludes women from places and spaces though (Jordan & Aitchison, 2008). Places and technologies are deeply political and due to the structural exclusion of minority groups from their development, masculinised and heterosexually informed (Mackenzie & Wajcman, 1999; Valentine, 1993). The combination of masculinised digital-material spaces therefore, can be conceptualised as collective determinants of women's capacity to 'be' in tourist spaces in the same way that men can. William's (25–29, heterosexual man, England) recount of a visit to India with his fiancé demonstrates how places that are inherently gendered, when combined with men's harassing behaviour, can greatly affect women's experiences:

> India for example is a lovely place, but if I was a single female traveller I'd be weary. Because even walking around with my fiancé, she'll be next to me, and there'll be Indian men just staring at her, and I'm right next to her the entire time ... and there's guys that are walking along with the umbrella and they're literally ducking down to have a look under and see her—very creepy. But it's that type of thing—as a male I just don't have to deal with it and it's much easier for me and there's much less risk involved if I were to go to random places.

If we conceive that masculinised activities (travel) that take place in masculinised spaces and places (tourist settings) objectify and alienate women, then we must also conceive that women's empowerment is not likely to be sought through the attribution of masculinised technological artefacts that, described by Tinder's creator as "your most dependable wingman" (Tinder on the App Store, 2018), sexualise, objectify and alienate them further. As MacKenzie and Wajcman (1999) describe, "Even if it is mistaken to see technologies as requiring particular patterns of social relations to go along with them, some technologies are, in given social circumstances, more compatible with some relations than with others" (p. 4). And this is, we argue, applicable to Tinder.

Travelling with Tinder: The 'Wing*man*' in Your Pocket

As with travel, much of what we know about Tinder and its heteropatriarchal roots can be traced back to where and how it was created, how it is represented in social discourses and how it is used and by whom. Having been designed by a group of men to reflect the frat house dating culture of American college campuses and launched through a series of college parties in 2012 (Bosker, 2013), Tinder has become a sexual sphere of heteronormative interactions. Armed with a design that combines speed and familiar micro-actions with visual politics (David & Cambre, 2016), Tinder transforms contemporary dating into a game (David & Cambre, 2016), which journalists claim has led to the rejection of traditional monogamy in favour of casual sex (Sales, 2015). As Hobbs, Owen, and

Gerber (2017) argue, these claims about Tinder's 'liquification' of love (Bauman, 2003) do not reflect its reality; many people still engage with the platform in the hope of forming meaningful long-term partnerships. Tinder's users, however, are not all using the platform for the same reason. Our survey data reveals that men are using Tinder for 'casual sex' or 'hook-ups' when travelling, and/or meeting travellers in their place of residence, far more frequently than women. In fact, men and women often have conflicting ideas about what Tinder is as a social space and what it should be used for during travel. Expectations often did not match reality:

> So all I'd heard [about Tinder] was obviously from my guy friends and one of them who sort of pushed me toward using it, he actually met people and he goes for the hook-ups, never relationships kind of, but he does it pretty obviously, so I guess going in that was the expectation going in, that people that were using the app were mostly all like that. But I guess I realised like, my expectation changed from that to, after talking to a couple of people that I matched with it really didn't seem like that was what was going on. Like, I actually haven't met any girl that I thought was just looking for casual sex. (Hong, 25–29, heterosexual man, China)

While Tinder's reputation might shape the social discourses that surround it, social media platforms are also shaped by the mediated practices and communicative habits of their users (Gibbs, Meese, Arnold, Nansen, & Carter, 2015) who adopt, resist or appropriate their affordances (Duguay, 2017). Tinder is better understood as a space where meanings are not static but consistently negotiated by users. Differing interpretations can be problematic for several reasons but are most problematic if you are a woman using Tinder to make platonic connections in a foreign country. As researchers have noted before, sharing a space with people using a dating app for different reasons can create tension (Blackwell, Birnholtz, & Abbott, 2014). Some people resist the capacity for sexual spaces to be neutralised and continue to assume others within that space are seeking out casual sex (Blackwell et al., 2014; Shield, 2017). As such, 'looking for friends' can be interpreted to mean 'looking for friends with benefits' (Blackwell et al., 2014). While street harassment that is unwanted and uninvited was classed by our participants as sexual harassment, men's unwanted sexual advances on Tinder, or after meeting someone from Tinder, were normalised and written off as a miscommunication between two people who were simply "not looking for the same kind of relationship" (Kate, 21–24, bisexual woman, France). Yet, it is women who are burdened by the normalisation of this sexualised behaviour, and not men who often saw sex as "a bonus" (Hayden, 35–39, heterosexual man, Australia).

Women are, by designed default, made responsible for their own safety if they use Tinder during travel. Tinder's response to complaints about women's harassment on the app instigated the introduction of a designed-in feature entitled 'Menprovement', which asks women to respond to men's offensive behaviour with a series of 'wrap on the wrist' GIFs. With such moves, Tinder continues to serve a heteropatriarchal function by trivialising women's safety concerns. By positioning men as in need of only light-hearted reprimand, GIF responses reinforce that women are responsible for their own safety. Many of our women participants inferred that it is their job to ensure they clearly communicate to men if sex and sexual dialogue is unwanted. As Aria (21–24, heterosexual woman, Canada) explains, women should place disclaimers in their bios such as "I'm just using this for travelling" to avoid "an individual [perceiving that] you're putting yourself out there for a hook up". This behaviour is normalised within the context of male participants knowing that "girls don't want to meet with travellers on Tinder … because [Tinder] has the reputation of … boys who are just looking for hook-ups" (Hong, 25–29, heterosexual man, China).

Female participants acknowledge that when they did make their intentions clear, they were often met with sarcasm: "I found that sometimes, people would match with me only to be able to chat with me to criticize the fact that I was trying to make friends on a 'dating app'" (Laura, 25–29, queer woman, USA). This pressure could have serious consequences for women, who are socialised in a way that makes it more difficult for them to say no to men (Motley & Reeder, 1995) and more vulnerable both physically and emotionally to sexual risk-taking (Impett & Peplau, 2003). Furthermore, the social policing of Tinder as a 'sexual space' had implications for women that extended well beyond their initial attempts to manage their personal safety.

Women who found themselves in unsafe situations often believed they were at fault for disrupting the sexual space of Tinder with their attempts to form platonic connections. Men largely characterise staying safe on Tinder as a "girl concern" (Hong, 25–29, heterosexual man, China) whereas women tend to blame Tinder and not the men themselves for unwanted sexual encounters: "it is Tinder so I don't have high expectations of the men I talk to" (Leah, 21–24, heterosexual woman, Canada). Further, fears about having to engage in casual sex would often inform women's decisions not to meet up with men at all. As Anna (25–29, heterosexual woman, Australia) tells us:

> I was travelling through Europe solo for 4 weeks, and was interested in meeting like-minded men who would be interested in sharing a meal or coffee with me. While my Tinder profile was active the entire time, and I had over hundreds of invitations from men enthusiastically offering to show me around, I decided not to meet up with anyone. Primarily because, upon pondering over it a while longer, I felt that there was something inadvertently transactional about this kind of arrangement—in that if they take me out and show me around, I would be expected to reciprocate the generosity through casual sex, which I am in no way interested in. I felt that men were probably aroused by the fact that I was temporary.

While Anna's testament demonstrates how men perceive women's temporality in travel as novel, it also elucidates how Tinder speeds up the time-compressed nature of the holiday and eliminates the formative steps for building trust and closeness (David & Cambre, 2016). Unlike in social sharing networks (such as CouchSurfing, Ridesharing, and WWOOFing), where meaningful connections arise quickly due to the sharing of personal stories in face-to-face encounters (Bialski, 2012; Germann Molz, 2014), Tinder's architectural erosion of the time-distance necessary for creating meaningful human relationships (David & Cambre, 2016) disrupts the formative factors of the 'sexual script', which governs who women should have sex with, when and what sexual activities they should engage in (Thomas, 2005). As Thomas (2005) describes, although the 'sexual script' is typically sped up during travel, sexual intercourse is typically seen as the 'ultimate' point of the relationship trajectory in holiday romances (p. 578). Macy's (25–29, heterosexual woman,

Australia) experience, for example, demonstrates how the 'sexual script' plays out where tourists use Tinder to mediate their sexual engagements during travel:

> When I was travelling it was really just for casual sex. I was on-campus, like lived in a dorm, and the guy that I met with a couple of times, he was staying in a motel because he was working so we went and got take away beers and hung out there. But the other guy who I slept with, the first time I met him between two bins [laughs] … we just like met halfway walking along the river trail, which is like the main road and I was drunk and so then there was these two industrial bins so we just went between there so I gave him a blow job and left [laughs].

With the acceleration packaged into Tinder's swipe-activated UI (David & Cambre, 2016), various aspects of the 'sexual script' are skipped almost entirely. This might explain why women find it frustrating to negotiate the architecture and culture of Tinder amidst their embedded understanding of how sex and relationships should work. William's (25–29, heterosexual man, England) recounting of a conversation he had with a female friend illustrates the disconnect between men and women's understanding of dating on Tinder:

> She didn't want to use Tinder because she thought it was all about one night stands, because that is what it's synonymous with now … she was saying that she met this guy and she thought it was going quite well, but then she found out he was dating like 3 other people. It's like that's kind of typical. After like 3 or 4 dates I wouldn't say sleep with this person during this period anyway but after 3 or 4 dates, before you sleep with them, have that discussion and go hey, I like you, I want to be exclusive and move forward. You can't and she was actually saying oh he was cheating on me. And I'm like oh well not really, he was just dating 3 or 4 people much as I probably would have at the time.

As William's story suggests, men and women have different ideas about how the 'sexual script' should play out with Tinder. This is likely why women who use Tinder report feeling disrespected, and why researchers have criticised Tinder for exacerbating the 'predator-unsafety prey dynamic' (Lopes & Vogel, 2017) that women already experience in public spaces (Pain, 1991, 1997; Valentine, 1989).

While our male participants championed Tinder's speeding up of time, which made finding women "endlessly more practical and accurate than stumbling your way through a bar trying to meet a fitting match" (Aleksander, 21–24, heterosexual man, Belgium), they also acknowledged Tinder's capacity to make women less trusting of them. In turn, Tinder made it more difficult to meet tourist women in travel and tourism settings:

> There are some girls, I think they go into it thinking I'm not going to meet with a guy, unless something drastic happens. Whereas I'm more like, OK like swiping right and matching is just the beginning and just the kick-start to the meet up that is going to happen soon. I take it like that, and I tell them, yeah I get to know people better in person, like that is just how I interact, so I ask people to meet up fairly early, compared to anyone else I've talked to and um, there are people who just stop talking to you after I ask, because I guess they don't want to say no. (Hong, 25–29, heterosexual man, China)

By the logic that anonymity and liminality, described as the transcendence of the "classifications that normally locate states and positions in cultural space" (Turner, 2002; van Gennep, 1960), enable women new freedoms to engage in sexual risk-taking during travel, women should be able to swipe, match and meet as liberally as men can. Yet, Hong's attestation that women often stopped talking because they 'don't want to say no' tells us much about how embodied forms of self-surveillance still operate in digital-material tourist spaces. While anonymity might enable women new opportunities for making social connections in travel without having to worry about social surveillance (Berdychevsky & Gibson, 2015), Tinder's reputation as a hook-up app (David & Cambre, 2016; Duguay, 2017) and its amplification of (and dismissal of) sexist behaviours maintains that travelling with Tinder is not experienced equally by women. This is deeply problematic when we consider that "physical travel not only has the potential to transform travellers, but can also have significant impacts upon the social collectives to which a traveller returns" (Lean, 2016).

Conclusion: Technology Is Not a Travel-Equaliser

Travel is a deeply colonial, heteropatriarchal practice that, constituted by the intra-action of human and non-human forces (Condie et al., 2018), continues to position local and tourist women as commodities to be consumed by men. As such, the sexualised language of tourism and the problematic power dynamics that come with it should be challenged. So too should the co-option of heavily gendered, sexualised tourist discourses by Tinder and other mobile dating technologies that closely associate travel with sex. As more sexist technologies become deeply intertwined with the continuum that ranges from commercial (sex tourism) to non-commercial (holiday romances) sex, we disagree with Ryan and Hall (2005) who take the stance that there is no point challenging the sexual discourses of tourism. When the dehumanisation of women within tourism is furthered by gamified socio-sexual encounters with Tinder, problematic power relations are maintained and perpetrators remain unaccountable for their actions. As we have elsewhere argued, "Tinder provides more than snapshots into contemporary social life and its networked intimacies: it is a way-finder, knowledge-generator, friendship-giver, sex-sorter, game-changer, time-passer, soul-destroyer, esteem-giver, self-depressor, sushi-train, love-machine" (Condie et al., 2018, p. 112).

What Tinder is not however, is a travel-equaliser. With a more progressive mindset, tourism and the technologies that now accompany the traveller could be orientated towards more productive and respectful encounters. However, before we can investigate the opportunities that exist to degender technologies, we must seek to investigate opportunities to decolonise them, which can only be achieved by decolonising our research practices, centring issues of race and nationality, and speaking to women living in countries where Western travellers visit and interact with them via new dating platforms. Following Jeffrey's (2018) call to stop conceptualising "women in the West as 'guest' and women in the rest as 'host'", we aspire to employ anti-colonial, new materialist modes of inquiry (Condie et al., 2018) and a "feminist research ethics of care" (Condie, Lean, & Wilcockson, 2017, p. 153) to generate knowledge and responses that serve the best interests of 'host' women who, commonly positioned in hegemonic tourism discourses as commodities to be consumed by men from wealthy, powerful countries, are also using Tinder to enable new social connections during travel.

References

Barad, K. (2003). Posthumanist performativity: Toward an understanding of how matter comes to matter. *Signs: Journal of Women in Culture and Society, 28*(3), 801–831.

Bauman, Z. (2003). *Liquid love: On the frailty of human bonds*. Cambridge: Polity.

Berdychevsky, L., & Gibson, H. J. (2015). Women's sexual sensation seeking and risk taking in leisure travel. *Journal of Leisure Research, 47*(5), 621–646.

Bialski, P. (2012). *Becoming intimately mobile*. New York: Peter Lang.

Blackwell, C., Birnholtz, J., & Abbott, C. (2014). Seeing and being seen: Co-situation and impression formation using Grindr, a location-aware gay dating app. *New Media & Society, 17*(7), 1117–1136.

Bosker, B. (2013). Here's one of the college kids helping Tinder take over campuses. *Huffington Post* [online]. Retrieved May 20, 2018, from http://www.huffingtonpost.com.au/entry/tinder-app-college-kids_n_3530585

Condie, J., Lean, G., & James, D. (2018). Tinder matters: Swiping right to unlock research fields. In C. Costa & J. Condie (Eds.), *Doing research in and on the digital: Research methods across fields of inquiry* (pp. 102–115). London: Routledge.

Condie, J., Lean, G., & Wilcockson, B. (2017). The trouble with Tinder: The ethical complexities of researching location-aware social discovery apps. In *The ethics of online research* (pp. 135–158). Bingley: Emerald Publishing Limited.

Craik, J. (1997). The culture of tourism. In C. Rojek & J. Urry (Eds.), *Touring cultures: Transformations of travel and theory* (pp. 113–136). London: Routledge.

David, G., & Cambre, C. (2016). Screened intimacies: Tinder and the swipe logic. *Social Media + Society, 2*(2). https://doi.org/10.1177/2056305116641976

Duguay, S. (2017). Dressing up Tinderella: Interrogating authenticity claims on the mobile dating app Tinder. *Information, Communication and Society, 20*(3), 351–367.

Elsrud, T. (2001). Risk creation in traveling: Backpacker adventure narration. *Annals of Tourism Research, 28*(3), 597–617.
Enloe, C. (1989). *Bananas, beaches and bases: Making feminist sense of international politics*. London: Pandora.
Falconer, E. (2011). Risk, excitement and emotional conflict in women's travel narratives. *Recreation and society in Africa, Asia and Latin America, 1*(2). Retrieved from https://journal.lib.uoguelph.ca/index.php/rasaala/article/view/1511
Fox, N. J., & Alldred, P. (2013). The sexuality-assemblage: Desire, affect, anti-humanism. *The Sociological Review, 61*(4), 769–789.
Fox, N. J., & Alldred, P. (2015). New materialist social inquiry: Designs, methods and the research-assemblage. *International Journal of Social Research Methodology, 18*(4), 399–414.
Germann Molz, J. (2014). Toward a network hospitality. *First Monday, 19*(3). https://doi.org/10.5210/fm.v19i3.4824
Germann Molz, J., & Paris, C. M. (2015). The social affordances of flashpacking: Exploring the mobility nexus of travel and communication. *Mobilities, 10*(2), 173–192.
Gibbs, M., Meese, J., Arnold, M., Nansen, B., & Carter, M. (2015). #Funeral and Instagram: Death, social media, and platform vernacular. *Information, Communication and Society, 18*(3), 255–268.
Graburn, N. H. (1983). The anthropology of tourism. *Annals of Tourism Research, 10*(1), 9–33.
Hobbs, M., Owen, S., & Gerber, L. (2017). Liquid love? Dating apps, sex, relationships and the digital transformation of intimacy. *Journal of Sociology, 53*(2), 271–284.
Hobbs, J. D., Pattalung, P. N., & Chandler, R. C. (2011). Advertising Phuket's nightlife on the internet: A case study of double binds and hegemonic masculinity in sex tourism. *Sojourn: Journal of Social Issues in Southeast Asia, 26*(1), 80–104.
Impett, E. A., & Peplau, L. A. (2003). Sexual compliance: Gender, motivational, and relationship perspectives. *Journal of Sex Research, 40*(1), 87–100.
Jeffrey, H. L. (2018). Tourism and gendered hosts and guests. *Tourism Review*. https://doi.org/10.1108/TR-02-2017-0024
Jeffreys, S. (2003). Sex tourism: Do women do it too? *Leisure Studies, 22*(3), 223–238.
Jordan, F., & Aitchison, C. (2008). Tourism and the sexualisation of the gaze: Solo female tourists' experiences of gendered power, surveillance and embodiment. *Leisure Studies, 27*(3), 329–349.

Lean, G. (2016). *Transformative travel in a mobile world*. Boston, MA: CABI.
Lean, G., Condie, J., & James, D. (forthcoming). *Around the world in 80 (000) Tinder swipes: The use of location-aware social discovery applications during travel and tourism*.
Leheny, D. (1995). A political economy of Asian sex tourism. *Annals of Tourism Research, 22*(2), 367–384.
Lopes, M. R., & Vogel, C. (2017, August). Women's perspective on using Tinder: A user study of gender dynamics in a mobile device application. In *Proceedings of the 35th ACM international conference on the design of communication* (p. 12). ACM.
MacKenzie, D., & Wajcman, J. (1999). *The social shaping of technology* (2nd ed.). Buckingham: Open University Press.
Morgan, N., & Pritchard, A. (2012). *Advertising in tourism and leisure*. Oxford: Routledge.
Motley, M. T., & Reeder, H. M. (1995). Unwanted escalation of sexual intimacy: Male and female perceptions of connotations and relational consequences of resistance messages. *Communications Monographs, 62*(4), 355–382.
Nuttavuthisit, K. (2007). Branding Thailand: Correcting the negative image of sex tourism. *Place Branding and Public Diplomacy, 3*(1), 21–30.
Oppermann, M. (1999). Sex tourism. *Annals of Tourism Research, 26*(2), 251–266.
Pain, R. (1991). Space, sexual violence and social control: Integrating geographical and feminist analyses of women's fear of crime. *Progress in Human Geography, 15*(4), 415–431.
Pain, R. H. (1997). Social geographies of women's fear of crime. *Transactions of the Institute of British Geographers*, 231–244.
Paris, C. M., Berger, E. A., Rubin, S., & Casson, M. (2015). Disconnected and unplugged: Experiences of technology induced anxieties and tensions while traveling. In I. Tussyadiah & A. Inversini (Eds.), *Information and communication technologies in tourism* (pp. 803–816). London: Springer.
Pritchard, A., & Morgan, N. J. (2000a). Constructing tourism landscapes-gender, sexuality and space. *Tourism Geographies, 2*(2), 115–139.
Pritchard, A., & Morgan, N. J. (2000b). Privileging the male gaze: Gendered tourism landscapes. *Annals of Tourism Research, 27*(4), 884–905.
Pruitt, D., & LaFont, S. (1995). For love and money: Romance tourism in Jamaica. *Annals of Tourism Research, 22*(2), 422–440.
Ryan, C., & Hall, M. C. (2005). *Sex tourism: Marginal people and liminalities*. London: Routledge.

Sales, N. J. (2015). Tinder and the dawn of the "dating apocalypse". *Vanity Fair*. Retrieved from http://www.vanityfair.com/culture/2015/08/tinder-hook-up-culture-end-of-dating
Sanchez Taylor, J. (2001). Dollars are a girl's best friend? Female tourists' sexual behaviour in the Caribbean. *Sociology, 35*(3), 749–764.
Sanchez Taylor, J. (2006). Female sex tourism: A contradiction in terms? *Feminist Review, 83*(1), 42–59.
Shield, A. D. (2017). New in town: Gay immigrants and geosocial dating apps. In A. Dhoest & L. Szulc (Eds.), *LGBTQs, media and culture in Europe* (pp. 244–261). New York: Routledge.
Sirakaya, E., & Sonmez, S. (2000). Gender images in state tourism brochures: An overlooked area in socially responsible tourism marketing. *Journal of Travel Research, 38*(4), 353–362.
Sparke, M. (1996). Displacing the field in fieldwork: Masculinity, metaphor and space. In N. Duncan (Ed.), *Bodyspace: Destabilising geographies of gender and sexuality* (pp. 212–233). London: Routledge.
Taylor, A. (2017). Tinder tourists: 'Quick sex app' replaces Lonely Planet as tool for travellers. *The Sydney Morning Herald*. Retrieved from https://www.smh.com.au/lifestyle/life-and-relationships/tinder-tourists-quick-sex-app-replaces-lonely-planet-as-tool-for-travellers-20171004-gyugo5.htm
Thomas, M. (2005). 'What happens in Tenerife stays in Tenerife': Understanding women's sexual behaviour on holiday. *Culture, Health and Sexuality, 7*(6), 571–584.
Tinder on the App Store. (2018). Retrieved from https://itunes.apple.com/au/app/tinder/id547702041?mt=8
Turner, V. (2002). Liminality and communitas. In M. Lambek (Ed.), *A reader in the anthropology of religion* (pp. 358–374). Malden, MA: Blackwell.
Tyson, G., Perta, V. C., Haddadi, H., & Seto, M. C. (2016, August). A first look at user activity on Tinder. In *2016 IEEE/ACM international conference on advances in social networks analysis and mining (ASONAM)* (pp. 461–466). IEEE.
Valentine, G. (1989). The geography of women's fear. *Area, 21*, 385–390.
Valentine, G. (1993). (Hetero) sexing space: Lesbian perceptions and experiences of everyday spaces. *Environment and Planning D: Society and Space, 11*(4), 395–413.
van Gennep, A. (1960). *The rites of passage*. Chicago: University of Chicago Press.
Wilson, E., & Little, D. E. (2005). A "relative escape"? The impact of constraints on women who travel solo. *Tourism Review International, 9*(2), 155–175.

5

'I get my lovin' on the run': Digital Nomads, Constant Travel, and Nurturing Romantic Relationships

Beverly Yuen Thompson

Introduction

In 1997, Tsugio Makimoto and David Manners published their future-looking manifesto *Digital Nomad* at a moment when the internet—and its possibilities—were just entering the popular imagination. The authors present a vision of how the new technology could revolutionise modern life—especially by inverting work and leisure. No longer would residential location be based on commuting distance to cubicles—workers could disperse around the globe, to more temperate climates, and work the hours they wanted, with the magic of logging on to the computer. The authors envision a lifestyle that would (eventually) spark a movement—'digital nomadism.' Digital nomads are location-independent workers who use their freedom from office commuting to travel internationally. While digital nomadism is a popular topic for travel blogs and business magazines, empirical research on the lifestyle has lagged behind (Thompson, 2018). This chapter explores the leisure side of the digital

B. Y. Thompson (✉)
Siena College, Albany, NY, USA
e-mail: bthompson@siena.edu

C. Nash, A. Gorman-Murray (eds.), *The Geographies of Digital Sexuality*,
https://doi.org/10.1007/978-981-13-6876-9_5

nomad lifestyle; in particular, the dating and love lives of those who are constantly on the move. As digital nomads' work-lives are dependent on and managed through technology, the parallel uses of the internet to organise their social and dating lives are explored, focusing on their use of online meet-up groups and dating websites. Using a sociological approach to explore the concept of digital nomadism, this chapter will briefly overview how the lifestyle has been defined in the academic literature. The sociological literature on family and online dating will prove useful to understand how technology has intersected with dating patterns.

This chapter contributes to the empirical research on the leisure side of the digital nomadism phenomena as well as the literature focusing on online dating applications and how these have shifted dating patterns in Western contexts. As the digital nomad participants lack a deeper connection to the locations in which they reside and search for love, online dating applications provide an easy avenue for finding potential dates. However, since their stays in any one location tend to be of a shorter duration, such relationships are also short-lived, as potential partners may be location *de*pendent. Such dating patterns are also strongly influenced by the demographic identities of the participants, with women and LGBT individuals managing the most complex challenges as nomads. The ethnographic data is based on interviews with 38 self-identified digital nomads, or aspirants, primarily women, who were found through three conferences aimed at an (aspiring) digital nomad audience. The empirical findings of this research present a contingent lifestyle where constant travel contributes to feelings of rootlessness and loneliness. The majority of the participants were single, and this loneliness contributed to their desire to seek out a romantic companion. Participants who were already in a relationship had the most emotional support.

Digital Nomads in the Gig Economy

Digital nomads are workers whose primary employment (e.g., digital marketing, web design, and software engineering) takes place on the internet—they are 'location independent.' Digital nomads travel frequently; both domestically and internationally. It is difficult to estimate the number of digital nomads, but there are some measures that can provide context. The US Bureau of Labour Statistics reported in 2014 that there are 14.4 million self-employed workers in this country (comprising roughly 10% of the US workforce). As well, the number of full-time US employees who work primarily from home has risen to over 3.3 million (cited in Garrett, Spreitzer, & Bacevice, 2017, p. 822). Such numbers of freelancers in Europe were estimated at 15% of the workforce, according to Gandini's (2016a) research on freelancers in Milan and London. Gandini (2016a) also finds that the popular freelance website Upwork has a registered nine million users, four million clients, and one million jobs posted each year for the exchange of $1 billion dollars (loc 1224). While well-compensated technology workers are predominantly men, women comprise the aspirational social media and low-level marketing workers that make very little, if any, money. Duffy (2017) labels this 'aspirational labour,' which she notes, "is a mode of (mostly) uncompensated, independent work that is propelled by the much venerated ideal of getting paid to do what you love" (p. 4).

Gigs are one-time jobs that can be acquired by workers who are members of a particular employment website. Once the work is completed, the client rates the work performance and this contributes to the worker's overall rating (Gandini, 2016a, 2016b; Gandini, Pais, & Beraldo, 2016; Luce, 2017). Gig work does not come with benefits—freelancers must cover their own retirement, health-care, and operational costs. Juliet Schor is one of the few critical sociologists examining the impacts of the gig economy on workers. According to a Pew survey that Schor and Attwood-Charles (2017) cite, "gig workers disproportionately earn less than US$30,000 annually, however, because many are in school, part timers, or not in the labour force; this is not surprising" (p. 9). This is similar to Gandini's (2016a) findings, where his interviewees earned an average of £38,257 for London-based workers, and €32,487 for those in Milan. Gandini (2016a) also found that a significant number of workers relied on financial support from family to supplement their meagre incomes.

Seeking Community: Leisure and Online Dating in a Liquid World

Digital nomads spend a large percentage of their life online—not only for work but also for leisure and love. Participants report pursuing this lifestyle to intensify their leisure, experiences, and social lives, yet a prominent emotional outcome is a sense of social disconnection and loneliness. With their isolated work-life, only relieved by co-working spaces and meet-ups, nomads have difficulty establishing community. This question of community is, of course, a central theme in sociological literature, from Emile Durkheim's (1893/1997) concept of organic versus mechanical forms of solidarity, to Robert Putnam's (2001) classic *Bowling Alone*.

According to Durkheim, organic solidarity arises in technologically advanced societies in which individuals are reliant on the interconnected webs of labour, supplies, and service for consumption. Alexis de Tocqueville (1835, 1840) focused on the democratising of American culture and its lively civic society organisations that brought the masses together in public forums, and yet he critiqued the homogenising process of mass culture. The liveliness of civic society at the turn of the century that de Tocqueville describes is reliant on the physical coming together of bodies in conversation with neighbours and townsfolk, not likely translated to the contemporary online forums in which nomads communicate, but still remain anonymous, apart from their constructed online personas. Contemporary theorists, such as Robert Putnam (2001, 2016), note a decline in social cohesion loosely associated with the rising neoliberal economy and precarious employment. Putnam's writing demonstrates that this decline in community is not specific to digital nomads alone but part of the larger social context in which urban communities are becoming isolated in general, with social interactions often limited to the service economy.

Zygmunt Bauman (2000) conceptualises the post-modern era as 'liquid'—unstable, adaptive, or combining irreconcilable differences. 'Community' belongs to the solidity of the past, which Bauman (2000) calls "the last relic of the old-time utopias of the good society; it stands for whatever has been left of the dreams of a better life shared with better neighbours all following better rules of cohabitation" (p. 92). Bauman describes this community as an idealised "short-cut to togetherness," a grouping of people with sheer, comforting sameness (p. 99). Bauman (2000) also labels these moments of collective sameness as 'carnival communities,' or states that "explosive communities are events breaking the monotony of daily solitude." Besides the outmoded aspiration towards an embodied community, Bauman makes the distinction that contemporary society is based on "their capacity as consumers," positing our significant identity markers as nothing more than fashion objects purchased in the marketplace (p. 76). The online marketplace of dating fosters a mentality of objectifying people, another consumable item in the hyper-consumption and temporal lifestyle of the nomad, and the larger, unstable society (Bauman, 2000, p. 121; Henderson, 2014, p. 71). Bauman's 'carnival communities' closely represent the ways in which digital nomads gather for a short period of time with a specific group of people, never lasting long enough to forge real connections. As digital nomads focus so much on the freedom that their remote work-life offers, it may be at the price of sacrificing social connections, especially romantic love.

Leisure, Privilege, and Power

It is important to understand how one's demographics relate closely to homogeneous partner selection, even while travelling in different countries. Nomads' interactions with locations are often bracketed off from local life, and the nomads remain at a distance from local culture. They overwhelmingly choose partners with demographics very similar to their own, rather than marrying local citizens. Unlike some ex-pats, who may settle in a new country and marry a local citizen, digital nomads are often looking for other travellers to join their nomadic adventures, rather than seeking a permanent home in a new location.

Nomads lack perspective on their privileged positioning within the global economy, including those based on citizenship, race, gender, dis/ability, and sexual orientation (Spracklen, 2013). In the copy written by digital nomad bloggers, one finds little recognition of these power imbalances, as they write that anyone can take up the lifestyle (Solomon, 2017).

Some nomads participate in 'volunteer tourism' and 'travelling with a purpose,' which ultimately may have little outcome other than a few selfie photos with the local people. Indeed, in their critique of volunteer tourism, Bandyopadhyay and Patil (2017) compare a key dimension of colonial tourism with that contemporary practice: travel writing. Digital nomads often capture their experiences on travel blogs with an intended audience of other nomads, tourist, and ex-pats, not the local community in which they are embedded.

Online Dating, Gender Roles, and Sexual Orientation

Online dating has quickly transformed the landscape of courtship, with large swaths of society using such websites, and yet there continues to be associations of deceit and lingering stigma with the practice (Freedman, 2011; Sautter, Tippett, & Morgan, 2010). Comedian Aziz Ansari (2016) teamed up with New York University sociologist Eric Klinenberg to interview people globally about their experiences with technologically enhanced contemporary dating, on topics ranging from sexting to cyber-cheating. Ansari's main thesis is that people historically met their partners based on extreme proximity—they lived in the same apartment building or within a few blocks of each other (hence, the 'girl next door'). People met through family introductions, friends, or church acquaintanceships. This data reflects historian Stephanie Coontz's (1992) research on the history of marriage wherein she argues that throughout most of modern history, marriage was about tying socially equivalent families together, and very little to do with romantic love. With the advent of online dating, the supermarket of potential partners seems limitless, and it can create a sense that there is always someone else to 'swipe right' upon. Christian Rudder (2015) founder of OkCupid, uses his exclusive access to the company's database to report the actual patterns of behaviour of the website users, not just personally reported behaviour. One of the most important findings that Rudder (2015) presents is the extreme homophilia exercised by a presumably cosmopolitan clientele. Online daters wrote to potential partners who were very similar to themselves in race, religion, education, income, and even key-terms use (Skopek, Schulz, & Blossfeld, 2011). Other researchers have shown the nuances of how multiracial users maintain some benefits over their monoracial non-white counterparts in this highly racialised context in which whiteness continues to be prioritised (Curington, Lin, & Ludquist, 2015).

With each shifting new context of technological or lifestyle development, there is a hope to open the opportunity for gender equality, yet that is rarely the outcome—rather, gender norms continue to be entrenched in new ways. Rudder (2015) shows that the gender dynamics of who writes the first message follows traditional patterns of male pursuers. Pei and Ho (2008) find that Chinese women's sexual behaviour online mirrors their offline behaviour, in that they preferred "relationally-oriented activities" (p. 204). While recognising the pleasure that online dating and flirting brought to the women, Pei and Ho (2008) caution that the perspective of online dating as an equal space for women is exaggerated and ignores the embedded structural power of gender relations. Once couples are living together, gender imbalances of power in the household continue to reflect different opportunities in the home and in leisure choices. Gorman-Murray (2013) finds that gender dynamics alter the ways in which masculinity is performed within the domestic environment, by observing the spatial and embodied dynamics of men's bodies in the home. Haworth (2014) finds that how couples can individually exercise choice in their leisure practices is highly contingent upon the couple's negotiation and communication skills. Unequal gender dynamics continue to play out in all aspects of heterosexual coupling, from online dating, co-habitation, and selecting how one's leisure time is spent. Nomadic couples often have male partners earning more money, and therefore, leading the decision on location selection and leisure pursuits.

For gay, lesbian, and queer identified nomads, issues of coming out, and finding partners in the online environment, were prevalent, especially for lesbians. The process of coming out is an ongoing one, and in a heteronormative travel and leisure environment, reaffirming one's sexuality can be a constant process (Weston, 1991). Consideration of sexual orientation may play a role for nomads in selecting their travel itinerary as human rights protections are unevenly developed globally (Corrales,

2015; Thoreson, 2014). While queerness and space may have been defined by gay neighbourhoods in past decades, the mobility of people and their interactions with locations is more fluid now, and less defined by space, but by temporal gatherings (Nash & Gorman-Murray, 2014). However, there is a correlation between the world's richest cities and LGBT-friendly cities (Corrales, 2010).

Methodology

I began this research by attending three major digital nomad events. The first event was the third annual DNX Conference for Digital Nomads & Life Hackers in Lisbon, Portugal, on 9–10 September 2017. The DNX hosts events in both German (the founders are German) and English, thereby representing the large German digital nomad community. This event was aimed towards aspiring nomads, with speakers presenting their personal, inspirational stories, often tracing a popular narrative arch: from corporate job to digital freedom. Next, I attended the Digital Nomad Girls retreat in Javea, Spain, from 18 to 27 September 2017. As an immersive, ten-day retreat, with a full agenda, and even shared rooms, the 15 participants bonded in a way reflective of such intensive time spent together. Half of the attendees were already nomads, while the other half were aspiring. I was able to bond with, and secure interviews with, the majority of attendees—including the founder Jenny Lachs and her partner Simon. Jenny then connected me with the founders of 7in7, a conference for experienced digital nomads. 7in7 took place from 3 to 9 October 2017, in Barcelona, Spain, and attracted approximately 70 participants. The title of the conference signified that it would take place each year for seven years on seven different continents—yes, including Antarctica. I interviewed all of the organisers, many of the main speakers, and quite a few of the participants during follow-up Skype interviews over the next three months. The 7in7 conference focuses on 'invisible nomads,' and centres on women, people of colour, and the LGBT community.

Participant Demographic Information

There were 38 participants in this study. All of the participants were from strong passport countries, and those who had citizenship in weaker passport countries had dual passports—thus paired with a stronger one. A passport's strength is measured by how many visa-free countries one can enter. The participants overwhelmingly spoke only English. Those who spoke two or more languages were primarily of non-English speaking national background (n = 7). Rarely did white English speakers learn a second language (n = 4). Nearly all participants bemoaned their lack of bilingual abilities, but few put sustained effort into learning another language, and instead relied on the prevalence of English in the countries they visited. Thirteen participants spoke two or more languages, and five spoke three or more. Twenty-two participants spoke only English.

Their ages ranged from 21 to 49, with the majority in their thirties. In total, 12 of the participants were in their twenties, 22 were in their thirties, and 4 were in their forties. Twenty-eight of the participants were racially white (including one Arab and two Hispanic whites). Five participants were of African descent, two were Asian, and three were mixed race Asian and white. Thirty of the participants were heterosexual, three were bisexual, and five were lesbian, gay, or queer-identified. Six of the participants were married (with two in the process of divorce), while the majority of them were single (n = 32), with ten in significant relationships. Only 1 participant out of 37 had children (now grown). Only 6 participants hoped for children in the future, with 15 unsure, and 13 were adamant to remain child-free. Only six participants held a religious identity: including one Hindu, one Muslim, and four Christians. Some qualified themselves as 'spiritual.'

Most of the participants held Bachelors' degrees (n = 23). Nine participants had graduate degrees (MA = 6; JD = 1; PhD = 2). Six participants did not complete college. Four had some college education, and one participant graduated with a high school degree. Half of the participants had no student debt (n = 20) and the other half had student debt (n = 18). Criminal records pose barriers for travel. Only one of the participants had a minor misdemeanour criminal charge, which had been expunged.

This study was based primarily on female participants ($n = 33$), in addition to interviews with five male participants.

The three empirical themes below emerged from questions based on the academic and popular literature on digital nomads, as well as dominant themes covered at the conferences and in the interviews. Open questions based on lifestyle, motivation, dating, and romantic partnerships were asked of the participants. All interviews were conducted on Skype, audio recorded, fully transcribed, and codes were developed for themes that emerged from their stories. As two of the three conferences marketed their events for demographic minorities in the community (women, people of colour, queer), identity was central for this group of participants. The majority were single women, and therefore, questions and themes in the data related to their romantic searches were coded, based on their motivation and process of seeking partners. A few nomadic couples were interviewed, and their experiences provide important lessons for single nomads who aspired to be in a partnership.

Findings: Digital Nomad Dating

Social Distancing from the Stereotype of the 'Digital Bro-Mad'

When asking participants about dating within the digital nomad community, the first image to emerge is the stereotype of the 'digital bro-mad'—a privileged, heterosexual white male, located on the beach next to his laptop and surfboard, and who stays in Thailand where his socio-economic status empowers him. Such images of nomads overlap with those of sexual tourists or men seeking 'traditional women' (Taylor, 2001; Wonders & Michalowski, 2001) or of those acting in a 'colonialist tourist' manner (Bandyopadhyay & Patil, 2017). Two of the participants mentioned this stereotype in order to distance themselves from it. Nicole, a lesbian from the United States, states:

> Because of the temporariness—especially for men—there is a mindset that they're here for a good time, not to be caged in or held down by dating

someone. They are like Tinder culture. They just want to have fun, hook up at night, go to the beach in the morning, work on their business in the afternoon, and party. They are like, 'I'm here being better than a tourist. I'm here having fun living my life and this is how I want to do it.' There are some couples that travel together, but they are very couple-y. Then, there is a very large subsection of people who are hooking up on the road. There is not a lot of dating. I think that that informs their behaviour, they think, 'I can treat women like shit because I'm leaving.'

Nicole found herself outside of these options as a lesbian and also as someone who was not interested in dating, but mostly looking for friendships, or at least a serious relationship developing out of an established friendship. Because of her isolation in this regard, and the continual process of coming out (Weston, 1991), she established her own queer women's digital nomad Facebook group to meet others. For US citizen Alexis, who has worked for years in Hong Kong and other countries, this stereotype did impact her dating life, as she found herself in second place to this imagined 'traditional' and submissive Asian woman, from which she deviated as a Western, mixed-race Asian-white, successful lawyer, with an outgoing personality:

> I find that a lot of ex-pats are really privileged, at least male expats ... A lot of people move to southeast Asia and think, 'Oh, look at me, I can do whatever I want here because all the women want a white husband.' That really turns me off, so that's why I don't normally date other expats or nomads ... I saw this all the time in Asia with western guys ... They said when you meet an Asian woman who has been brought up in Asia, she treats you like a god who can do no wrong. It actually made dating as an expat western female hard. As a mixed-race person who has some Asian blood, I thought I would clean up with the dudes in Asia, much more so than in New York ... I thought Asia would be really refreshing, but they said, 'You are too western for me.'

None of the participants in this study presented themselves in a stereotypical 'bro-mad' manner where they discussed dating local women, which could be attributed to the particular conference demographics I attended, and to my identity as a female and feminist researcher.

Searching Online for an Ideal Match

The nomads who were single and looking had romantic ideals about their perfect match—someone who could travel with them and form an independent unit. Frequent travelling to new places provides nomads with an ostensibly endless supply of potential partners, reflecting Ansari's (2016) and Rudder's (2015) findings of the seemingly endless prospective stream of partners contributing to a selective, consumerist mindset. Marie Clark, a mixed-race Japanese/white heterosexual woman from London, who is actively looking for a partner, states:

> I would love to meet someone while travelling. Somebody that can come with me to America, who shares this lifestyle. In Portugal, I met this 24-year-old typical surfer. Totally bad for me! In my head, 'no.' In my heart, 'no, no, no.' But there was an incredible attraction. In my 20s, I was very spiritual. I didn't have many experiences with guys. It was only in my 30s that I thought, 'Right. Fuck it.' So, yeah, it was a great experience. Kind of heart-breaking, but fun. If you meet someone, you need to commit pretty early on to be with them. To change your travel plans to be with them. I realise that I would love to be the sort of girl or person that could not get attached, but I get incredibly attached.

Marie's potential dating partners seem to announce their interest in her just as they are leaving town, offering her nothing but missed opportunities with fleeting acquaintances. Both Alexis and Marie Clark are not using dating applications such as Tinder. Marie socialises through co-living spaces, Bauman's (2000) 'carnival communities' that bring a very specific demographic grouping of people together on a 'fun,' curated, and temporary basis. Finding a partner within the same lifestyle was one of the biggest challenges for nomads. Many worried about finding a partner that was location *de*pendent, and who may ask them to stop travelling. Even when finding another nomad to partner with, their travel itineraries, work commitments, and desires, may differ significantly. Only US-born Taylor specifically stated that she dates local men in Guatemala, where she has settled. But even Taylor, who speaks fluent Spanish, still spends the majority of her time with ex-pats and nomads:

> I'm one of those people who is all about living like a local, even though, most of my friends are ex-pats or international. In Antigua and Guatemala specifically, the two populations that make up the city are ex-pats and native Guatemalans. They are very welcoming. I really love having Guatemalan friends. They're kind of my vice; I need to stay away. I've been in way too many casual relationships.

For the majority of nomads seeking romantic relationships, they find their community—like the other parts of their lives—online. They network in digital nomad Facebook groups, attend nomad conferences, and there is even a dating site called nomadsoulmates.com. For LGBT folks, online dating is even more prevalent. American Kyrie did use Tinder during her travels before she met her current UK-born partner Hannah, another digital nomad with whom she travels. Once Kyrie partnered up, she no longer felt such a need to connect with other queer women online:

> I met them on Tinder, mostly. But only like one or two people would come through Cambodia every month! It was an ongoing joke for me and my friends. 'Oh! There's one in town! I have a date this week!' Dating kind of fell into my lap in Bangkok with Hannah. I am in a couple of queer nomad groups. I don't engage much. Once you're in a relationship, it's a little less necessary to meet people. Before I met Hannah, I was travelling alone. She's the longest relationship I've had. It's such a contrast travelling with a person because you have your built-in community, and your built-in support system. I really enjoyed 7in7 for the fact that it has allowed me to meet a handful of queer digital nomads.

Now, instead of putting her energy into finding dating partners, Kyrie and Hannah spend their time considering which countries are more LGBT friendly. Homophobic episodes have not been a common occurrence for the couple, outside of the harassment of women on public streets. Kyrie states:

> We're pretty aware of the countries we are in, their views on GLBTQ folks, and what kind of public displays of affection are tolerated. The typical harassment of women is what we get. You come across that travelling, regardless of being queer. We were in Bangkok together, that was fine. It is

very open, you can hold hands and walk down the street. In Budapest, we wouldn't. It is just about being aware of your surroundings.

US-based Jessa finds dating as a lesbian nomad quite challenging to navigate—both the sparsely populated queer online dating environment, as well as the responses she gets from potential partners to her lifestyle. Jessa reports:

I think part of it is just the lack of a critical mass of nomads, especially queer women nomads. Being queer reduces the dating pool by about 90%. I have been using sites like OkCupid when I'm in a location. I would get people who say, 'I'm up for a fling.' And, I say, 'No. I actually want a relationship.' Or, they would say, 'I want a relationship. Maybe I can convince you that you don't want to be a nomad anymore.' So, neither of those are really great options. I have been continuously updating my profile on the sites: 'I'm a nomad. I don't plan to stop. I move every 2–3 months. Ideally, I am looking for somebody who wants to do that with me.' But I'm open to the idea of having a home base.

Nicole asked her Facebook group of lesbian nomads about their dating experiences. She reports the group consensus that online dating was a challenge, if not 'a mess':

Basically, the consensus is that they are not necessarily meeting people through these online platforms. Or not happily. I think a lot of people have said they've met friends. I think a lot of people have hooked-up, but I think people aren't going to post about that as much because it's a public group.

Deb is a Chinese American lesbian who works in the field of medical technical writing and makes a six-figure salary each year, but works long, intense days, and balances her work with activities such as extreme mountain climbing. She has experienced both, travelling with a girlfriend for a year-long stint, as well as her current single and dating nomadic lifestyle:

Queer dating can be interesting, but also extremely challenging. You are really limited to only a few geographic areas in the world where you can really have fun as an out queer, and still get dates. Some queers avoid the

> less friendly countries, but I try not to let it put me off. Maybe the Middle East is my threshold, as the laws are particularly bad, and I find the homophobia, culture, and being female a potentially challenging combination. And even then, I'm going to Uganda where there's a 'jail gays for life' law and interest in a 'kill the gays' law. I try to balance it out with periodic stops in friendlier countries now, to be able to 'top up on the gay,' as I jokingly call it. For the immediate future, it looks like jaunts to less tolerant places (i.e., Uganda, Rwanda, and Kenya), are going to be interspersed with visits to Norway or Sweden, because it's easier to get dates, I can kiss a woman in public, and I feel safe. As for the actual dating and my style of travelling, which tends to be fast, it can deter people from trying to meet me. On the other hand, if I can manage to meet up with someone somewhere, it seems like I meet more badass, interesting, and unconventional women who are more daring and risk-taking.

For LGBT nomads, such concerns as the safety and homophobic climate of national laws, as well as the ability to find a date, are more of a problem than for their heterosexual counterparts. Human rights organisations and researchers have brought attention to the uneven development of LGBT rights globally. Such organisations find uneven rights, with most of the LGBT-friendly cities overlapping with the richest world cities, and protective laws increasing in some places (e.g., South America), while violence against LGBT communities remains relatively high (e.g., Brazil) (Corrales, 2010, 2015; Thoreson, 2014).

Challenges for Nomadic Couples

Finding a partner was not the end of challenges for nomadic romance. Both partners needed to find a happy compromise between their travel itineraries, their location-independent or -dependent work contracts, and when they decided to settle down for a period or indefinitely. When I spoke with Mariza, she was married to a man whom she met while she spent several years working in Brazil:

> I met my husband during the second year I was in Brazil. We were together for a couple of years. He is a programmer. ... My husband ended up getting

> a contract in Brazil until November of this year, so he stayed. I decided in June that I would go back and try to figure something else out with a start-up that I was working with.

Her husband's contract grounded him in Brazil, and Mariza was less than enthusiastic to return to Brazil for the indefinite future, but she was willing to try. However, a few months later, the couple engaged in a Facebook-public divorce in which Mariza had to quickly establish residency in the state of Nevada in order to complete the divorce proceedings. Alexis has a digital nomad partner, but they travel separately and come together for shorter periods of time. She states:

> I have a partner and he is in a similar situation. We have a location-independent partnership. He is based somewhere else right now and the lifestyle seems to work for us. We don't want to totally merge, but we still love being there for each other … We're going to Panama City in a couple of weeks. That's going to be fun.

Gender dynamics were still prevalent with the heterosexual digital nomad couples. When the decision to go nomadic comes from the male partner, the decision is mostly affirmative, even when the female partner disagrees with the decision. This reflects the differential power dynamics related to job type and income, as the male digital nomads had more computer design employment, whereas women had much lower paid and aspirational social media gigs that provided little income to use for travel and more expensive country visits (Duffy, 2017; Gandini, 2016a; Schor & Attwood-Charles, 2017). For Marta from Poland, her boyfriend decided to become a digital nomad and resented Marta's financial dependency on him, which strained their relationship. They temporarily broke up, only to have her submit to his lifestyle decision in order to remain a couple:

> It was not my idea, to be absolutely fair. My fiancé is a real nerd—in work and life. He lives online. He started encountering articles about the digital nomad movement. We had these conversations over wine and I was always supportive. I loved travelling for holidays, but I never took it seriously. We had some problems in our relationship. I had left my job and stayed at home. That didn't work very well for our interactions because I became

> dependent on him. At some point, he decided that he was going to travel. I said, 'I don't want to.' So, we broke up. It was for about 2 or 3 weeks. I decided to travel on my own. With a lot of drama, we decided that we loved each other very much and actually wanted to build a life together. We created a 1-year plan to prepare ourselves for this financially. We bought tickets a year in advance to Chiang Mai. We decided to go to a place where we will meet nomads.

For Mirtha, originally from the Dominican Republic and currently working as a computer technician, she is excited about the possibility of becoming nomadic, but her boyfriend is not. She states:

> He learned about [the lifestyle] from me. He is very reluctant. He was born and raised in Barcelona. Of course, it's something that I want, but I also love him. He's insecure because all his clients are in Barcelona. Any time I bring this subject to the table, he is like, 'Ah, but no. My clients are here. There is no possibility for me to work remotely.' But he can have meetings on Skype. I would like to have a person to share this adventure with. I hope things work out and we can stay together. I understand that if it has to end because of that, then I will just have to accept it and move on.

Mirtha took time at the Digital Nomad Girls' retreat to gather the advice of the other attendees who supported her decision to choose her nomadic freedom over her established relationship, which Mirtha was reluctant to leave.

Finally, considering the difficulties of dating as a digital nomad, many simply give up on the prospects and enjoy their curated digital nomad community, with whom they gather in popular tourist destinations. For many nomads, the lifestyle proves to be temporary, and establishing and maintaining relationships are one aspect of the challenges that pressure people to once again become location *de*pendent. The majority of the nomads interviewed were single, only a few were (still) married, and only one-third of the unmarried nomads had significant relationships. Therefore, the challenges of an established relationship, especially those including childrearing, were a strong impediment to a nomadic lifestyle.

Conclusion

Digital nomads have adopted a lifestyle in which they attempt to blend their passion for travel with remote work. Critiques of freelance work point to its precarious nature, in which workers must bid for each small 'gig' or job, for which they are remunerated without benefits or security, which academics are beginning to examine. Because of this financial situation, many nomads move to affordable locations, such as Thailand, where such income can still pay the rent. The digital nomads interviewed here are primarily of the Millennial generation, and as such, at a time in their lives before they have married or have children, and they are often dating or in relationships. However, the digital nomad lifestyle does not lend itself easily for dating and establishing relationships. The participants primarily sought the company of other nomads, travellers, and expats of their own country, or those of other English speaking, developed countries—not locals in the places in which they travel. Their dating targets were of this similar demographic. Therefore, they used online meet-up groups and dating websites to find their social and romantic company. Some, like Marie Clark from the United Kingdom, utilised co-living spaces that were populated with this target demographic from which to select friends and romantic partnerships. In her case, by the time potential partners expressed interest, it was always at the end of their stay in the co-living space, and thus, a missed opportunity, falling through the cracks of both of their travel itineraries. For nomads to find a romantic partner among those of the same group was a challenge in itself. But for them to agree to travel together and harmonise their travel plans—a fast or slow pace, country selection, or accommodation type—provides a real challenge. Furthermore, finding a partner that is not remote and pressures the nomad to establish a base with them is yet another challenge. And finally, for those who eventually would like to have children, that will most likely force them to find a base, as none of the digital nomads interviewed had minor-age children (although managing such a challenge is often a topic covered at digital nomad conferences, such as 7in7 and DNX).

Conferences such as 7in7 attempt to address demographic-based inequalities inherent in the digital nomad community. Such inequality is represented by the 'bro-mad' stereotype—a financially secure, heterosexual white male travelling to beach resort town such as Chiang Mai, Thailand, where he can drink, surf, and indulge with local women without repercussion for bad behaviour. 7in7 advertises that its conference speakers are overwhelmingly comprised of women, people of colour, and people of diverse sexual orientations. Gender inequalities arise in the nomadic community based on the more powerful position men have with higher-paying employment and thus more power to make lifestyle decisions, whereas their female partners are often in lower-financial tier jobs that provide little security (Duffy, 2017).

LGBT folks were most likely to find community at the 7in7 conference, which addressed their specific demographic needs in the nomadic community, unlike more established conferences such as DNX. LGBT folks reported paying more attention to the social climate of homophobia in destination countries and managed their travel and self-presentation accordingly. For lesbians, they report encountering more gender-based harassment than homophobia, but they were cautious about expressing affection in certain countries perceived as less tolerant than others. As Deb expressed, she alternates her travel between intolerant and tolerant countries, so she can "top up on the gay." LGBT folks were the most likely to rely on dating applications and websites as they were less likely to encounter other sexual minorities in the general nomad community. Nicole has established a Facebook group for lesbian nomads in order to create her own community and bring others together to network, make friends, and discuss issues specific to their concerns.

Overall, while the digital nomad lifestyle branding had the feel of a pyramid scheme being sold on popular websites, where individuals may try and sell the lifestyle via their e-books and video courses, there were many lifestyle challenges that were unaddressed—particularly around the topic of loneliness and maintaining romantic partnerships. The challenges of establishing and maintaining a long-term partnership provide an impetus for becoming less nomadic and more location-based.

References

Ansari, A. (2016). *Modern romance*. New York, NY: Penguin Books.

Bandyopadhyay, R., & Patil, V. (2017). 'The white woman's burden'—The racialized, gendered politics of volunteer tourism. *An International Journal of Tourism Space, Place and Environment, 19*(4), 1–13.

Bauman, Z. (2000, reprint 2012). *Liquid modernity*. Malden, MA: Polity Press.

Coontz, S. (1992). *The way we never were: American families and the nostalgia trap*. New York, NY: Basic Books.

Corrales, J. (2010). *The politics of sexuality in Latin America: A reader on lesbian, gay, bisexual, and transgender rights*. Pittsburgh, PA: University of Pittsburgh Press.

Corrales, J. (2015). The politics of LGBT rights in Latin America and the Caribbean: Research agendas. *European Review of Latin American and Caribbean Studies, 100*, 53–62.

Curington, C. V., Lin, K. H., & Ludquist, J. H. (2015). Positioning multiraciality in cyberspace: Treatment of multiracial daters in an online dating website. *American Sociological Review, 80*(4), 764–788.

de Tocqueville, A. (1835 & 1840, reprint 2003). *Democracy in America and two essays on America*. New York, NY: Penguin Classics.

Duffy, E. B. (2017). *(Not) getting paid to do what you love: Gender, social media, and aspirational work*. New Haven, CT: Yale University Press.

Durkheim, E. (1893, reprint 1997). *The division of labour in society* (W. D. Halls, Trans.). New York, NY: Free Press.

Freedman, E. (2011). *Transient images: Personal media in public frameworks*. Philadelphia, PA: Temple University Press.

Gandini, A. (2016a). *The reputation economy: Understanding knowledge work in digital society*. London: Macmillan Publishers.

Gandini, A. (2016b). Digital work: Self-branding and social capital in the freelance knowledge economy. *Marketing Theory, 16*(1), 123–141.

Gandini, A., Pais, I., & Beraldo, D. (2016). Reputation and trust on online labor markets: The reputation economy of Elance. *Work Organization, Labor and Globalization, 10*(1), 27–43.

Garrett, L. E., Spreitzer, G. M., & Bacevice, P. A. (2017). Co-constructing a sense of community at work: The emergence of community in coworking spaces. *Organizational Studies, 38*(6), 821–842.

Gorman-Murray, A. (2013). Urban homebodies: Embodiment, masculinity, and domesticity in inner Sydney. *Geographical Research, 51*(2), 137–144.

Haworth, J. (2014). Leisure, life, enjoyment and well-being. In S. Elkington & S. J. Gammon (Eds.), *Contemporary perspectives in leisure: Meanings, motives and lifelong learning* (pp. 39–53). New York, NY: Routledge.

Henderson, K. A. (2014). The unsustainability of leisure: The sustainability of just leisure. In S. Elkington & S. J. Gammon (Eds.), *Contemporary perspectives in leisure: Meanings, motives and lifelong learning* (pp. 67–78). New York, NY: Routledge.

Luce, E. (2017). *The retreat of Western liberalism*. New York, NY: Atlantic Monthly Press.

Nash, C. J., & Gorman-Murray, A. (2014, May). LGBT neighbourhoods and 'new mobilities': Towards understanding transformations in sexual and gendered urban landscapes. *International Journal of Urban and Regional Research, 38*(3), 756–772.

Pei, Y., & Ho, S. Y. (2008). Sex and life politics formed through the internet online and offline dating experiences of young women in Shanghai. In K. E. Kuah-Pearce (Ed.), *Chinese women and the cyberspace*. Amsterdam: Amsterdam University Press.

Putnam, R. D. (2001). *Bowling alone: The collapse and revival of American community*. New York, NY: Simon & Schuster.

Putnam, R. D. (2016). *Our kids: The American dream in crisis*. New York, NY: Simon & Schuster.

Rudder, C. (2015). *Dataclysm: Love, sex, race, and identity-what our online lives tell us about our offline selves*. New York, NY: Broadway Books.

Sautter, J. M., Tippett, R. M., & Morgan, S. P. (2010, June). The social demography of internet dating in the United States. *Social Science Quarterly, 91*(2), 554–575.

Schor, J. B., & Attwood-Charles, W. (2017). The "sharing" economy: Labor, inequality, and social connection on for-profit platforms. *Sociology Compass, 11*(8), 1–16.

Skopek, J., Schulz, F., & Blossfeld, H. P. (2011, April). Who contacts whom? Educational homophily in online mate selection. *European Sociological Review, 27*(2), 180–195.

Solomon, T. (2017, October 16). *How to become a digital nomad*. Retrieved from The Self Employed website: https://www.theselfemployed.com/find_work/become-digital-nomad/

Spracklen, K. (2013). *Whiteness and leisure*. New York, NY: Palgrave Macmillan.

Taylor, J. S. (2001, August). Dollars are a girl's best friend? Tourists' sexual behavior in the Caribbean. *Sociology, 35*(3), 749–764.

Thompson, B. (2018). Digital nomads: Employment in the online gig economy. *Glocalism: Journal of Culture, Politics and Innovation*, (1).

Thoreson, R. R. (2014). *Transnational LGBT activism: Working for sexual rights worldwide*. Minneapolis, MN: University of Minnesota Press.

Weston, K. (1991). *Families we choose: Lesbians, gays, kinship*. New York, NY: Columbia University Press.

Wonders, N. A., & Michalowski, R. (2001, November). Bodies, borders, and sex tourism in a globalized world: A tale of two cities—Amsterdam and Havana. *Social Problems, 48*(4), 545–571.

Part II

Dating and Intimacy at the Interface

6

"There's no one new around you": Queer Women's Experiences of Scarcity in Geospatial Partner-Seeking on Tinder

Stefanie Duguay

> [W]hen you get to the end of Tinder and it's like, "There's no one new around you." And it does refresh all the time—new people come on, but still—and you're like, "There's no more." You've got to think, like, "Of course there are lesbians and people that don't have Tinder and they're still out there." But you're like, "That's it. I know all of them. There's only this many that are interested in me within this range. These are my only options." So yeah, I get that feeling sometimes. (Danaë, 19, student)

Danaë is describing her use of the popular dating app, Tinder, to find other women around her to date. Tinder is known for its "swipe" configuration (David & Cambre, 2016), whereby users are presented with profile cards that they can swipe left to dismiss or right to "like." When two users swipe right on each other, they form a "match" and gain access to the app's chat functionality. However, what Danaë terms the "end of Tinder" is a screen that appears when a user has swiped through all available profiles in an area. The screen declares "There's no one new around

S. Duguay (✉)
Concordia University, Montreal, QC, Canada
e-mail: stefanie.duguay@concordia.ca

C. Nash, A. Gorman-Murray (eds.), *The Geographies of Digital Sexuality*,
https://doi.org/10.1007/978-981-13-6876-9_6

you" and prompts users to invite their Facebook friends to join the app. Users searching for previously unknown potential partners have limited options when this happens. They can reconfigure their search criteria, relocate to a different area in hopes of uncovering profiles that were not previously in range, or wait for new people to come into proximity, refreshing the screen in anticipation that new profiles will appear.

Despite these recourses, Danaë and several other queer women[1] who I interviewed encountered this screen frequently. Their experiences gave rise to a shared and deep-seated feeling of scarcity in relation to other queer women, both on the app and in physical space. This feeling of scarcity was precipitated not only by these queer women's interactions with the app but also by Tinder's technological arrangements. This chapter demonstrates how these social and technological influences combined with regard to key factors that intensified notions of scarcity. These factors included embodied constraints on search criteria, the propensity for unwanted recognition on the app and in physical space, and the abundance of accounts that did not belong to queer women. All of these sociotechnical conditions increased the frequency with which participants reached "the end of Tinder," especially in smaller cities and rural locales.

This chapter's findings augment existing scholarship regarding mobile apps, and dating apps in particular, through the addition of queer women's experiences with a particularly popular dating app. While scholars have often discussed how mobile technology seamlessly co-situates users by overlaying physical and digital space (Blackwell, Birnholtz, & Abbott, 2015; de Souza e Silva, 2006; Hjorth & Lim, 2012), the experiences included here reflect social and technological hindrances to co-situation. They also highlight a difference between co-situation with other Tinder users in general and desired

[1] I adopt Gray's (2009) definition of "queer" as "the action of identity work" (p. 26), which involves "the collective labor of crafting, articulating, and pushing the boundaries of identities" (p. 26). Queer encompasses identities in tension with presumptions that individuals are heterosexual and cisgender. I refer to "women" as female-identified individuals, aligning with how participants identified their gender, including androgynous and genderfluid women. For lack of a neutral umbrella term for people of diverse sexual and gender identities (Barker, Richards, & Bowes-Catton, 2009), I refer to lesbian, gay, bisexual, transgender, and queer people in aggregate as LGBTQ people.

co-situation with potential partners. While some men seeking men (MSM) on dating apps experience similar difficulties finding desired long-term partners (Cassidy, 2016), this chapter identifies a sense of scarcity that encompassed these queer women's use of Tinder.

Digital and Geographic Co-situation

With the widespread adoption of geolocation-enabled mobile phones, this technology has shifted individuals' relationships with physical locations and digital *spaces* (communities, platforms, and networked infrastructures through which individuals connect). As de Souza e Silva (2006) explains, mobile technologies give rise to "hybrid spaces" that blur the borders between physical and digital spaces, bring digitally connected social networks into physical spaces, and alter interactions within urban spaces. In these hybrid spaces, mobile apps—ranging from location-based games to social network sites—invoke emotional and social engagement from users (Hjorth & Lim, 2012). This can generate forms of "mobile intimacy," bringing individuals together through the "overlaying of the material-geographic and electronic-social" (Hjorth & Lim, 2012, p. 478). While this understanding of mobile intimacy attends to the materiality of geographic spaces and their digital enhancement, scholars have highlighted that the digital is also material (Dourish, 2016). Material elements of mobile phones and apps (e.g. features, interfaces, devices) shape social connections and physical interactions (Bucher & Helmond, 2017; McVeigh-Schultz & Baym, 2015). The research presented in this chapter attends to the way participants' social interactions and geographic contexts intersected with the app's technological arrangements to form experiences linked to feelings of scarcity.

Mobile dating technologies present an apt case where social and emotional intentions are intensified in the pursuit of sexual and romantic partner-seeking. Since in-person encounters are often the aim,[2] a range of technologies have long mediated dating in attempts to facilitate this,

[2] Race (2015) has discussed how some dating app users may only aim to engage with others through the app to exchange sexual photos or entertain fantasies without acting on them.

from newspaper personals to telephone hotlines, video dating, and online websites (Duguay, Burgess, & Light, 2017). Long before the uptake of dating applications, MSM used digital technologies to catalyse physical encounters by establishing mutual proximity through local chatrooms on Internet Relay Chat (IRC) (Campbell, 2004), Bluetooth technology on early mobile phones (Mowlabocus, 2010), and even the installation of computing terminals in gay venues (Fletcher & Light, 2007). With MSM's rapid uptake of dating apps, led by Grindr but accompanied by a range of others to suit varying tastes (Gudelunas, 2012), these apps have shifted MSM's perceptions of social and physical space.

Prior to Tinder's swiping functionality, the most common dating app interface used by Grindr and other apps for MSM provided a grid-like view of other users' profile pictures, displayed in order of proximity. The ability to easily identify others on the app alongside their locational information co-situates users in a common digital space across multiple physical spaces (Blackwell et al., 2015). This allows users who are physically embodied in heteronormative surroundings to be co-present with other MSM on the app. While few users of apps for MSM report that this co-situation gives them a sense of community, especially since much app activity is focused on sexual encounters, some men feel that it fosters familiarity with other non-heterosexual men nearby (Miles, 2017). This familiarity can give rise to spaces of gay sociability, often occurring in individuals' homes or at parties (Race, 2015), and help MSM to gather information and social connections when they are new to a city (Shield, 2016). Therefore, these apps facilitate a sense that MSM are not alone in urban landscapes where physically denoted non-heterosexual spaces, such as gay bars and venues, have dwindled and become dispersed (Ghaziani, 2014; Nash, 2013). Although studies of MSM note their discontent with how dating apps often frame encounters as sexual transactions (Licoppe, Riviere, & Morel, 2016), sort men's bodies into hypersexualised masculine categories (Bonner-Thompson, 2017), and can preclude the formation of romantic connections (Cassidy, 2016), men rarely speak of a lack of other men available through these apps. Instead, the apps showcase an abundance of potential partners—a "catalogue of men," as one participant in Brubaker,

Ananny, and Crawford's (2016) study articulated. The co-situation of MSM on dating apps provides a sense that there is a volume of nearby users who share similar sexual desires.

A similar history of hybrid spaces is missing for queer women. Early technologies, such as the French Minitel (a precursor to the internet) and bulletin board services (BBS), connected lesbians across geographical space (Chaplin, 2014; Correll, 1995). Chaplin (2014) notes how the Minitel "made possible new forms of lesbian identity untethered to specific locations, organizations, embodiment, or proximity" (p. 452). While these connections over shared sexual identity facilitated the formation of online communities and fuelled activism, their geographically untethered connections did not frequently facilitate meeting in person. This theme of connecting online with physically disparate others is common throughout scholarly accounts of queer women's use of web portals, chat rooms, and social media (Cooper, 2010; Cooper & Dzara, 2010; Gray, 2009).

The rise of dating apps marketed towards queer women has drawn attention to how mobile technologies may (or may not) co-situate these users. Murray and Ankerson (2016) identify the branding and design labour put into the lesbian dating app "Her" in attempts to accelerate temporal rhythms of lesbian dating to fit with the mobile marketplace. However, the success of these measures in the app's North American and United Kingdom markets has yet to be determined. On the other hand, Butterfly, a social networking app marketed to lesbian and bisexual women in Hong Kong, seems to have achieved this. Studies show that it facilitates mobile intimacy among users (Tang, 2017) and co-situates them across digital and public space, leading to sexual and romantic encounters (Choy, 2018). Similar to Blackwell et al.'s (2015) study of MSM on Grindr, Choy (2018) found that lesbian and bisexual women could connect through Butterfly even when in public spaces that were hostile towards homosexual people. However, Hong Kong's high population density and tremendous uptake of mobile technology (Tang, 2017) may contribute to the co-situation among queer women reported in these studies. This chapter examines a different set of digital and geographic influences with respect to the co-situation of queer women on Tinder.

Investigating Queer Women's Experiences of Tinder

As Tinder gained popularity following its launch in 2012, media outlets heralded it as "Grindr for straight people" (Muston, 2013). By 2014, Tinder's CEO Sean Rad reported that users were swiping through 1.2 billion profiles per day and generating more than 15 million matches per day (Bertoni, 2014). Surveys of Tinder users have found that their main motivations for using the app include entertainment and sexual partner-seeking (Carpenter & McEwan, 2016; Ranzini & Lutz, 2016), with women tending to use Tinder more for friendship and self-validation and men focused more on sexual encounters (Ranzini & Lutz, 2016). Newett, Churchill, and Robards (2017) found that for Australians aged 18–30, Tinder was a commonplace tool in their intimate lives, overlaying physical space with a shared digital space to facilitate the formation of connections and meeting face-to-face. While the app's marketing and uptake has generally encompassed a heterosexual user base, it is possible for individuals to switch their search criteria to "seeking" partners of the same gender, enabling LGBTQ people to use it as a tool in their intimate lives.

The methods I used to investigate queer women's use of Tinder were twofold. First, I conducted an app walkthrough (Light, Burgess, & Duguay, 2018) as an examination of Tinder's digital material influences on user experiences. The walkthrough first involved establishing the app's environment of expected use by ascertaining its vision, operating model, and governance processes from a scan of Tinder's policies, promotional materials, and ancillary media. Then I executed the technical walkthrough, moving step-by-step through Tinder's screens to identify the mediator characteristics (interface design, features, symbols, and discourses) through which it guides user activity. The swipe is Tinder's central functionality (Duguay, 2018), which focuses user activity on sorting through profiles one-by-one. Departing from the grid interface of apps like Grindr, Tinder presents profiles for swiping based not only on proximity but also on personalised algorithms tailored to a user's search criteria, profile information, and past swiping behaviour (Carr, 2016). Through the walkthrough, I established a foundational knowledge of Tinder's framing and functionality in which I grounded my subsequent research with users.

Secondly, I conducted interviews with ten queer, female-identified Tinder users. I recruited participants through LGBTQ communities and social media networks. Participants varied in age (from 19 to 35), job status (from student to service industry and white-collar workers), and sexual identity (with three identifying as gay, three as lesbian, one as bisexual, one as queer, one as pansexual, and one as "homoflexible"—interchangeably identifying as bisexual and pansexual). Eight participants were located in Australia and two were in Canada. Since all participants were living in sizeable urban centres, their experiences of using Tinder did not differ greatly based on their country, but participants noted specific aspects of physical locations that impacted their Tinder use. I conducted interviews in person and by Skype, asking participants to lead me through their Tinder profiles and swiping behaviour in a way that combined the walkthrough's attention to digital materiality with interviewee input (Light et al., 2018). Interviews lasted 60–90 minutes each and, following transcription, I iteratively coded them to identify descriptive, topical, and analytic themes (Morse & Richards, 2002). Participants' names have been replaced with their chosen pseudonyms. These methods posed some limitations, with recruitment leading to a sample of participants that was largely urban-dwelling, cisgender, and white. Therefore, this study only partially and initially addresses the need for research that explores the diversity of dating app users and their experiences. But for its part, this chapter examines the experiences of these ten women, which have been shaped by their varied sexual identities, ages, employment statuses, and encounters in physical and digital spaces.

Scarcity: Not Zero Feet Away

Participants were motivated to use Tinder through the promise of co-situation with other queer women on the app. Upon setting their search criteria to include women, they could sometimes identify other women using the same criteria. Julia (28, accountant) explained, "You can see them nearby, how many kilometres they are away. So yeah, and you can see some girls are obviously gay by their photos. It gives you a good indication." While Julia did not assume that every profile Tinder presented belonged to a queer woman, she picked up indicators through individuals' appearances and biographies. For Phyllis (23, student), installing Tinder in her densely populated neighbourhood was an eye-opening experience:

> I didn't realise there's actually a lot of gay people in my building, and I didn't realise that until I got the app. I figured out they must be screening [against] heterosexuality in my building because there's actually so many gay people.

She joked and continued her reflection, "I must be running into them in the elevators a lot. I don't see them unless they're on Tinder—not that I'm recognising any of them … maybe eventually if I run into them enough." Tinder provided Phyllis with a sense of co-situation by displaying queer women nearby and indicating they were close enough to live in the same building as her. However, her failure to encounter these women in shared physical space raised suspicion over the reliability of Tinder's co-situational information.

Several participants complained that Tinder was an unreliable tool for actually establishing co-situation with other queer women. ThunderGoddess (35, consultant) stated, "I don't find the location is nearly as accurate as Grindr." Identifying as bisexual, she frequently went to LGBTQ dance clubs with her gay male friends whose Grindr searches were more effective than Tinder at helping them find nearby potential partners. Grindr's marketing boasts of the app's ability to enable hook-ups at "zero feet away," giving it a reputation of being effective for initiating spontaneous sexual encounters despite sometimes compromising users' safety (Cook, 2014). In contrast, ThunderGoddess explained of Tinder:

> It's a location-based app but not a proximity-based app. It's not like going on Zomato—aka Urbanspoon—and being like, "Find the closest restaurant to me, stat!" "Find the closest hot guy or hot girl next to me, stat!" I don't use it at clubs.

She compared Tinder to Zomato, an app that identifies nearby restaurants. Although both Tinder and Zomato indicate a target's distance in kilometres or miles, Tinder's location accuracy was not reliable enough to enable ThunderGoddess to co-situate herself with other queer women in dance clubs.

More common than uneven experiences of digital but not physical co-situation were instances where participants swiped to "the end" of Tinder with no further profiles presented. Laura (34, project manager) identified this problem:

> My friend and I would just sit beside each other on a quiet Sunday night and be like, "Let's play Tinder together." … She was interested in men only, and at the time, I was women only, and I'd be done in ten minutes and she could go on, and on, and on.

Some participants again blamed the scarcity of profiles on Tinder's unreliable geolocation information, while others, like Bec (30, unemployed), questioned Tinder's uptake:

> The lesbians I do find on Tinder aren't usually that close to me … but then I can jump on that Brenda app or whatever it's called now, Whack Off or whatever, and they're 0.1 of a mile [away]—a lot of people. So, I know they're around but I don't think they're on Tinder.

She referred to Wapa, marketed as a "gay dating app for women" (Wapa, n.d.), which has a grid sorting interface similar to that of Grindr and displays women by proximity alongside specific location information. Along with conjecturing about Tinder's inaccurate location detection, ThunderGoddess also thought that the sparseness of queer women in her searches could be attributed to Tinder's saturation with heterosexual male users and queer women's hesitancy to use the app:

> I swipe through so many men to find so few women that it just gives me the impression that there really aren't that many queer ladies in [city]. Or at least [there aren't that many] that are really using it, because I know there are plenty of queer ladies in [city].

These women's experiences reflect that Tinder's technological mechanisms and its variable uptake among queer women contributed to a strong sense that queer women were scarce. This feeling of scarcity on the app, as announced by the "There's no one new around you" message, overlaid their experience of physical space to shake their hope of meeting nearby queer women. The factors explored in the following sections intensified this sense of scarcity.

Embodied Partner-Seeking

With the rise of location-based dating apps, partner-seeking has increasingly become focused on meeting people in close proximity (Quiroz, 2013). Participants reflected this preference to meet nearby others in their Tinder search criteria. While searches varied, from as near as 20 km to as far as 117 km, no participants expanded their search to Tinder's maximum radius of 160 km. Their reasons for finding partners within this limited range were practical: for Caitlin (24, nurse), meeting locations needed to be "accessible via public transport." Phyllis asserted, "I don't want to have to drive too far or to Skype anyone." It was of utmost importance to ThunderGoddess that matching on Tinder could lead to meeting in person: "I just sort of like hanging out with people in real life." She concurred, "I don't want to meet somebody on Tinder that I can't be with in person." In contrast to the geographically untethered lesbian communities that older technologies facilitated, these women used Tinder's geolocation features with the intent of meeting face-to-face.

A small search radius also enabled participants to meet with matches more rapidly. Laura described:

> Much like if you run into someone on the street and decided to go for coffee right then and there on the spot. So [Tinder] is more of an opportunity … to connect with someone, like have a spontaneous, kind of, drink or coffee, or go for a walk, or something.

Participants' desire to meet in person with little hindrance or delay departs from conceptions that lesbian dating is necessarily temporally slow (Murray & Ankerson, 2016). Their focus on in-person activities to increase familiarity also contrasts with the fast, transactional sexual encounters that MSM often arrange through apps (Licoppe et al., 2016). Instead, several participants wanted to connect through the app and meet face-to-face, after exchanging messages and background information, to determine if their connection would develop into a dating relationship. Danaë, who had set her radius the widest, was aware that her willingness to travel to meet her matches was exceptional. She planned to drive about 100 km to meet a woman with whom she felt an intense connection, "I matched her, like, two weeks ago and I'm seeing her for the first time on the weekend … So, she's special because I'm making that journey. I think I'm a little bit in love with her." By setting a narrow radius, based on the logistics of meeting in-person and a preference for spontaneity, most of the participants precluded the chance of meeting someone "special" for whom they would be willing to travel.

Although dating apps have rapidly increased in uptake (Smith, 2016), there remains some stigma around their use (Ahlm, 2016; Race, 2015). Participants were conscious of this when deciding where to access Tinder. Phyllis was wary of others spotting her using the app:

> I'm not one of those people that stands out in public and like, "Yeah, I'm using Tinder. I don't care." Because if I'm using it on the train or something, like I'm messaging someone, I'll be like, "Is there a security camera behind me? … Are they watching me on Tinder and laughing at me?"

She was concerned not only about the privacy of her messages but also about being seen as actively looking for dates on Tinder. For HotChocolate (35, secretary), Tinder helped her to pass time in her workplace, but she worried about homophobic colleagues seeing her using the app. She hid her Tinder use and did not discuss dates at work: "I didn't feel that it was necessary to openly out myself at work because I'm there to work as a secretary. I'm not a lesbian secretary; I'm just a secretary." These participants did not want to be situated in physical space with unknown others or formal acquaintances while looking for more intimate connections in the app's digital space. This contributed to a tendency to swipe on profiles from home or other regular, fairly private locations, which constrained the volume of women they encountered.

Tinder Tourism, Rural Locales, and Recognisability

Several participants engaged in Tinder tourism, using the app to meet people and arrange social and intimate encounters while travelling (Lean & Condie, 2017). On a trip across Europe, Julia paid for the premium version of Tinder so she could swipe on users in advance of arriving in her next location, "If I waited till I got there and was swiping, then it'd be too late because I'd match with someone and wouldn't have enough time to talk to them and try to organize a time to see them." Using the premium version added a temporal dimension to the app that allowed for arranging co-situated encounters in the future. Similarly, Briana (28, student) used Tinder while travelling through Hong Kong and Bangkok, "I got a few invites to a pool party; another [match] was a DJ. It was kind of cool to see that there was a queer community over there." Making connections with women on the app enabled her to enter a queer social scene and gave her a sense of community. Gertie (34, accountant) could see how Tinder would be useful for queer women travelling through her city because there was no gay village demarcating the LGBTQ social scene, "It's not in tourist books [to] go down this street and that's the gay street … there's no fricking rainbow on the bloody road." Similar to how MSM use dating apps not only for intimate encounters but also to find friends, employment, and accommodation when arriving in a new city (Shield, 2016), participants formed these sorts of connections through Tinder.

Despite their experiences with Tinder tourism, some participants also felt that tourists just passing through their cities highlighted the lack of local queer women. ThunderGoddess sighed, "I've connected with so many people—probably a third of the people on that [match] list are people who don't live here." Phyllis also felt like she was close to swiping through all the queer women who lived in her city, "I think there's so few gay people in [city] … it's sort of a challenge to get every single gay person in [city] on my Tinder—I'm going to do it eventually." She was certain she could map out her city's small queer community simply by swiping through the profiles of users who were not just travelling through.

However, participants found it was easier to meet women on Tinder in urban centres than in less populated areas. Julia's travels took her to small cities and towns where Tinder was useless, "[The] Greek islands, Ibiza—there were a few people but not many at all, and then I went to the South of France and there was none." While MSM in less populated areas often still use Grindr and await new users to enter their proximity (Blackwell et al., 2015), several of the women I spoke with were reticent to use Tinder in rural locations. Imminently moving to a small town, Caitlin was undecided, "It could be useful to meet people ... but there's no privacy when you're using social media in a small town." She felt a lack of control over who would see her Tinder profile, and she believed that most people would recognise her from the app in physical spaces around town. Phyllis was adamant that it was not a useful tool in her small hometown:

> There's no one, and everyone knows everyone there too, because it's just a small city. There [are] three lesbians there so you can't use Tinder. If you want to date someone there, you go down to the bar and you find that other lesbian and you date that lesbian. That's what you do. Everyone will know in five minutes, and then if you've got to break up with [her], you've got to move cities.

Phyllis was concerned not only with a lack of Tinder users in her town but also with how well everyone there knew each other. In contrast to Tinder, which necessitates swiping to get a sense of whether others are nearby and places a 160 km limit on non-paying users' searches, Grindr displays users across a broad radius, giving the sense that other MSM exist even if they are fairly distant (Blackwell et al., 2015). Grindr's ads for its premium version promise users that they will be able to see "6x the guys"[3] if they pay, providing certainty that there are indeed more men on the app. Tinder only allowed Phyllis to see the limited number of lesbians situated in her hometown and, like other participants, she did not want to be recognisable both on a dating app and in that familiar physical space when she may not want to pursue a relationship with these particular women.

---

[3] In-app Grindr advertisement from the 2018 version for iPhone.

This unevenness of co-situation posed a problem for several participants. They were wary of Tinder when they were likely to be recognised in physical spaces by app users in whom they were disinterested or prior to confirming mutual interest. Bec's profile photos were older snapshots from before she cut her hair "because I've been to some lesbian events where I can tell people recognise me from some of the dating apps and that's a little bit awkward." She preferred to surprise Tinder matches with her short hair rather than be instantly recognisable to women with whom she had not sparked a connection in physical spaces. When Danaë encountered an acquaintance from an in-person context on Tinder, she attempted to intensify their connection through the app, "I swiped her and turned out, she swiped me, and then I said something like, 'Well, now we matched on Tinder, I guess we're obligated to flirt.'" But Danaë was embarrassed when the woman did not flirt back, "I felt so disappointed … Like, now I'm going to have to see you again IRL [in real life] and we've matched on Tinder but not had a conversation. So, that failure's just going to loom above us." With this woman already in her social network, Danaë was concerned about seeing her again in physical space when their encounter on Tinder had not worked out. In instances when these queer women did not want to be recognisable to others, whether because of failed flirtations or the airing of their dating desires across contexts, co-situation on Tinder became a problem rather than a sought-after outcome. Scarcity in these situations was experienced as a surplus of acquaintances but a lack of viable (often equated with previously unknown) dating or sexual partners.

Intrusions in Co-situated Space

Queer women's scarcity on Tinder was highlighted by the volume of profiles in participants' searches that belonged to other kinds of users. Even participants who set their search criteria to show "only women" often encountered three other types of profiles. First, participants spoke about "fake" profiles, which were unlikely to be operated by the individual depicted in the profile photos. Julia recounted:

> There was this one [user] that was a girl and then they're like, 'Can you send me some photos? Send it to this number.' And then I got my housemate to call the number and it was a guy's voicemail.

Several participants noted that sexually aggressive conversations and photoshopped pictures were often indicators of fake accounts (those with deceptive intentions). Julia became an expert at spotting these users, noting that they often had few Facebook friends, and warned, "If they start talking dirty straightaway or they ask for nudes, then it's a guy. That's happened to me probably five times—probably more than that actually." Profiles operated by men were common in participants' searches and sometimes appeared forthrightly as such. Participants assumed this was a glitch in the app or a user purposely invading searches by switching gender settings.

The second type of account that frequently appeared in participants' searches belonged to heterosexual couples looking to match with bisexual women. Caitlin found that most of these accounts stated in their profile, "We're looking for someone to have some fun with," and she found it easy to "just screen them out." However, Julia noted that some couples' accounts were challenging to identify, "There's a lot of those and some of them you can't tell from the profile. It might just be photos of the girl and not a girl and a guy. Yeah, or single—if they just said single." Although some Tinder users may be looking for sexual or romantic arrangements with multiple partners, couples' accounts that omitted their intentions perpetuated a form of deception similar to that of the aforementioned fake accounts. Since Tinder does not have options to specify non-monogamous relationship formats, the app also contributes to these accounts appearing out-of-place in queer women's searches for other single women.

Third, participants encountered several accounts belonging to heterosexual women looking for friends or to engage in flirtatious behaviour without the intention to start a relationship. Danaë spotted these accounts by the women's "duck face selfies," posing with a pouty mouth to emphasise their femininity, and explained:

> The *straight girl look* is like the, "I'm going to go out tonight and get drunk and have sex with a guy and it's going to be so much fun. And I'm just on Tinder for friends/sleep with me and my boyfriend."

She noted an overlap between "straight girls'" profiles and those of couples looking for threesomes, since these women were often looking to temporarily experiment with their sexuality. Briana suggested that Tinder could provide a filter regulating the visibility of these profiles by including a "sexuality" field in the search criteria. This would help her to "know if that person is going to swipe on me or whether they're just looking for—like, if they're straight and looking for friends." Tinder has since acquired the app Hey! VINA, which it markets as "Tinder for (girl) friends!" but also promotes its original app as a place where users can meet new people for a range of purposes including friendship (Recode, 2016). Altogether, men, couples, and heterosexual women crowded the digital space on Tinder where participants attempted to co-situate themselves with other queer women.

Conclusion

This chapter has illustrated that these queer women's notions of scarcity in relation to other queer women on Tinder stemmed from two outcomes of the app's technological arrangements, user choices, and social context. These outcomes involved Tinder's failure to co-situate participants with other queer women and, when co-situation occurred, the common experience of unintended or undesirable co-situation. With regard to technological arrangements, failure to co-situate emerged from Tinder's reportedly unreliable locational information, constraints on search proximity, and the swipe interface that displayed others one-by-one with a finite supply of users due to its 160 km cut-off. Social factors precipitating failed co-situation included the app's variable uptake among queer women, their reluctance to meet women who were not in close proximity, and their tendency to swipe in repeated and private locations. Through these sociotechnical arrangements, these queer women did not experience Tinder in the same way that some MSM experience dating apps as catalogues of men or tools for indicating possible hook-ups that are zero feet away. Instead, participants' lack of co-situation with queer women on Tinder contributed to feelings of despair and scepticism that they would meet potential partners located near them in physical space. None of them spoke about Tinder fostering familiarity or a sense of community among queer women. Rather, their queer communities convened in physical spaces where recognition through Tinder posed awkward complications of uneven co-situation. In these instances, participants felt a lack of control over who might have seen their profile and whether rejection in one space would bleed into the other.

This kind of undesirable co-situation and other forms of it were also subject to sociotechnical influences, with social norms and meanings playing a large role. Participants often felt that co-situation was undesirable when they were recognisable to broad audiences both on the app and in physical space. This sort of co-situation was experienced as potentially reputation-damaging, reflected in Caitlin's worries about having her sexual desires disclosed as she settled into a small town. Recognisability in digital and physical space impeded participants' ability to first make an impression either on Tinder or in person and then carefully guide the melding of these spaces. Participants were also co-situated with deceptive accounts, couples, and heterosexual women, which they often found undesirable since these users complicated their search for other queer women. While MSM sometimes encounter heterosexual women on apps like Grindr (e.g. Beusman & Sunderland, 2015), Tinder's widespread user base makes co-situation with a range of users highly likely, without providing controls for users to limit their visibility to these audiences or more finely filter their searches.

Tinder's failure to co-situate these queer women with desired potential partners on the app and in physical space had a tangible impact on their views towards the geographical proximity of other queer women. While some participants expressed that they knew other queer women were located in the same city based on their experiences in queer spaces and connections they had already made, participants also often responded with despair. This chapter's opening quote demonstrates this oscillation, as Danaë wavered between the sentiment "Of course there are lesbians ... that don't have Tinder" and the feeling of "That's it." While this chapter has outlined both social and technological influences on queer women's digital co-situation, it is clear that there are tangible aspects of Tinder's design (e.g. search options, profile fields, and interface layout) that could help to alleviate this sense of scarcity. Any dating app seeking to include queer women in its user base should recognise the importance of these design considerations for making users feel less alone on the app and in their surroundings.

Acknowledgements Thank you to Jean Burgess and Elija Cassidy, who contributed insights into the analysis that has taken shape here. Thanks also to those at the McGill Queer Research Colloquium where I presented some of these conclusions. I would like to convey deepest thanks to the participants who discussed their Tinder use with me.

References

Ahlm, J. (2016). Respectable promiscuity: Digital cruising in an era of queer liberalism. *Sexualities, 20*(3), 364–379. https://doi.org/10.1177/1363460716665783

Barker, M., Richards, C., & Bowes-Catton, H. (2009). "All the world is queer save thee and ME …": Defining queer and bi at a critical sexology seminar. *Journal of Bisexuality, 9*(3–4), 363–379.

Bertoni, S. (2014). *Tinder swipes right to revenue, will add premium service in November*. Retrieved from http://www.forbes.com/sites/stevenbertoni/2014/10/20/tinder-swipes-right-to-revenue-will-add-premium-service-in-november/

Beusman, C., & Sunderland, M. (2015). The girls who use Grindr. *Broadly*. Retrieved from https://broadly.vice.com/en_us/article/pg79qm/the-girls-who-use-grindr

Blackwell, C., Birnholtz, J., & Abbott, C. (2015). Seeing and being seen: Co-situation and impression formation using Grindr, a location-aware gay dating app. *New Media & Society, 17*(7), 1117–1136. https://doi.org/10.1177/1461444814521595

Bonner-Thompson, C. (2017). "The meat market": Production and regulation of masculinities on the Grindr grid in Newcastle-upon-Tyne, UK. *Gender, Place and Culture, 524*(November), 1–15. https://doi.org/10.1080/0966369X.2017.1356270

Brubaker, J. R., Ananny, M., & Crawford, K. (2016). Departing glances: A sociotechnical account of "leaving" Grindr. *New Media & Society, 18*(3), 373–390. https://doi.org/10.1177/1461444814542311

Bucher, T., & Helmond, A. (2017). The affordances of social media platforms. In J. Burgess, T. Poell, & A. Marwick (Eds.), *The sage handbook of social media* (pp. 233–253). London and New York: Sage.

Campbell, J. E. (2004). *Getting it on online: Cyberspace, gay male sexuality, and embodied identity*. New York: Routledge.

Carpenter, C. J., & McEwan, B. (2016). The players of micro-dating: Individual and gender differences in goal orientations toward micro-dating apps. *First Monday, 21*(5), 1–10.

Carr, A. (2016, January 11). I found out my secret internal Tinder rating and now I wish I hadn't. *Fast Company*. Retrieved from https://www.fastcompany.com/3054871/whats-your-tinder-score-inside-the-apps-internal-ranking-system

Cassidy, E. (2016). Social networking sites and participatory reluctance: A case study of Gaydar, user resistance and interface rejection. *New Media & Society, 18*(11), 2613–2628. https://doi.org/10.1177/1461444815590341

Chaplin, T. (2014). Lesbians online: Queer identity and community formation on the French Minitel. *Journal of the History of Sexuality, 23*(3), 451–472. https://doi.org/10.7560/JHS23305

Choy, C. H. Y. (2018). Smartphone apps as cosituated closets: A lesbian app, public/private spaces, mobile intimacy, and collapsing contexts. *Mobile Media and Communication, 6*(1), 88–107. https://doi.org/10.1177/2050157917727803

Cook, J. (2014, August 29). Security flaw in gay dating app Grindr reveals precise location of 90% of users. *Business Insider*. Retrieved from http://www.businessinsider.com/exploit-reveals-location-of-grindr-users-2014-8?

Cooper, M. (2010). Lesbians who are married to men: Identity, collective stories, and the Internet online community. In C. Pullen & M. Cooper (Eds.), *LGBT identity and online new media* (pp. 75–86). New York: Routledge.

Cooper, M., & Dzara, K. (2010). The Facebook revolution: LGBT identity and activism. In C. Pullen & M. Cooper (Eds.), *LGBT identity and online new media* (pp. 100–112). New York: Routledge.

Correll, S. (1995). The ethnography of an electronic bar: The Lesbian Cafe. *Journal of Contemporary Ethnography, 24*(3), 270–298. https://doi.org/10.1177/089124195024003002

David, G., & Cambre, C. (2016). Screened intimacies: Tinder and the swipe logic. *Social Media + Society, April–June*, 1–11. https://doi.org/10.1177/2056305116641976

de Souza e Silva, A. (2006). From cyber to hybrid: Mobile technologies as interfaces of hybrid spaces. *Space and Culture, 9*(3), 261–278. https://doi.org/10.1177/1206331206289022

Dourish, P. (2016). Rematerializing the platform: Emulation and the digital-material. In S. Pink, E. Ardevol, & D. Lanzeni (Eds.), *Digital materialities: Design and anthropology* (pp. 29–44). London: Bloomsbury.

Duguay, S. (2018). Tinder - Swiped: A focal gesture and contested app visions. In J. W. Morris & S. Murray (Eds.), *Appified: Culture in the age of apps* (pp. 127–135). Ann Arbor, MI: University of Michigan Press.

Duguay, S., Burgess, J., & Light, B. (2017). Mobile dating and hookup app culture. In P. Messaris & L. Humphreys (Eds.), *Digital media: Transformations in human communication* (2nd ed., pp. 213–221). New York: Peter Lang.

Fletcher, G., & Light, B. (2007). Going offline: An exploratory cultural artifact analysis of an internet dating site's development trajectories. *International Journal of Information Management, 27*(6), 422–431. https://doi.org/10.1016/j.ijinfomgt.2007.08.001

Ghaziani, A. (2014). *There goes the gayborhood?* Princeton: Princeton University Press.

Gray, M. L. (2009). *Out in the country: Youth, media, and queer visibility in rural America*. New York: New York University Press.

Gudelunas, D. (2012). There's an app for that: The uses and gratifications of online social networks for gay men. *Sexuality & Culture, 16*(4), 347–365. https://doi.org/10.1007/s12119-012-9127-4

Hjorth, L., & Lim, S. S. (2012). Mobile intimacy in an age of affective mobile media. *Feminist Media Studies, 12*(4), 477–484. https://doi.org/10.1080/14680777.2012.741860

Lean, G., & Condie, J. (2017). The curious case of Tinder tourism. *Critical Tourism Studies Proceedings, 69*. Retrieved from http://digitalcommons.library.tru.ca/cts-proceedings/vol2017/iss1/69

Licoppe, C., Riviere, C. A., & Morel, J. (2016). Grindr casual hook-ups as interactional achievements. *New Media & Society, 18*(11), 2540–2558. https://doi.org/10.1177/1461444815589702

Light, B., Burgess, J., & Duguay, S. (2018). The walkthrough method: An approach to the study of apps. *New Media & Society, 20*(3), 881–900. https://doi.org/10.1177/1461444816675438

McVeigh-Schultz, J., & Baym, N. K. (2015). Thinking of you: Vernacular affordance in the context of the microsocial relationship app, Couple. *Social Media + Society, 1*(2), 1–13. https://doi.org/10.1177/2056305115604649

Miles, S. (2017). Sex in the digital city: Location-based dating apps and queer urban life. *Gender, Place and Culture, 524*, 1–16. https://doi.org/10.1080/0966369X.2017.1340874
Morse, J., & Richards, L. (2002). *Read me first for a user's guide to qualitative research*. Thousand Oaks, CA: Sage.
Mowlabocus, S. (2010). *Gaydar culture: Gay men, technology and embodiment in the digital age*. Farnham: Ashgate.
Murray, S., & Ankerson, M. (2016). Lez takes time: Designing lesbian contact in geosocial networking apps. *Critical Studies in Media Communication, 33*(1), 53–69. https://doi.org/10.1080/15295036.2015.1133921
Muston, S. (2013). *Meet Tinder – aka the "shy Grindr"*. Retrieved from http://www.independent.co.uk/news/media/online/meet-tinder-aka-the-shy-grindr-8460863.html
Nash, C. J. (2013). The age of the "post-mo"? Toronto's gay Village and a new generation. *Geoforum, 49*, 243–252. https://doi.org/10.1016/j.geoforum.2012.11.023
Newett, L., Churchill, B., & Robards, B. (2017). Forming connections in the digital era: Tinder, a new tool in young Australian intimate life. *Journal of Sociology*, September. https://doi.org/10.1177/1440783317728584
Quiroz, P. A. (2013). From finding the perfect love online to satellite dating and "loving-the-one-you're near": A look at Grindr, Skout, Plenty of Fish, Meet Moi, Zoosk and assisted serendipity. *Humanity & Society, 37*(2), 181–185. https://doi.org/10.1177/0160597613481727
Race, K. (2015). Speculative pragmatism and intimate arrangements: Online hook-up devices in gay life. *Culture, Health & Sexuality, 17*(4), 496–511.
Ranzini, G., & Lutz, C. (2016). Love at first swipe? Explaining tinder self-presentation and motives. *Mobile Media & Communication, 5*, 1–22. https://doi.org/10.1177/2050157916664559
Recode. (2016). *Full video: Tinder CEO Sean Rad at Code 2016*. Retrieved from http://www.recode.net/2016/6/17/11966748/sean-rad-tinder-full-video-code
Shield, A. (2016). New in town: Gay immigrants and geosocial dating apps. In A. Dhoest, L. Szulc, & B. Eeckhout (Eds.), *LGBTQs, media, and culture in Europe: Situated case studies*. London: Routledge.
Smith, A. (2016). *15% of American adults have used online dating sites or mobile dating apps*. Retrieved from http://www.pewinternet.org/2016/02/11/15-percent-of-american-adults-have-used-online-dating-sites-or-mobile-dating-apps/

Tang, D. T. S. (2017). All I get is an emoji: Dating on lesbian mobile phone app Butterfly. *Media, Culture and Society, 39*(6), 816–832. https://doi.org/10.1177/0163443717693680

Wapa. (n.d.). *Wapa: The fresh gay dating app for women*. Retrieved from http://wapa-app.com/

7

Going the Distance: Locative Dating Technology and Queer Male Practice-Based Identities

Sam Miles

Introduction

> *'Michael'*[1] *loads his Grindr app with a shiver of anticipation. He has been stuck in meetings for most of the afternoon, followed by an underground commute that temporarily cut off his 4G connection, but he is now back at home. He is once again connected, and ready to connect. The app opens with a yellow glow, and the bright screen fills with faces and bodies, all within his district of south London. He navigates straight to his new clutch of unread messages and replies to each with the same catch-all response: 'good thx, u?'*

This quotidian hybrid routine, as practised by 'Michael', is a fictional snapshot, but one that has been amalgamated from the narratives of several respondents in a research project exploring male–male locative dating app use amongst men living and working in London, UK. The snapshot

[1] Pseudonyms are used throughout this chapter.

S. Miles (✉)
London School of Hygiene and Tropical Medicine, London, UK
e-mail: s.miles@qmul.ac.uk

C. Nash, A. Gorman-Murray (eds.), *The Geographies of Digital Sexuality*,
https://doi.org/10.1007/978-981-13-6876-9_7

functions as a metaphor for one typology of practice amongst many more for queer technology users seeking social and sexual relationships in the contemporary city. This chapter develops scholarship in both geographies of sexualities and digital geographies by exploring how digital–physical hybridisation mediated by locative dating apps shapes queer male practice-based identities, and how these typologies might in turn inform physical queer encounters.

Drawing from a qualitative research project involving in-depth interviews with 36 'MSM' (men who have sex with men—a definition that includes, but is not limited to, gay and bisexual men), I explore the impact of online connection on different 'routes' to physical meeting, analysing how practice-based online identities inform subsequent physical encounters. I argue that certain modes of behaviour help to identify a particular range of users, and that these practice-based identities are implicitly linked to different forms of hybridisation. This chapter draws on recent scholarship in hybridisation as well as my own empirical research results in order to sketch three typologies of queer male app user that function as examples of different practice-based identities: the 'embracer', the 'time-waster' and the 'minimalist'. These typologies offer a snapshot into a larger diversity of use, and are by no means objective or essentialist categories: indeed, my own research has muddied definitional categorisation, demonstrating the imbrications between different 'types' of use from the same user at different times, depending on personal motivation, the 'market' of available online matches and the genre of the app in question (Miles, 2017). Instead, what these typologies illustrate is the intriguing variety in modes of user engagement that become bound up in, and mediated by, the digital and physical hybridisation enabled by popular mobile media platforms.

This study of typologies of practice is important because it generates implications for how identities are practised through hybrid technologies that incorporate digital practices into physical realms, which in a contemporary context of ubiquitous, personalised and pervasive technology increasingly informs interpersonal communication. I argue that whilst different user typologies are differently represented in online locative media, it is the mode of use, as well as the 'type' of user, that underpins the nature of technological involvement. What follows is a proposal that we use these sketched-out case studies as a way into understanding typologies of *practice*, which in turn generate distinctive practice-based identities that can be extrapolated beyond thinking about online, offline and hybrid spaces to wider questions about identities, sexualities and digital geographies.

The Irresistible Hybridisation of Locative Media

Given that online and offline lives are increasingly interwoven, hybridisation is now a reality for geographies of sexualities in the digital age. Hybridisation provides a useful way of thinking about the interconnected dimensions of all sorts of spaces and practices as types of assemblage (following Latour, 2006, amongst others), used in this chapter as a descriptive rather than conceptual tool for exploring practice-based identities. Yet hybridisation represents a particularly intriguing way to think about the incorporation of technology into human sexual experiences. This is because sex and sexuality have been so tangibly mediated by technological apparatus over recent years, from internet pornography to virtual reality environments, and from online chatroom communities to niche-interest matchmaking portals. GPS-mediated partner-seeking apps hosted by mobile phones, such as Grindr, Tinder and Hornet, represent a distinctive (and sometimes provocative) chapter in this ongoing relationship by collapsing established understandings of time and space into an altogether more intense sensory user experience.

Developments in mobile phone software over the past decade have made hybridity a key feature of internet access, collapsing historical separations between physical and digital terrain. Online or 'virtual' space has progressed from an entity distinct from the real world into a more haptic environment predicated on more extensive entanglements with physical or 'real' human experiences (Brubaker, Ananny, & Crawford, 2014; Davis, Flowers, Lorimer, Oakland, & Frankis, 2016; Farman, 2012; McGlotten, 2013). Practice-based identities are constituted through the circulations between persons, objects, digital environments and material environments that make up this technological hybridisation as performed via mobile technology. Beyond the established sense of a meshing of digital and physical terrain, hybridisation is understood here to synthesise relationships established online with physical meetings realised offline.

One way in which mobile media technology has been popularised is via GPS-enabled, or locative, mobile phone dating and hook-up platforms. These platforms utilise the mapping software built into contemporary smartphone software to locate the phone, and therefore the app user, with cartographic specificity. The app then shares these coordinates with other users to build up a sophisticated snapshot of spatial proximity. These apps provide a valuable way to interrogate technological hybridity because they overlay physical terrain with an online map of potential social or sexual partners. They go beyond providing a 'new layer of virtual sites superimposed over geographic spaces' (Kitchin, 1998, p. 403), to invite the almost seamless hybridisation of virtual and embodied domains, which in turn expedites new online and offline encounters for locative app users. These users can communicate remotely with others virtually whilst moving around their own physical environment, but then shift that virtual communication into its own embodied encounter in physical space, thanks to sophisticated GPS algorithms that parse potential partners by geographic distance.

Long considered 'early adopters' of new technologies (Mowlabocus, 2010; see also Miles, 2018; Skeggs, Moran, Tyrer, & Binnie, 2004), MSM have colonised locative dating and hook-up apps such as Grindr, Tinder and Hornet in particularly high numbers compared to heterosexual populations, and done so across a range of age groups, ethnicities and socioeconomic backgrounds. Prestage et al. (2015) find that in Australia, for example, men meeting same-sex partners online for either casual or romantic relationships has now replaced other methods of encounter *across every age group*. This disproportionate adoption by MSM within a single decade (market leader Grindr was released late in 2009, and was not even initially internationally available) is perhaps less surprising given the historical affinity between MSM and online dating and chat communities (Campbell, 2004; Grov, Breslow, Newcomb, Rosenberger, & Bauermeister, 2013; Rosenfeld & Thomas, 2012). Grindr now boasts over 10 million users in 192 countries worldwide, and, along with its competitor apps, seems to generate affection and frustration in equal measure amongst its subscribers. The ability of these platforms to connect hundreds or even thousands of plugged-in users simultaneously based on physical coordinates is also the source of much popular media debate about how these networks are best navigated and how users present their identities online.

Research into locative technology has tended to overlook hybridisation itself in favour of thinking about what virtuality signifies for representation, masculinities and display (see McGlotten, 2013; Woo, 2013 amongst others). Yet the emphasis of these locative products lies in shifting online communication to physical encounter. For example, sending one's geographical 'pin' to another user online in the virtual 'space' of an app in anticipation of meeting mediates this intensely hybrid physical and digital space via spatial cartography, blending a social media network approach with something more erotically charged. The need now is to consider locative media not just in terms of online presentation and effect (and indeed in terms of affect too) but how these online presentations inform lived behaviour. In the case of this chapter, that journey is explored through online user typologies that variously expedite or impede the route to offline physical queer encounter. Unpacking in more detail this journey from virtual communication to embodied meeting is key to understanding how technology users are subject to—or actively participate in—the sociotechnical relations that mediate contemporary geographies of sexualities.

Let's (Not) Get Physical

Parallel to the growing popularity of locative media as a broker for queer male (and increasingly, female) intimacies, queer-coded spaces that historically constituted sites for community are becoming fragmented by changing patterns of sociality. The decline, or at least deconcentration, of physical queer venues (Campkin & Marshall, 2017; Nash & Gorman-Murray, 2014, 2016) is in part the result of macro-level economic shifts (Andersson, 2011; Delany, 1999; Hubbard, 2011), as well as a sense of detachment from the gay community, not least for those historically less represented within its environs (Nash, 2013). Yet the convenience offered by locative partner-seeking apps, and their seamless domestication into the home of what were formerly public encounters, plays no small part in this shift to privatised sex and socialisation. Whilst unlikely to be the sole driver for deconcentration of physical sites for same-sex encounter, there is evidence to suggest that the use of locative dating and hook-up apps by MSM does impact on queer physical spaces, particularly in urban settings (Collins & Drinkwater, 2016; Ghaziani, 2014; Nash, 2013; Nash & Gorman-Murray, 2014; Race, 2015). This impact is significant, given the valorisation of urban environments for the particular affordances they have historically offered for forging connection and encountering difference (Young, 1990). Of course, safety in public space is not guaranteed, as a long history of 'gay-bashing' and police scrutiny demonstrate (Andersson, 2011; Turner, 2003), but over the past half-century, these public city spaces have come to represent 'new visions of cosmopolitanism whereby plural and accommodating subject positions could be fostered amidst the tolerance and diversity of urban life' (Koch & Latham, 2012, p. 145).[2] The net result is a rapidly changing environment for sexual minorities that increasingly mediates encounter virtually whilst struggling to demarcate queerness publicly.

The burgeoning popularity of MSM locative apps certainly testifies to extensive male–male social and sexual encounter, with a significant proportion of these encounters now brokered by apps rather than more traditional embodied scenarios in gay bars or community venues, or comparatively older technological apparatus such as desktop websites Gaydar or GayRomeo (platforms that themselves cohered a space for a far greater range of 'spectators' than the average real-life gay bar (Mowlabocus, 2010, p. 192)).[3] It is my belief that the outcome of this different assemblage may see spontaneous sociability, in the guise of chance encounters in physical space, being replaced by more focused networking. The impact may be ambiguously experienced—for some,

[2] Notwithstanding valid critiques of the restricted access to these sites predicated on ethnicity, class or income (see for example Bassi, 2006; Jaspal, 2017; Lewis, 2016).

[3] Nevertheless, it is worth acknowledging the many commonalities, as well as obvious differences, between contemporary locative media apps and their immediate predecessors on static landline computers. As Mowlabocus argues, physical and virtual concepts on desktop platforms 'are not discrete but pervade one another, with digital communications often structuring physical practices, identities and experiences' (Mowlabocus, 2010, p. 2).

the digitally mediated encounter expedites a specific and desired goal; for others, the streamlined algorithm inhibits the potential for spontaneous introductions predicated upon physical co-presence. The sheer diversity in MSM populations, whether in terms of self-defined sexuality, age, socioeconomic background or ethnicity, might presuppose fragmentation regarding any meaningful sense of queer community, but MSM app users do still valorise a sense of community (Hubbard, Collins, & Gorman-Murray, 2015), and to some extent exercise this via intense sociality in their locative app use (Miles, 2017). It may be that one consequence of the rapid growth in MSM locative media apps is that the hybridised spaces these platforms produce can cohere entirely new composite environments that compete with established, embodied spaces for queer male socialisation; or conversely that MSM locative apps succeed in areas with an established 'critical mass' of interested parties—whether comprised of traditional 'gay villages' or more diffuse queer populations, or generally cosmopolitan locales (Gorman-Murray & Nash, 2017; Nash & Gorman-Murray, 2016).

What is uncontestable is that the progressive foregrounding of online platforms for physical encounter in queer male culture provokes consideration of online identity, practice and even ethics. Locative hybridisation alters the parameters of the encounters that constitute sociality or community, for example through processes of selection that improve user efficiency in scoping potential partners. Aside from the debates pitting locative media against physical encounter already explored in this chapter, some scholars have argued that mobile technology commodifies intimacy itself, replacing committed relationships with more fleeting connections (Badiou, 2012; Bauman, 2003; Turkle, 2011). This is a well-rehearsed form of dissent against the creeping incorporation of digital technology into every aspect of contemporary lived experience, exemplified by socio-technical hybridisation more effectively than perhaps any other scenario. In reality, there is nothing to suggest that these hybridised and expedited digital connections are necessarily less valuable in their own form than the more orthodox relations that preceded them and which humanistic scholarship tends to valorise. Nevertheless, looking more closely at how MSM app users practise their identities online and how this impacts on 'real'-life intimacies as they are brokered by locative technology can prove valuable, not just for thinking about changing queer male sexual practices, but as a way into larger debates about hybridised life for *any* contemporary technology user. Identifying three user typologies as exemplars for practice-based identity work helps us to conceptualise digital–physical hybridisation through embodied practices that we can recognise and digest.

The Research Project

Thirty-six participants were involved in the research project on which these results are based. Semi-structured interviews were conducted in public spaces including cafes, libraries and meeting rooms across London, UK, over the course of one year. Participation in the study was voluntary, and recruitment, data collection and analysis all adhered to institutional ethical requirements.

App users became involved in the project by either responding to recruitment posters in public spaces around London, contacting a passive recruitment profile[4] on Grindr, Tinder and Hornet, or becoming involved as 'snowball' volunteers who learnt about the study from their peers. The eligibility criteria utilised in recruitment were left deliberately broad in order not to narrow focus to subgroups of male users channelled by age, background or ethnicity but instead to ensure that empirical outcomes captured the commonalities and differences typical of this diverse cross-section of use. Twenty-five participants were white/Caucasian, six were 'BAME' (Black, Asian and Minority Ethnic) and five were mixed heritage, and participants ranged in age from 18 to 65 years old. Thirty-two participants identified as gay, three as bisexual or bi-curious, and one as straight but sexually involved with men. The majority of participants were single at the time of interview, but five were partnered, of whom three were in open relationships. The sheer diversity of users, and their corresponding approaches to the hybridised practice central to locative technologies, invites us to sketch out several typologies of user amongst many more modes of use described by participants.

[4] That is, a deliberately general invitation for involvement rather than actively approaching users.

Three User Typologies

The following section argues that the hybridisation of digital and physical environments enabled by locative media has the effect of producing distinct practice-based identities, which are demonstrated here via three fictionalised vignettes amalgamated from real-life users. These typologies are informed by data collected, but they are not the only three, and being aligned to one typology does not invalidate commonalities with another. Nevertheless, these clusters of behaviours provide a fitting reflection of the way in which participants tended to categorise or 'sort' other online users into groups as a way to ascertain their availability and interest in offline partnering. Approximately one third of the total participant group expressed 'embracer' traits, another third expressed 'time-waster' traits and a smaller proportion—about one-fifth—demonstrated 'minimalist' traits (see Fig. 7.1). The paucity of 'minimalist' typologies amongst the group logically correlates with the comparative reluctance of this type of user to volunteer for involvement in a research project about app use. An overlap between 'embracer' and 'time-waster' traits suggests changing

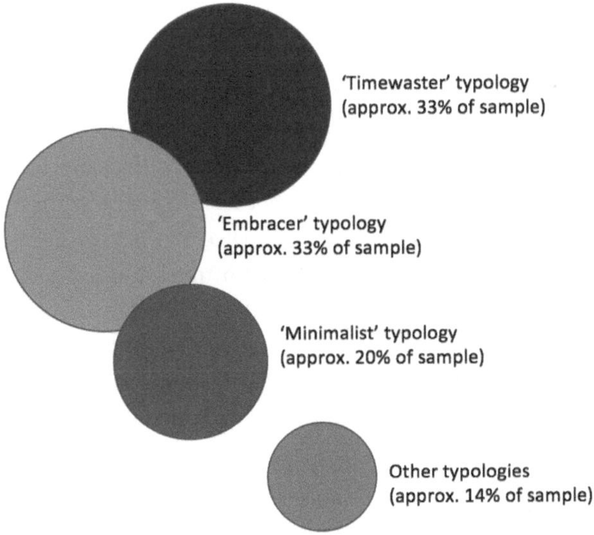

Fig. 7.1 Visualisation of different male–male dating app user typologies

appetites within each user for app-mediated encounters over time, but more surprising were small overlaps between 'minimalist' and 'embracer' traits, emphasising the flexible, rather than rigid, nature of these practice-based identities. These overlaps also serve to emphasise that it is *type* of use, rather than user, that informs each profile (after Gorman-Murray, 2009).

The Embracer

Mikori, 29, is a long-time user of Grindr, Tinder, Hornet, Jack'd and Scruff. He logs into all five of these apps every day, reasoning that each app brings with it a different (and sometimes overlapping) selection of potential matches. Grindr, he points out, features the users of almost every other app he uses, and some more besides. Mikori works as an advertising executive for a global brand and has no qualms about displaying his smiling face in his profile picture, along with his age, weight, interests and hobbies. He is looking for dating and longer-term relationships, but is happy to meet for sex too, and has in the past cycled between these goals as and when he meets other users. He sometimes uses the app in his workplace and shares particularly exciting matches with his (female) colleagues, as well as debriefing them after his weekday evening dates at gay bars in Soho, London.

The 'embracer' as a type of app user (recognising the elasticity inherent in that labelling) is able to adapt quickly to the hybrid experience of locative media, and uses the apps in a manner that broadly reflects the idealised mode of use promoted in the way in which these apps are marketed. The embracer is happy to include a photo of their face in their online profile and furnishes that profile with an honest and extensive biography that may include metrics such as height and weight, location, interests, HIV status and a description of who (as well as what) they are looking for. This is a consumer who willingly participates in, rather than refutes, the entangled public–private model of hybrid digital–physical engagement promoted by MSM locative apps. Amongst the sample for this project, whilst around half of participants' narratives suggested 'embracer' traits, only one third of participants actually evidenced 'embracer' traits in relaying their online practices to the researcher (Fig. 7.1). Whilst these attributes can only ever be subjectively categorised, it does suggest an intriguing disconnect between self-perceived and actualised identity practices in the sample, since the 'embracer' is arguably seen to be the most confident or socially secure typology.

The openness with which these apps operate for those opting into the semi-public app environment is especially striking compared to predecessors in online MSM dating and hook-up culture. Indeed, Tinder—an app that dominates the heterosexual matchmaking scene in the UK and US—goes as far as to connect the user's account to their Facebook profile, with the neat (or unnerving) result being a list of friends held in common with hitherto unknown potential partners in the vicinity. The assumption made by Tinder that integrating an ostensibly private dating or hook-up profile with a vastly more public social media outlet should be *de rigueur* is telling in terms of the kind of hybridisation that is taken for granted in this scenario. It also reveals those practice-based identities who participate, or are able to participate, in this public assemblage, where for queer users 'outness' is both assumed and socially accepted. Given that queerness is highly visible in public space by dint of its very existence as an exception to heteronormativity (Skeggs et al., 2004), the embracer is likely to self-define as gay or bisexual, and be 'out' to friends, family and colleagues, because their queerness is made public by their technological involvement and therefore visibilised. They are in turn less likely to self-police their online identity for fear of it affecting their lived reality.

The embracer conceptualises the contemporary offering of MSM locative media products as helpful tools to broker new encounters, and they tend to balance online conversation with a willingness to meet up with other users for embodied encounter too. Whether these encounters are uniformly successful or smooth is another matter entirely, given that the reality of hybridisation may diverge from what the online introduction promises (Miles, 2017). Being a user who embraces the hybridising qualities of locative apps for the efficiency of their scoping abilities or their assistance in meeting new partners does not necessarily protect that user from the complex and sometimes confusing social realities of a physical meeting.

The Time-Waster

José is 21, studies at a London university and came out to close friends and family as gay just over a year ago. He uses a range of MSM dating and hook-up apps, is happy to sketch out what he sees as the differences between their intended use and finds all of them to be interesting, even educational, environments. It is here that he has learnt about other users—their likes and dislikes, their relationship formats (monogamous, poly, open) and their sexual interests. He has gathered from different users the best places to go gay clubbing in central London and hopes in time to make use of these recommendations. However, he has only met one user from Grindr in real life, and found the experience as confusing as it was exciting. He uses the apps every day and strikes up conversation with a whole range of people, but when they move the conversation to hooking up (the minimalist), he blocks them, reluctant to commit to such a significant meeting with so little preamble. Others chat online for a night or two and then invite him on a date (the embracer), but José worries that the chatty person he is online will translate to a stuttering, shy guy who can't keep up with the English or know what to say when his date asks about his previous relationships.

The 'time-waster' represents perhaps the most maligned trope of online dating: the user who is, intentionally or unconsciously, in the opinion of other participants, somehow 'misusing' the app against a collectively conceived mode of practice amongst the user base. As project participant Liam explains: 'it's just chatting, chatting, chatting'. The active hybridisation of the user experience on MSM partner-seeking apps, in which users are able to go about their daily routines in physical space whilst simultaneously communicating with men on a virtual platform provided by the apps, means that apps should speed up time spent searching for potential matches and shorten the distance needed to encounter those matches. However, the time-waster complicates this 'ideal' hybridised experience because they are so comfortable in the online space of the locative platform (or conversely so *un*comfortable in the 'real' world of physical encounter) that they communicate with other app users for long stretches of time, seemingly without any desire to progress virtual conversation to a physical encounter. Their motivations are overwhelmingly negatively interpreted by participants, and they are commonly criticised for their (perceived) selfishness, given that they waste others' time without committing to a real-life meeting. We see, then, that online space has a tendency to replicate the very same divisions that often demarcate offline spaces (Gross, 2007), even where the hybridising abilities of the platform in question could logically invite the user to think differently about how bodies might be categorised or conceptualised.

In short, the time-waster is not complying with the hybridisation that enables these apps to collapse virtual and physical space. Yet their tendency to prevaricate is not necessarily alien to any of us, given that a successful offline encounter is mediated by online rapport. Despite the ease with which different 'types' of use (and user) can be corralled into different practice-based identities, every app user is different, and whilst a user might feel attracted to one conversational partner and pursue a physical encounter, they may in turn be repelled by the over-direct or unappealing approach of a different user. For example, Liam, having identified the traits of time-wasters, reflects on his own aimlessness online: 'most of the time I go there I think "why am I even coming here?" I'm not *looking* for anything'. This behaviour could constitute exactly the same prevarication that frustrates him in conversation with others. The reality is that the time-waster represents a *mode* of use, flexibly inhabited by a range of users, rather than a concrete identity of a subset of users. This is made even more apparent given the striking recurrence of time-wasting narratives from a range of participants who criticised others for precisely the time-wasting behaviour that they themselves admitted to exhibiting at other times in their conversation with other users.

Data from this research project also shows that the time-waster personality is overrepresented amongst younger app users, and users who are not yet 'out', or users who are new to the locative media platform itself. For this subset of users, what might be conceived of by others as interminable delays to in-person meet-ups, or aimless prevarication, may actually be more accurately described as a 'testing the water' of the online environment before committing more fully to the hybridisation that the app prioritises as the intended progression for its user interactions. José's narrative suggests that the time-waster typology should not be dismissed for its inability to effectively realise hybridisation, but considered more carefully for what it means in the larger assemblage. There is much that José can gain from the rich queer network of locative media; the bigger question here is which variables influence willingness to participate in the invited hybridisation.

The Minimalist

Jason, 40, sometimes has sex with men but does not identify as gay. When he wants to hook up with someone, he downloads Grindr, surfs it only for long enough to find someone local to come over to his apartment and then deletes the app again until the next time he wants to hook up, in a cyclical pattern that repeats every month or so. He is not interested in chatting online, nor in dating or meeting in gay bars, pubs or nightclubs. He prefers not to spend too long getting to know a 'match' in person, preferring to prioritise sex. To this end when he messages another user online, he opens with the question 'what are you into?' and, after establishing they are interested in 'no strings' sex, he checks what specific sexual practices they prefer and whether they are free immediately. Jason reasons that sex is the primary intended use for these apps, and that to think otherwise is naïve.

Contrary to popular assumptions, the minimalist user may well be aware of a range of MSM locative media products and enrolled on several, even if only intermittently. Their restricted participation does not necessarily foreclose any experience with this technology. It merely suggests that their use is oriented to their goal of expediting offline sexual encounter. One could even argue that this approach reflects Sherry Turkle's (2011) concern that technology inhibits embodied communication, although Turkle's anxieties centre on the intensification of online communication as a substitute for meaningful socialisation, whereas for the minimalist, emotional rapport is not required for sexual encounter (indeed, it may even inhibit the erotic potential of precisely this kind of meeting). In this dataset, many participants demonstrating 'minimalist' identity traits are comfortable with operating apps precisely *because* they prioritise physical encounter over online communication; moreover, they prioritise casual, non-intimate sexual encounters over dating, relationships or even repeat encounters with previous partners. After all, by logging into an online platform such as Grindr, the user is committing his spatial coordinates to the algorithms of a programme that prioritises spatial proximity over any other variable for partner matching.

The minimalist user is often typecast by others as closeted, sexually opportunistic or more generally as obstructive to collectivist notions of queer community, but the fact that their mode of engagement is more fleeting, more goal-oriented and less interested in socialised paths to encounter is moot. The minimalist is using these apps in their simplest sense, as a networked assemblage of people and devices. For users like Jason, the hybridisation that results from the assemblage is distinctive only in that it makes meetings happen, and if a new apparatus becomes available that scopes potential partners more efficiently (eliminating the time-waster typology, perhaps), the minimalist would switch without hesitation. In short, for the minimalist, there is no collectively imagined community or meaningful space fostered by the hybrid app environment, but that is not an issue because the minimalist's mode of use remains viable.

Despite the logical assumption that MSM locative dating apps are able to overlay heteronormative physical space with a queerer virtual network or 'skin' of men seeking other men for erotic encounter, and therefore construct a place for the queer bodies who are normally 'out of place' (Cresswell, 1996) in heteronormative society, as a practice-based identity the minimalist user is himself 'out of place' in this app-mediated online network because his focus remains in the physical environment. For this kind of user, the app provides a means to an end rather than a tenable environment for meaningful connection in or of itself. From the point of view of the minimalist however, the time-waster, and even to an extent the embracer, are both typologies that are antithetical to how MSM locative technology platforms are best utilised. The embracer is comfortable with the hybridisation of public and private, online and offline, which does not suit the low-key approach of the minimalist; meanwhile, the time-waster squanders their own and others' time online by pursuing virtual rapport at the expense of a commitment to physical meeting. This perception is ubiquitous even though, as José's narrative demonstrates, the reality may differ altogether.

Equally, this is not to say that the minimalist's approach to the assemblage is wrong; on the contrary, he efficiently utilises the affordances of contemporary hybridisation. Theoretically, technological hybridisation enables users to attend to both physical and virtual environments at the same time, ideally generating richer interpersonal connection (Gordon & de Souza e Silva, 2011). Locative male–male partner-seeking apps evidence this ability with an ostensibly undirected but widely practised focus on accelerated encounter to sexual contact. On Grindr for example, matches are ranked by proximity, with the 'grid' of available men rearranging in real-time as both the mobile app user and others move around their physical environment in order to expedite localised encounter based on shared desire. Apps can therefore evaluate the local topography in order to save time in having to scope out ideal partners, and cater both to those users seeking social or dating connections with those looking to expedite 'hook-ups' in their own or a nearby partner's home. A user like Jason therefore epitomises the dichotomy of these locative media platforms: he is using the GPS function of the technology to seamlessly hybridise his online scoping with offline sexual encounter, and he does so extremely efficiently. Yet at the same time, his style of use jars with other users and also the officially marketed image of these apps as constituting devices for neighbourliness or a similarly subjectively experienced queer community.

Conclusions

The embodied experience of technological involvement in everyday life is key to understanding geographies of sexualities now and in the future. This chapter has posited that locative MSM dating and hook-up apps demonstrate one way in which 'people incorporate digital media into their routine practices of relating' (Baym, 2010, p. 5), but it has also pursued the less-asked question of what this form of technological assemblage looks like in practice, and how digital identities, with all their quirks and subjectivities, are implicated in this involvement. Focusing on the *use* of apps as platforms that cohere different practice-based identities, rather than their more obvious post-human qualities alone, offers an insight into how technological mediation interplays with lived spatial and social concerns. We have seen that different practice-based identities enact different forms of hybridisation, with 'embracers' and 'minimalists' moving comfortably between online and offline spaces, whilst 'time-wasters' may resist moving offline. Demonstrating how hybridisation functions via mobile technologies not just theoretically, but as it pertains to practice-based identities, valuably extends work by Angela Meah (2014) in interrogating masculinities, identities and practices to understand how they combine (or resist combination) in the circulations of technology, people and spaces. These are circulations that look set to dominate social and sexual communications for years to come.

My aim in this chapter has been to illustrate how MSM apps help to develop quite distinctive practice-based identities, and do so in ways that encourage both scrutiny of other queer users and self-reflection for the user's own position in a complex and novel technological assemblage. As Meah (2014, p. 205) notes, scholarly interpretations based on qualitative observations in fieldwork 'must be considered provisional' since they are based on a limited sample and may not reflect the experiences of others outside that scope. Nevertheless, the 'provisional' picture built up by the typologies identified in this chapter is striking for what they tell us about how technology users pursue different routes to embodied connection. Therefore, although different 'types' of users understand their participation in technological hybridisation in different ways and with different outcomes, it is the *mode* of use, rather than inherent characteristics of a person, that informs engagement in digital–physical sexual encounter. The typologies I have described in this article reflect the ongoing tendency of MSM app users to categorise online bodies into assumed groups. However, by understanding these typologies as flexible modes of use rather than describing 'types' of persons, they come to constitute practice-based identities. The practice-based identities on display here refer not to the individual user but to certain modes of behaviour that can identify a certain range of users, or a quality or tendency *in that use*. For any user, app use evolves over time; indeed, it *must* if mutually satisfying social or sexual encounters are to develop. These locative media also represent different things for different queer bodies at different times—as a tool for encounter, an educational resource, a drug trading platform or even a virtual lifeline on a lonely night. Locative app users must navigate tensions between the possibilities offered by the platforms and more ambiguous or problematic experiences when practising technological hybridisation.

A key point of exploration in this chapter has been how technological hybridisation shapes embodied encounter. Digital–physical hybridisation is differently practised by different bodies at different times, and the socio-sexual environment of queer locative dating and hook-up apps is no exception. As we have seen, hybridity is realised not just in the tantalising overlaying of virtual queer networks onto neutral geographical space, but also in the transition from online conversation to physical meeting. The sophistication of the locative technology in use invites this constantly-in-production hybridity, but generates its own inefficiencies when these practice-based identities meet in physical space. The newness of these platforms means that commonly held social codes for use are still under-established. Such issues may include incompatibility (sexually or socially) between two users only realised through physical encounter, or uncertainty regarding the social codes that should mediate physical encounter. The sheer plurality in modes of use impacts on established social norms for intimate relations, with the end result revealing an ambiguity in agreed models for interpersonal communication both online and offline. The fact that different users engage with the platforms in different ways is further complicated by the tendency of each user to approach each app differently and search for different outcomes on each. In this contextual flux, satisfying sexual encounter is far from guaranteed. There is therefore real value in continuing critical debate that interrogates how technology mediates real-life social and sexual encounters in embodied space, and what this will come to mean for queer technology, identity and belonging.

References

Andersson, J. (2011). Vauxhall's post-industrial pleasure gardens: 'Death wish' and hedonism and 21st century London. *Urban Studies, 48*(1), 85–100.

Badiou, A. (2012). *In praise of love*. London: Serpent's Tail.

Bassi, C. (2006). Riding the dialectical wares of gay political economy: A story from Birmingham's commercial gay scene. *Antipode, 38*(2), 213–235.

Bauman, Z. (2003). *Liquid love: On the frailty of human bonds*. Cambridge: Polity Press.
Baym, N. (2010). *Personal connections in the digital age*. Malden, MA: Polity Press.
Brubaker, J., Ananny, M., & Crawford, K. (2014). Departing glances: A socio-technical account of 'leaving' Grindr. *New Media and Society, 18*(3), 373–390.
Campbell, J. (2004). *Getting it on online: Cyberspace, gay male sexuality, and embodied identity*. New York: Harrington Park Press.
Campkin, B., & Marshall, L. (2017). LGBTQ+ cultural infrastructure in London: Night venues, 2006–present. *UCL UrbanLab*. London, UK. Retrieved from https://www.ucl.ac.uk/urbanlab/docs/LGBTQ_cultural_infrastructure_in_London_nightlife_venues_2006_to_the_present.pdf
Collins, A., & Drinkwater, S. (2016). Fifty shades of gay: Social and technological change, urban deconcentration and niche enterprise. *Urban Studies, 54*(3), 765–785.
Cresswell, T. (1996). *In place/out of place: Geography, ideology, and transgression*. Minneapolis: University of Minnesota Press.
Davis, M., Flowers, P., Lorimer, K., Oakland, J., & Frankis, J. (2016). Location, safety and (non) strangers in gay men's narratives on 'hook-up' apps. *Sexualities, 19*(7), 836–852.
Delany, S. (1999). *Times Square red, Times Square blue*. New York: New York University Press.
Farman, J. (2012). *Mobile interface theory: Embodied space and locative media*. New York: Routledge.
Ghaziani, A. (2014). *There goes the gayborhood?* Princeton: Princeton University Press.
Gordon, E., & de Souza e Silva, A. (2011). *Net locality*. Chichester: Wiley-Blackwell.
Gorman-Murray, A. (2009). Intimate mobilities: Emotional embodiment and queer migration. *Social & Cultural Geography, 10*(4), 441–460.
Gorman-Murray, A., & Nash, C. (2017). Transformations in LGBT consumer landscapes and leisure spaces in the neoliberal city. *Urban Studies, 54*(3), 786–805.
Gross, L. (2007). Foreword. In K. O'Riordan & D. Phillips (Eds.), *Queer online: Media technology and sexuality* (pp. 7–11). New York: Peter Lang.
Grov, C., Breslow, A. S., Newcomb, M. E., Rosenberger, J. G., & Bauermeister, J. A. (2013). Gay and bisexual men's use of the internet: Research from the 1990s through 2013. *Journal of Sex Research, 51*(4), 390–409.

Hubbard, P. (2011). *Cities and sexualities*. Abingdon: Routledge.
Hubbard, P., Collins, A., & Gorman-Murray, A. (2015). Introduction: Sex, consumption and commerce in the contemporary city. *Urban Studies, 54*(3), 567–581.
Jaspal, R. (2017). Coping with perceived ethnic prejudice on the gay scene. *Journal of LGBT Youth, 14*(2), 172–190.
Kitchin, R. (1998). Towards geographies of cyberspace. *Progress in Human Geography, 22*(3), 385–406.
Koch, R., & Latham, A. (2012). Inhabiting cities, domesticating public space: Making sense of the changing public life of contemporary London. In A. Madanipour, S. Knierbein, & A. Degros (Eds.), *Public space and the challenges of urban transformation in Europe* (pp. 144–154). New York: Routledge.
Latour, B. (2006). *Reassembling the social: An introduction to actor-network-theory*. Oxford: Oxford University Press.
Lewis, N. (2016). Canaries in the mine? Gay community, consumption and aspiration in neoliberal Washington, DC. *Urban Studies, 54*(3), 695–712.
McGlotten, S. (2013). *Virtual intimacies: Media, affect, and queer sociality*. Albany: SUNY Press.
Meah, A. (2014). Reconceptualising 'masculinity' through men's contributions to domestic foodwork. In A. Gorman-Murray & P. Hopkins (Eds.), *Masculinities and place: Gender, space and society* (pp. 191–208). Farnham: Ashgate.
Miles, S. (2017). Sex in the digital city: Location-based apps and queer urban life. *Gender, Place & Culture, 24*(11), 1595–1610.
Miles, S. (2018). Still getting it on online: Thirty years of queer male spaces brokered through digital technologies. *Geography Compass*. https://doi.org/10.1111/gec3.12407
Mowlabocus, S. (2010). *Gaydar culture: Gay men, technology and embodiment in the digital age*. Abingdon: Routledge.
Nash, C. J. (2013). The age of the "post-mo"? Toronto's gay village and a new generation. *Geoforum, 49*, 243–254.
Nash, C. J., & Gorman-Murray, A. (2014). LGBT neighbourhoods and 'new mobilities': Towards understanding transformations in sexual and gendered urban landscapes. *International Journal of Urban and Regional Research, 38*(3), 756–772.
Nash, C. J., & Gorman-Murray, A. (2016). Digital technologies and sexualities in urban space. In K. Browne & G. Brown (Eds.), *Routledge research companion to geographies of sex and sexualities* (pp. 399–405). London: Routledge.

Prestage, G., Bavinton, B., Grierson, J., Down, I., Keen, P., & Bradley, J. (2015). Online dating among Australian gay and bisexual men: Romance or hook-up? *AIDS and Behaviour, 19*(10), 1905–1913.

Race, K. (2015). 'Party and play': Online hook-up devices and the emergence of PNP practices among gay men. *Sexualities, 18*(3), 253–275.

Rosenfeld, M., & Thomas, R. (2012). Searching for a mate: The rise of the internet as a social intermediary. *American Sociological Review, 77*(4), 523–547.

Skeggs, B., Moran, L., Tyrer, P., & Binnie, J. (2004). Queer as folk: Producing the real of urban space. *Urban Studies, 41*(9), 1839–1856.

Turkle, S. (2011). *Alone together*. New York: Perseus.

Turner, M. (2003). *Backward glances: Cruising queer streets in New York and London*. London: Reaktion books.

Woo, J. (2013). *Meet Grindr*. Retrieved from https://books.google.co.uk/books/about/Meet_Grindr_How_One_App_Changed_The_Way.html?id=Aq7Zf4HBe6EC&redir_esc=y

Young, M. I. (1990). *Justice and the politics of difference*. Princeton: Princeton University Press.

8

Online Dating Practice as a Perfect Example of Interwoven Worlds? Analysis of Communication in Digital and Physical Encounters

Emiel Maliepaard and Jantine van Lisdonk

Introduction: Hybridisation of Virtual and Physical Spaces?

In 2002, Alexander introduced a guest editorial on digital spaces with the following words: "it is worth asking how computer technology is being used by queers to communicate, make contact with others, create community, and tell the stories of their lives" (Alexander, 2002, p. 77). Nash and Gorman-Murray (2014) observed that the internet and social media have potential widespread effects on traditional meeting spaces for lesbian, gay, bisexual, and trans (LGBT) individuals (see also Blackwell,

E. Maliepaard (✉)
Atria, Institute on Gender Equality and Women's History,
Amsterdam, The Netherlands
e-mail: e.maliepaard@atria.nl

J. van Lisdonk
Rutgers Centre of Expertise on Sexual and Reproductive Health and Rights,
Utrecht, The Netherlands
e-mail: J.vanLisdonk@rutgers.nl

C. Nash, A. Gorman-Murray (eds.), *The Geographies of Digital Sexuality*,
https://doi.org/10.1007/978-981-13-6876-9_8

Birnholtz, & Abbott, 2015). It goes unquestioned nowadays that computer technology has a profound impact on our daily routines, habitual activities, and everyday experiences. As Miles (2017) observes, scholarship on the spatial impacts and qualities of developments in computer technology has rapidly moved from viewing virtual spaces as having transcendental and liberating effects (e.g. Kitchin, 1998), to thinking about hybridisation to analysing "the multiple, simultaneous and interconnected dimensions of spaces and practices" (Miles, 2017, p. 1595). To paraphrase Jordan (2009), the interplay between software/code and actions that are predominantly rooted in offline practices creates new hybrid spaces and practices—the blurring of the real and virtual—and has profound effects on our embodied experiences (e.g. Cohen, 2007; Jordan, 2009; Miles, 2017; van Doorn, 2011).

Miles argues that online dating apps are an excellent example of the hybridisation of spaces as "the user is able to go about their work in physical space whilst also communicating with men on a virtual platform provided by the apps simultaneously and in an interconnected manner" (2017, pp. 1603–1604). Stempfhuber and Liegl use similar words to describe the hybridisation of spaces:

> Grindr's users are busy employing both their smartphones and their immediate senses to recreate their immediate surroundings. Grindr allows for the instantaneous creation of hybrid ecologies that mix physical and digital environments by constantly and swiftly switching between them. (2016, p. 67)

Many sites can become spaces for seeking contact with other men for online or physical, social or sexual connections through the use of location-based gay dating apps on smartphones (Blackwell et al., 2015). We agree with Blackwell et al. (2015), Miles (2017), and Stempfhuber and Liegl (2016) that online dating applications can be an interesting example of the hybridisation of spaces (see also van Lisdonk, Maliepaard, Oostrik, & Vermey, 2017). Nevertheless, the question remains whether users of these applications actually experience a hybridisation of online and offline spaces when participating in online dating practices. We discuss this question in this chapter by focusing on communication in the physical and digital encounters which together constitute the online dating practice.

Inspired by Brown, Maycock, and Burns (2005), in this chapter, we focus on different forms of (sexual) communication and scripts in order to understand people's experiences with, and understandings of, digital and physical (or IRL: in real life) encounters. By encounters, we mean meetings between two or more human bodies (Ahmed, 2000). Based on research with young men in the Netherlands, we first explore participants' understandings of online dating applications and compare specific communication scripts for digital and IRL encounters. Second, we analyse their experiences with communicating sexual preferences and boundaries to better understand how the young men experience the digital and physical encounters and spaces that are part of the online dating practice. Finally, we discuss whether participants' experiences with online dating practices, and the scripts for digital and IRL encounters, match our understandings of this as a practice that creates hybrid spaces.

Methods

This is an explorative study using face-to-face, in-depth interviews about people's experiences with online dating applications, and how men-who-have-sex-with-men (MSM) negotiate the sexual normativities of these apps and websites. Important topics included participants' understandings of the scripts (in particular the existing norms and ideal types), their position towards these scripts, their communication of sexual preferences and limits, norms regarding online chats and communication during physical encounters, and finally their experiences with (inappropriate) sexual behaviour. In line with our focus on participants' negotiations of the online dating scripts, we specifically looked at people's understandings of the dynamics between online and offline spaces.

We understand online dating as a practice that encompasses all doings, sayings, actions, moods, emotions, norms, and tasks, from opening an online dating application until "separating" after a sexual or social date (cf. Schatzki, 2002). Depending on understandings of practices, things or technology can be central elements of a practice. In this chapter, however, the focus is on the specific scripts of applications that guide or govern people's understandings and uses of these apps and subsequent IRL encounters (cf. Simon & Gagnon, 1984, 1986; Wiederman, 2005).

The target group of this study were young MSM, between 16 and 25 years old. The 16–25 age group is a quite common group in Dutch studies on the sexual experiences of men and makes this study relevant in debates on sexting and on the pros and cons of online dating. This study consisted of 21 research participants: one transgender and 20 cisgender male participants. Only one of them identified as bisexual, whereas all others, despite the fact that some participants had limited sexual experiences with women, identified as gay. In spite of attempts to work with organisations dedicated to supporting MSM of colour, we only managed to recruit three people of colour.

Interviews lasted between 60 and 105 minutes, averaging approximately 90 minutes. The first author and another male interviewer conducted all interviews. Interviews were transcribed, anonymised, and analysed in MAXQDA 12 using thematic analysis (Braun & Clarke, 2006). We deliberately choose to not use a grounded theory approach but to combine inductive and deductive analysis in order to both grasp the lived experiences of the research participants and apply sexual script theory to people's shared understandings of the online dating practice. All participants' names in this chapter are pseudonyms.

Scripts on Apps

Simon and Gagnon (1984, 1986) were the first to apply script theory to sexuality studies; nowadays, script theory is widely used to understand sexual behaviour between people as governed by scripts that work on three levels: societal, interpersonal, and intrapsychic (or intrapersonal). The theory of sexual scripts contends that sexual behaviour does not just happen but relies on sexual norms, symbols, and meanings, which may differ across cultures and contexts (Brickell, 2010; Simon & Gagnon, 1986; Wiederman, 2005). People acquire these scripts through imitation and learning from more experienced peers (Wiederman, 2005). Similar to practice theories, script theory argues that these norms, symbols, and meanings govern people's understandings of what is appropriate, acceptable, and just. Nevertheless, people retain their own agency to negotiate their position towards these scripts and whether to follow specific scripts in their sexual trajectories.

There are many online dating apps and websites for Dutch MSM, and the scripts vary between these apps and websites. In this study, online dating apps and websites that were used most frequently were Grindr, Tinder, PlanetRomeo, and Bullchat. Grindr and Tinder are only available on smartphones, Bullchat is web-based, and PlanetRomeo can be used in both modes. Online dating apps and websites that were mentioned but were less popular among the Dutch participants were Scruff, Growlr, Hornet, Hot or Not, OKCupid, Surge, Expreszo (Dutch), and Gay.nl (Dutch).

Meeting Other Men

> I believe it is quite interesting that there are two types of people on Grindr. (…) On the one hand you have the users who are looking for sex, the ones who fill in their sex stats and these kind of things. They also use these semi-nude pics. On the other hand, there are people who use Grindr for social contacts. These people clearly state "no sex" [on their profile]. So that's interesting. And both groups have a clear, distinct, understanding of Grindr. (Gerard, 24 years old)

Online dating applications, such as Grindr, are often marketed as social networking applications, which create online spaces for connecting with other MSM (e.g. *Miles*, 2017). Gerard is a frequent user of online dating apps such as Grindr, Tinder, and BullChat, and he often meets up with people for coffee, drinks, or to have sex. Gerard implies that people use online dating applications to facilitate IRL encounters between men. Despite the promise of these apps or websites to create a virtual community for non-heterosexual men, studies have shown that these applications predominantly function as mediators of social, sexual, and/or intimate encounters in public and private spaces (Miles, 2017; Raj, 2011; Stempfhuber & Liegl, 2016). Instead of community building or feeling part of a community (Miles, 2017), the primary reason our research participants use these applications is the perception that all users are "into men" and therefore they do not need to engage in all kinds of awkward situations to approach like-minded men. The use of these apps reflects a coping mechanism to deal with heteronormativity in everyday spaces and practices.

The nature of these digital and IRL encounters, however, may differ for users and depend on the specific scripts of the apps (Gudelunas, 2012; van Lisdonk et al., 2017). The research participants identified different types of meet-ups, in particular, social, sexual, and, of course, digital encounters. These digital encounters sometimes result in social and sexual encounters in physical space—the aforementioned IRL encounters—whereas others are limited to applications such as the dating apps and messenger apps (e.g. WhatsApp) for online socialising, sexting, or because people do not reply or are blocked.

Sex Script: Digital Encounters

> "Hey, what's up?" Very superficial, but that's how it always starts: "How are you doing?" "I'm okay, what about you?" Quite often people ask for pictures, that's really a big deal. It is quite convenient and easy nowadays to exchange pictures. Sometimes nude pics, but not always. I have been pretty careful with exchanging pics, in fact I never exchanged pics when I was younger. And then it is like "you wanna meet up?" And then you shift to WhatsApp. (John, 21 years old)

John introduces the sex script of Grindr, which he describes as superficial and functional. Grindr, and other apps with a clear sex script such as PlanetRomeo and Bullchat, can be nothing more than just virtual cruising spaces. Participants know exactly what they are doing: they approach strangers for quick, casual, sexual encounters (Licoppe, Rivière, & Morel, 2016). A social connection is not necessary. People who are familiar with these applications may know the exact functioning: one opens the application and sees a grid with profile pictures of users (for a vivid and visual description of Grindr, see Stempfhuber & Liegl, 2016), touches the picture to open the profile of the other user, and decides whether to approach or not. If we focus on the chats only, it becomes clear that the communication script for this app is straightforward and seems to have a predictable course: "How are you doing?", "what do you want?", "are you top or bottom?", and the final question "do you want to meet up?" People rapidly exchange phone numbers to continue the conversation on WhatsApp to arrange the technicalities before actually meeting up for sex: often to have sex in the house of one of the guys, sometimes outside for a car date or in a hotel if nobody is able to "host" others. People do not seem to use full sentences, many use some abbreviations such as BBS (Dutch abbreviation for *Baard, Bril, Snor*; Beard, Glasses, Moustache), and long conversations are a rarity. Miles' (2017) short discussion on the poor ratio of online conversations to in-person meet-ups also shows the importance of short and functional conversations during digital encounters. As such, there seems to be specific language that is used in online spaces that is different from the language used in everyday activities in offline space:

> Stats: your age, length, weight, penis size; they always want to know that. And if you're top or bottom. BBS. If you have no glasses, beard, or moustache, you add the G [*Geen*; No] before BBS. Yeah that is what they wanna know. You give the stats, get stats, or they are written down in the profile of the other one. Sometimes people exchange pictures, sometimes not at all. The next question is "Can you receive, can you come over?" "No, not really." I have a car, I can fetch you." "Okay, cool", "You know a nice place?", "Yes I do", "Okay". Then it, of course, depends on how far that person is away from you, but you may find yourself on the hood of the car within 30 minutes. (Ernst, 24 years old)

Ernst gives a detailed example of the communication on BullChat, which has a similar sex script to Grindr, but is understood as less personal because of the absence of a fixed profile. Ernst knows perfectly well how to engage in an online encounter and successfully organise a hook-up with another user. The language on BullChat is similar to the language on Grindr: functional and straightforward. Specific code language and abbreviations are limited to some well-known abbreviations as (G)BBS, sex roles such as top or bottom, and, in some cases, abbreviations for chemsex or other fetishes. As Ernst concludes in this excerpt, one can engage in sexual activities in a short time-frame.

More Social Script: Digital Encounters

> I can recall that one of my ex-partners wrote something on his profile about Smarties. So I started like "What is your favourite colour of Smarties?" That is not a very romantic start, but it breaks the ice and shows you've read into his profile. That you did some effort to not only send "Hi, how are you?" because normally the reply would be "Yeah, it's okay". (…) so you need to keep the conversation going. (Dave, 21 years old)

Dave predominantly used apps for socialising and finding a romantic partner. He discusses the more social script of Grindr, which seems incompatible with Grindr's emphasis on quick, casual, sexual encounters (Licoppe et al., 2016). Dave's example shows that in the more social script, people find it more important to use an icebreaker or at least show that they find someone, or a certain aspect of someone's profile, interesting. The communication is not focused on getting laid in the first place and could be characterised as less straightforward, more laidback compared to the communication in the sex script, and, most importantly, it is much more personal. Another important point is that one needs to keep the conversation going. As multiple men explain, a lot of conversations just end because someone is not interested anymore. It becomes clear that users often do not tell the other that they are not interested in someone—and explicitly reject them—but just stop replying to chat messages. The men reveal that they talk more about hobbies, interests, and daily life to keep these conversations going before possibly meeting up. These conversations can take hours, days, or even weeks, and participants find it important to feel a kind of chemistry in these chats. People's daily lives are introduced in the digital encounters on online dating apps or in messenger apps to foster a social connection:

I: So, can you tell me how these chats work? Is that something like "Hey, I want sex"?

P: No no. "Hi how are you?" blah blah. That's how I start. I mean, a lot of people just send "Hi, I'm horny". Yeah what they say depends on the person. The chat with the guy I met before was like "Hey how are you?" blah blah. A bit chitchatting. We shifted to WhatsApp.

Yeah, just casual conversations about everything: hobbies, normal conversations. And we met up like two weeks later.

I: So just talking about all kind of stuff, hobbies, and who you are?

P: Yeah, you make some sexual innuendo, but do not make it too obvious, no. (Johan, 19 years old)

Another example of a "more social script" is Johan's meet-up with a man he met on Surge, an online dating application that is similar to Grindr. Johan is not a person to explicitly and solely look for sex dates, but prefers to have more social dates or, in case he is single, to look for a romantic partner. Two things are remarkable in this excerpt. The first is that he does not like to be approached by people who just follow the sex script; he prefers to have a more casual conversation—some chitchatting—and talk about one's personal life to see whether there is a connection between him and the other. There is no explicit talk about sex roles, sexual preferences or whatsoever, but there is space for some subtle and playful hints. The second remarkable thing is that the actual meet-up took place two weeks after the first encounter on Surge. This gives time to get a certain idea about someone's personality and to feel if there is a social match; most people who follow the sex script meet-up the same day or at least very soon after the first encounter in digital space.

A final point is that most people quickly exchange numbers and switch to other digital technologies, in particular to WhatsApp. We expected that this would be to move away from a more sexualised environment to a more neutral environment. The majority of the participants who discussed using WhatsApp instead of other applications, however, simply argue that WhatsApp is more convenient and part of everyday life, thus fostering a hybridisation of online dating apps in one's daily life.

Pictures: Bridging Digital Space and Physical Space?

This section explores the position of pictures in communication scripts and whether pictures create more hybrid experiences. As John explains, when describing the Grindr sex script, pictures are very important. It is the first element of an online profile that attracts someone's attention on the dating app or website, and the main reason for people, in particular for the ones who follow the sex script, to approach someone or not. This means that pictures are the primary tool to advertise oneself on the virtual public (market)spaces and to communicate one's intentions for IRL encounters.

Internet spaces provide new opportunities for people to present oneself to others (e.g. Brown et al., 2005; Toma & Hancock, 2010). Our study confirms findings that people may choose to show different parts of their (unclothed) bodies and that particular meanings are attached to these decisions. The majority of research participants argue that face pictures communicate that someone is a "normal" person, whereas pictures of chests/torsos reveal that someone is explicitly looking for sex. Looks matter:

> Tinder is also about visuals, 'cause you also think like "okay, will I find this person attractive?". Because this person can be a great personality, but you also want to walk next to him on the streets and should be able to introduce him towards your parents. It would be unrealistic to argue that someone's looks don't matter. It would be great if it would work that way. (Dave, 21 years old)

Dave's quote shows the importance of someone's looks. Someone's looks are the first focus of the users of online dating apps. Someone needs to be "hot", or "attractive", or "good looking". Being a "twink" or being "sporty" were mentioned as the most desired men on online dating apps such as Grindr and Tinder, and therefore these mainstream apps reinforce societal norms—cultural scripts—on the desired or idealised male body: not hairy, young, slim, and, if possible, muscled (e.g. Bonner-Thompson, 2017; Casey, 2007). Dave argues that even on Tinder, an app often understood by research participants as a social app for MSM that resembles old-fashioned tea parties, people's looks are very important. Although several participants such as Dave felt unhappy with the emphasis on someone's looks instead of on someone's personality, they all feel like they cannot escape this focus on someone's looks and body type on any of the dating apps:

> Yeah, I think that you will always look at pictures first. So pictures are really important. I guess, when I started using Gay.nl, I saw a lot of things I

would not see on a normal first date. I saw nude pics of many men, even before we planned a date, to be honest. (Dave, 21 years old)

Dave is talking about his first visits to a Dutch online dating website, Gay.nl, and immediately notices how many men have nude pics on their profiles, and share nude pics via private messages or chats. These nude pics made him feel insecure: "help, this is too real, bye!!" (Dave, 21 years old). Exchanging (nude) pictures also adds to the experiences of online dating apps; this is when the human body itself, as an object of desire, and body language become part of digital encounters. Pictures create a whole range of emotions, from desire to disgust or even being scared as Dave was. Quite often people are already horny when they open their Grindr or PlanetRomeo app, but exchanging pictures via chat or WhatsApp definitely contributes to feelings of attraction and lust. Pictures of the human body, including the sexualised human body, create expectations for physical encounters with other men. Talking about one's preferences, some sexual innuendo, and hooking-up with someone can make someone yearn for meeting up; sexy or nude pics make online dating already more real, more intense, and more horny. Nevertheless, exchanging pictures is not equal to meeting up with men in IRL encounters, to which we now turn.

"Real" Encounters

I: So, when do you communicate your preferences. Is that online or when you actually see them?

P: No, that's something you do in the chat, as you want to know if it is worthwhile to go somewhere.

I: Could you tell me how you communicate that? Is there a certain moment in a conversation or does it differ every time?

P: Yeah, you just ask "What do you want?" Something like that. And the other replies and then you anticipate on that: "ehm, I want this, and this, and this". Then you have a match or not. (Maarten, 22 years old)

The majority of the research participants argue that when they arrange sex dates, they clearly state their preferences in the digital encounters. It is important to know what you want and what the other wants in order to arrange a satisfactory sex date via online dating apps, as Maarten's example shows. Some users state their preferences on their profile, in particular when they are into fetishes, while most of the men exchange their preferences via the chat function of the apps or via WhatsApp. Are you into vanilla sex, blowjobs, and do you have any fetishes? What is your role? Are you top or bottom? When there is a match between preferences, people can take the next step in planning their actual sex dates. These dates, contrary to more social dates that mostly happen in more public spaces such as a coffee bar, pub, or cinema, often take place in the bedroom of one of the app users, or at least in the private spaces of one of the participants (e.g. house, hotel room, or car). It seems that public and private spaces have a distinct role in the scripts present on online dating applications (see also Brickell, 2010).

Research participants, however, also note that they do not talk about their sexual limits during digital encounters. A few men suggest that stating one's limits while chatting with someone is not desirable as that may diminish the chances of actually arranging a sex date: it may exacerbate the poor ratio of online conversations to in-person meet-ups. In other words, if you want to be successful in online dating, you need to play the game and not deviate from the script. Not talking about your sexual boundaries on the online dating applications means, however, that people need to communicate their limits in the IRL encounters. As Brickell (2010) already noted, activities in spaces are informed by sexual scripts and, at the same time, spaces play a vital role in sexual scripts. The nature of communication is fundamentally different between digital and IRL encounters, and communication is a lot less scripted in IRL encounters:

P: Nah, I am a person who is sometime a bit too social. If someone says "I am very much into this", I say like "Okay as you are very much into this, I'm okay with it". That was me in the beginning and nowadays I am like "No, as everyone communicates what they want, I am gonna do that as well". That was quite difficult in the beginning.

I: Is that because you were uncertain?

P: Yeah, also. It's a bit like "What is normal and what can I can demand and what not?" Just learning when to say no. That was difficult in the beginning.
I: So trial and error?
P: Yea exactly. What is normal? Yeah also when it comes to sex you just get a certain image of what is normal. It can be quite difficult when you fall outside the norm. Penetration is something very normal and what to do when you don't like it? What to do? (Romeo, 25 years old)

This quote is exemplary of the experiences of the young men in this study. They need to communicate their sexual limits in the IRL encounters; however, that may be more difficult than expected for the participants. Contrary to online chats, people can literally smell, see, touch, hear, and taste their date partner(s). This proximity and the immediate encounter with another human body can make people more uncertain, in particular when they are not experienced in (online) dating. Digital encounters are experienced as more distant and anonymous according to the participants; in fact, several participants prefer approaching other men online instead of in a physical space such as a bar or public transport.

The men in this study explain that this proximity impacts their negotiations of what is acceptable for them and how to express their sexual boundaries. As Romeo argues, "What can I demand and what not?" It becomes clear that saying "no" to something becomes a lot more difficult for the men as they are still unaware of the scripts. Gerard, for instance, invited a man he met on Grindr for a sex date at his place. When this man showed up at his front door, he opened the door and the man appeared to look completely different from the pictures he sent. Despite Gerard's disappointment—this man was really unattractive and unhygienic in his experience—he did not dare to say no to having sex. Gerard, similar to Romeo in the above excerpt, explains that he did not want to disappoint or hurt his date, and therefore engaged in sexual activities. If he found someone unattractive or "not interesting" in online chats, Gerard (and others) would just stop replying to incoming messages or just end the conversation. In general, online rejection is understood and experienced as less painful or humiliating because it is less personal, more distant, and more anonymous.

The men argue that only through experience, through participating in hook-ups, people learn that they *can* communicate their boundaries in IRL encounters, and that they can say *no* to someone and still have a good time with this person. It literally is trial and error for the research participants to understand that saying no is part of a script, for example:

I: So we were talking about communicating your preferences and your limits…
P: Yeah that's something that you just do when you are doing stuff with someone. That's something you just notice or feel, in my opinion. If something is not pleasurable you just stop with them. If you don't want to do something, you just express that.
I: And how? How you do express that?
P: For instance, you're sitting on someone's lap. While you're kissing, that person moves his hand to your leg and your penis or ass … You can just grab his hand and put it away. Or you're saying like, "Can you please stop doing that?" There are just different ways [to communicate one's limits].
I: Is that difficult?
P: That's possible, it depends on how confident you are. It can be very difficult if you wanna please someone else … but it can also be like "Okay, I want this," and then notice that you don't want it after all. It can be difficult, but also be really easy. It's something you just learn from experience. (Jade, 21 years old)

Most participants argue that physical encounters are about "just having sex", but it is clear that "just having sex" is too simple and ignores the complexities of sexual encounters. As Jade explains, people also need to learn *how* to communicate their limits via body language and verbal expression. Most research participants, however, prefer expressing their boundaries via body language. This articulates the importance of the sensory experiences of encountering someone in physical space for sexual activities. People communicate their limits via touch, gestures, looks, and sounds. People's sensory experiences are vitally important to anticipate the body language of the other person/people involved in the sexual meet-up:

I: So it just goes on ... how do you communicate that you don't like something?
P: Yeah, it is pretty much taboo to talk about that, because it would ruin the magical atmosphere, but I sometimes think, like, "Yeah it would have been great to just ask someone 'Would you like to have sex?' instead of all this implicit communication and making things all exciting." So that may result in miscommunications, if you don't talk about it.
I: So it is mainly body language?
P: Exactly, body language. And, of course, when things really become extreme, you just tell something. But indeed, mostly body language. You just anticipate on what the other person does and does not do. Yeah some people really sense that, and some people really don't. (John, 19 years old)

John adds another difficulty to communicating one's limits during the hook-ups. He says that it is not done to talk about your limits as that may ruin the magical atmosphere of the hook-up; the flow of activities and sensations. People need to communicate their limits via body language: it is all about experiencing someone's movements, actions, and positions, whereas digital encounters are more about functional communication and getting what you want. John argues, however, that some people are more aware of the signals that the other person expresses. Sometimes it goes very smoothly, and with other sex dates, you need to explicitly tell people what you do not want to do. This may indicate that scripts for body language are less clear and can be experienced differently by the people present in that space, for example:

I: So you always propose safe sex?
P: Yes
I: Do people always respect that?
P: Yeah, nearly every time. Yeah, but it is like an issue when you are really horny at that moment, to get out of bed, get condoms and lube, and start over again. But that is what often happens. It is something you need to communicate at that moment, because it is not always straightforward. At least, that is the best way. I also have dates

> now and then when I just already get my condoms ready so you don't need to disturb that [the horny situation] to communicate what you want and not want. (Youri, 21 years old)

Most participants want to engage in safe sex practices as they are scared of contracting HIV or other sexually transmitted infections, and using a condom is a high priority for them. If their potential date expresses an interest in bareback sex on the online dating app, the research participants most likely do not want to meet up for sex. Youri is not an exception to this "rule". Nevertheless, he says that it can be really difficult to actually use condoms during sex as it requires an effort to leave the bed, get condoms and lube, put on the condom (which can be annoying), and start all over again. This example shows that someone's preferences *and* limits are negotiated during the IRL encounters; in this case, it may disrupt the horny atmosphere of the sexual encounter between Youri and his sex date. Youri is not the only participant who sometimes "chooses" not to use condoms so as to not ruin the horny atmosphere and the "flow of life" during IRL encounters; a large number of participants sometimes do not use condoms as they think that condom use could disturb the magical atmosphere and increase the chance of a failed date.

Several participants speak about the "magical atmosphere" or "flow" when talking about their experiences of sexual encounters in the bedroom. Encounters, as meetings between two (or more) human bodies in a particular space, create affective atmospheres: a transpersonal intensity that impacts people's embodied experiences and actions (e.g. Anderson, 2009; Duff, 2009). As Anderson (2009) notes, affective atmospheres appear and disappear, are concrete and vague, are collective and singular, and are suffused with both emotions and affects. These affective atmospheres are difficult to grasp in words—people use the above-mentioned words to make sense of these atmospheres—but have a strong and intense presence in the physical encounters; research participants did not speak about such magical atmospheres when discussing digital encounters. People need to negotiate their boundaries in the hook-ups, and their wishes and limits may change because of the flow of sayings, doings, moods, emotions, and the strong affective atmospheres that emerge in these IRL encounters. Also, as affective atmospheres emerge in encounters, they also differ in each encounter and will have a different impact on people's agency. To conclude, the normative structures of these scripts for communicating one's limits and preferences in the IRL encounters have a less governing impact on the doings, sayings, action, and experiences of the men involved compared to the scripts for digital encounters. There is no clear sexual script on what is acceptable and appropriate in these IRL encounters.

Discussion and Conclusion

Communication is a core element in online dating practices, and we highlighted three important issues: the structure of chats when following either the sex script or the more social script, the importance of pictures, and communicating one's preferences and limits during online and offline encounters. Focusing on communication in these physical and digital encounters may provide a tentative answer to the question of whether spaces that are part of the online dating practice are experienced as hybrid spaces for the people who use these apps to meet up with other men.

All research participants revealed that they know how to approach someone, respond to someone, and how to keep a conversation going in digital spaces. People familiarise themselves with the specific sex and more social communication scripts by doing and learning what is acceptable and appropriate in the chats. It is particularly helpful that these digital encounters are highly scripted, especially for people who participate in the sex script. The communication is functional, and exchanging pictures and preferences are the main objectives in order to organise the actual date in physical space. These scripts favour particular moods, emotions, ends, and tasks, and therefore seem to have a clear normative structure when it comes to the digital phase of online dating. As one research participant notices:

> I mean, if I'm on BullChat and someone approaches me like "Hi, how was your day?", I just ignore him. If I am on BullChat it is just about someone's cock or ass, or whatsoever, just what I fancy at that moment. So I just play along with the unwritten rules, and I appreciate that [particular script]. (Gerard, 25 years old)

The young MSM, however, strongly differentiate between communication in digital and actual physical encounters. Distance and sense of proximity (see also Cockayne, Leszczynski, & Zook, 2017) play a crucial role in people's experiences of online dating. Interestingly, several participants argue that they do not dare to approach men in bars or in other spaces, but do approach other men via online dating apps. Rejection is less harsh, less direct, and less humiliating online than on the dance floor, according to one participant. Despite the promise of apps to create virtual communities through profile pictures, exchange of sexy and/or nude pictures, and the chats, nonetheless people experience apps as more or less anonymous. Although some researchers may argue that computer-mediated communication can be more personal compared to face-to-face interaction (e.g. Walther, 1996), the use of mobile phones and apps creates a more impersonal experience for users in relation to communication and dating. Online dating apps without a fixed profile, such as BullChat, or profiles that are not connected to social media accounts, are experienced as even more anonymous and impersonal public spaces. Dating apps that are location-based already make it less distant from everyday life. Exchanging pictures is the activity that most clearly shows the bridging of digital and physical spaces, and how actions in digital encounters partially govern people's embodied experiences; however, this still does not meet the sensory experiences of actually meeting a body of flesh and blood at your front door.

While physical encounters between participants in online dating practices may be understood as impersonal, quick, or casual hook-ups in the sense of meeting with a stranger (e.g. Licoppe et al., 2016; Miles, 2017), it becomes clear that the hook-ups are everything but impersonal. MSM argue that online dating becomes "real" only when actually meeting up with another man and interacting with another male body. When online (sex) dating becomes "real", or hyperpersonal, people actually need to negotiate their wishes and preferences in a physical encounter with the other person, or more people. This is "where the magic happens" and people experience strong affective atmospheres that may guide people's experiences and actions. This also means that physical encounters, and the sexual activities that happen in these encounters, are not preconfigured during the digital encounter(s) between users but are the result of interpersonal and intrapersonal processes in these encounters.

Finally, we interpret this experience of "becoming real" as evidence that people do not necessarily experience online dating as creating hybrid spaces or as a blurring of the virtual and the "real" as suggested by Jordan (2009) or, in the context of online dating, Stempfhuber and Liegl (2016). This is confirmed by the young men's understandings of the very different scripts of the digital encounters and the physical encounters that often happen in the bedroom, or at least, private property (e.g. house or car) of one of the participants. Scripts are clearly spatialised and central to experiences of space (Brickell, 2010), including digital spaces, as shown in this chapter. As such, we conclude that the online dating practice itself consists of digital and physical encounters and creates the possibility to arrange encounters in all kinds of everyday spaces, but is experienced by its users as consisting of two different worlds or spaces with their own particular scripts: the digital encounter and the "real" encounter. Perhaps online dating is not the perfect example of hybridisation, it is the perfect opportunity to study hybridisation and its impacts on sexual scripts and people's embodied experiences of participating in practices that consist of both digital and physical spaces and encounters.

References

Ahmed, S. (2000). *Strange encounters: Embodied others in post-coloniality*. London: Routledge.

Alexander, J. (2002). Introduction to the special issue: Queer webs: Representations of LGBT people and communities on the World Wide Web. *International Journal of Sexuality and Gender Studies, 7*(2–3), 77–84.

Anderson, B. (2009). Affective atmospheres. *Emotions, Space, and Society, 2*(2), 77–81.

Blackwell, C., Birnholtz, J., & Abbott, C. (2015). Seeing and being seen: Co-situation and impression formation using Grindr, a location-aware gay dating app. *New Media & Society, 17*(7), 1117–1136.

Bonner-Thompson, C. (2017). 'The meat market': Production and regulation of masculinities on the Grindr grid in Newcastle-upon-Tyne, UK. *Gender, Place, and Culture, 24*(11), 1611–1625.

Braun, V., & Clarke, V. (2006). Using thematic analysis in psychology. *Qualitative Research in Psychology, 3*(2), 77–101.

Brickell, C. (2010). Sex, space and scripts: Negotiating homoeroticism in history. *Social and Cultural Geography, 11*(6), 597–613.
Brown, G., Maycock, B., & Burns, S. (2005). Your picture is your bait: Use and meaning of cyberspace among gay men. *The Journal of Sex Research, 42*(1), 63–73.
Casey, M. E. (2007). The queer unwanted and their undesirable 'Otherness'. In K. Browne, J. Lim, & G. Brown (Eds.), *Geographies of sexualities: Theory, practice, and politics* (pp. 125–136). Aldershot, UK: Ashgate.
Cockayne, D., Leszczynski, A., & Zook, M. (2017). #HotForBots: Sex, the non-human and digitally mediated spaces of intimate encounter. *Environment and Planning D: Society and Space, 35*(6), 1115–1133.
Cohen, J. E. (2007). Cyberspace as/and space. *Columbia Law Review, 107*, 210–256.
Duff, C. (2009). On the role of affect and practice in the production of place. *Environment and Planning D: Society and Space, 28*(5), 881–895.
Gudelunas, D. (2012). There's an app for that: The uses and gratifications of online social networks for gay men. *Sexuality & Culture, 16*(4), 347–365.
Jordan, B. (2009). Introduction: Blurring boundaries: The real and the virtual in hybrid spaces. *Human Organization, 68*(2), 181–193.
Kitchin, R. (1998). Towards geographies of cyberspace. *Progress in Human Geography, 22*(3), 385–406.
Licoppe, C., Rivière, C. A., & Morel, J. (2016). Grindr, casual hook-ups as interactional achievements. *New Media & Society, 18*(11), 2540–2558.
Miles, S. (2017). Sex in the digital city: Location-based dating apps and queer urban life. *Gender, Place, and Culture, 24*(11), 1591–1610.
Nash, C. J., & Gorman-Murray, A. (2014). LGBT neighbourhoods and 'New Mobilities': Towards understanding transformations in sexual and gendered urban landscapes. *International Journal of Urban and Regional Research, 38*(3), 756–772.
Raj, S. (2011). Grindring bodies: Racial and affective economies of online queer desire. *Critical Race and Whiteness Studies, 7*(2), 1–12.
Schatzki, T. R. (2002). *The site of the social: A philosophical account of the constitution of social life and change*. Pennsylvania: Pennsylvania State University Press.
Simon, W., & Gagnon, J. H. (1984). Sexual scripts. *Society, 22*(1), 53–60.
Simon, W., & Gagnon, J. H. (1986). Sexual scripts: Permanence and change. *Archives of Sexual Behavior, 15*(2), 97–120.
Stempfhuber, M., & Liegl, M. (2016). Intimacy mobilized: Hook-up practices in the location-based social network Grindr. *Österreichische Zeitschrift für Soziologie, 41*(1), 51–70.

Toma, C. L., & Hancock, J. T. (2010). Looks and lies: The role of physical attractiveness in online dating self-presentation and deception. *Communication Research, 37*(3), 335–351.

van Doorn, N. (2011). Digital spaces, material traces: How matter comes to matter in online performances of gender, sexuality and embodiment. *Media Culture Society, 33*(4), 531–547.

van Lisdonk, J., Maliepaard, E., Oostrik, S., & Vermey, K. (2017). *Weinig om het lijf? Ervaringen met online dating van jonge mannen die seks hebben met mannen*. Utrecht, Netherlands: Rutgers.

Walther, J. B. (1996). Computer-mediated communication: Impersonal, interpersonal, and hyperpersonal interaction. *Communication Research, 23*(1), 3–43.

Wiederman, M. W. (2005). The gendered nature of sexual scripts. *The Family Journal, 13*(4), 496–502.

9

'I didn't think you were going to sound like that': Sensory Geographies of Grindr Encounters in Public Spaces in Newcastle-upon-Tyne, UK

Carl Bonner-Thompson

Introduction

Digital screens and spaces have the capacity to reshape how bodies experience offline places. This capacity is made possible by the multiple spatial arrangements through which digital screens and spaces are made meaningful. Men who use Grindr can meet each other for different purposes. They meet for sex, hook ups, dates, friendship, to sell sex, or to experience a new place—to name a few. In this chapter, I explore the encounters that men have in public spaces (bars, cafés, and streets) in Newcastle-upon-Tyne, UK. I argue that, as Grindr does not enable the sounds of voices to be heard, users build up multiple expectations of other Grindr users and encounters. These expectations have been formed through digital pictures, conversations, and profiles and are closely tied to the expectations of public embodiment of masculinity in Newcastle. When these expectations are not met, desires are reshaped. In this sense, digital technologies

C. Bonner-Thompson (✉)
School of Geography and the Environment, University of Oxford,
Oxford, UK
e-mail: carl.bonner-thompson@ouce.ox.ac.uk

C. Nash, A. Gorman-Murray (eds.), *The Geographies of Digital Sexuality*,
https://doi.org/10.1007/978-981-13-6876-9_9

are shaping how people experience public spaces as their expectations are unmet or affirmed.

When people meet 'in the flesh', the sensory dimensions of bodies come to matter. This reshapes how Grindr users desire one another in ways that entangle with expectations that are formed in the digital environment alongside expectations of how gender should be performed and embodied in public spaces. These expectations are, in part, assembled through the regionally specific ways gender is imagined and understood—standards of masculinity that are specific to Newcastle. Men who use Grindr negotiate self/other in public spaces through sensory experiences that emerge through dominant discursive understandings of masculinities. I frame this chapter through sensory geographies, particularly drawing on visceral understandings of sound (Duffy & Waitt, 2013; Duffy, Waitt, & Harada, 2016; Waitt, Ryan, & Farbotko, 2014). I bring sensory geographies into conversation with digital geographies to contribute to materially grounded studies of digital environments and practices (Kinsley, 2014).

Grindr is a location-based dating app that is aimed at, and mainly used by, men. Grindr has become known as an app used for casual sex and hook ups, and has gained media attention for putting gay men in 'risky' sexual encounters (Crooks, 2013; Raj, 2013). Grindr has also been 'blamed' for the closure and decline of non-heterosexual bars and clubs, as dating apps are regarded as 'replacing' the need for LGBTQ+ people to use physical spaces to meet one another (Bitterman & Hess, 2016; Miles, 2017). Previous research on Grindr has sometimes pathologised the app (Jaspal, 2017; Landovitz et al., 2013; Rendina, Jimenez, Grov, Ventuneac, & Parsons, 2014; Rice et al., 2012), with some exploring the gendered, sexualised, and embodied experiences of using it (Blackwell, Birnholtz, & Abbott, 2015; Bonner-Thompson, 2017; Miles, 2017; Stempfhuber & Liegl, 2016). This chapter focuses on men who are using Grindr to meet people for dates and friendships. This is not to say that these participants do not wish to have sex. I am focusing on the encounters in public that may lead to sexual encounters in the future. Often when men meet in public, they are doing so for the first time. Many participants would comment that they are unable to hear how people sound or see how their bodies move through Grindr screens. Therefore, when Grindr users meet in public, the ways they understand and feel about people's bodies are reshaped through the spaces and places they meet in/across. This chapter, then, contributes to conversations that explore how digital technologies are reshaping how bodies feel in offline places, furthering understandings of the entanglements of online/offline.

The 30 men I interviewed lived in Newcastle or Gateshead at the time of the study (August–December 2015). Newcastle is a small, post-industrial city in the northeast of England with coal-mining and ship-building histories. Due to its industrial past, the city is predominantly working-class, with particular forms of working-class masculinity dominating the region (Mah, 2010; Nayak, 2006). The city is also predominantly white in terms of race and ethnicity, with masculinities being produced through notions of whiteness (Nayak, 2003). Since the decline of its traditional industries, the city has undergone investment and re-branding, focusing on retail, leisure, restaurants, and the night-time economy. It has a small 'gay scene' known as the 'pink triangle'. This is a zone in the city centre that is triangulated by non-heterosexual bars and clubs.

The industrial history has shaped the ways gender is understood, performed, and embodied in and across the city. Nayak (2003, 2006) has explored how young working-class men who live and work in Newcastle negotiate shifting regional identities. Unable to transition from school into 'hard', labour-intensive work, young working-class men often find it difficult to meet expectations of masculinities and construct masculine identities (McDowell, 2003; Nayak, 2003, 2006; Willis, 1977). 'Geordie' men can find it difficult to 'become' men as traditional forms of masculine labour have disappeared. Nayak (2003, 2006) has argued that men in Newcastle attempt to embody masculinity through consumption practices—drinking alcohol and buying branded clothes—whilst performing heterosexuality through the pursuit of sexual encounters with women. Nayak (2006) has explored how men's voices, whiteness, and regional dialect become entangled in the embodiment and construction of local masculinities. Class dynamics shape how men from Newcastle use ways of speaking to sometimes differentiate between themselves through a certain roughness and harshness on particular words. Here, sounds or words become important to help make sense of self and other as they engage in different places. Nayak's (2006) work does not think about how sounds of voices shape how bodies feel in places. Therefore, I use a visceral lens to further understand how bodies respond to the sounds of voices, especially when Grindr users have expectations formed through digital encounters that are closely tied to expectations of public performances of masculinity in Newcastle. In particular, I explore how this is unique to public spaces, as more 'manly' performances of masculinity *become* more important when some Grindr users are in public spaces in Newcastle. In the following section, I discuss the work in sensory geographies, particularly sound and touch, which informs the ways I conceptualise offline Grindr encounters.

Visceral Geographies of Sense and Sound

Taking a sensory approach to bodies and places enables an understanding of experiences beyond discourses and language (Rodaway, 1994). Human experiences are multisensory. Our senses are entangled in the ways bodies feel, experience, and perceive the world (Pink, 2012; Rodaway, 1994). Geographers have paid attention to how senses shape experiences of places, furthering understanding of how bodies and spaces are mutually constituted (Gallagher, 2016). This has involved exploring senses and homes (Duffy & Waitt, 2013; Kerr, Gibson, & Klocker, 2018; Morrison, 2012), nightclubs (Caluya, 2008; Misgav & Johnston, 2014), cities (Waitt & Stanes, 2015), festivals (Duffy, Waitt, Gorman-Murray, & Gibson, 2011), and beaches (Obrador-Pons, 2007).

Visceral geographies can be used as a frame to think through bodily sensory engagements. Visceral experience is understood as gut feelings (e.g. shame) that can shape how people create spaces (Probyn, 2000). Longhurst, Johnston, and Ho (2009, p. 334) suggest that a visceral geographical approach involves an exploration of:

> the sensations, moods, and ways of being that emerge from our sensory engagement with the material and discursive environments in which we live. Paying attention to the visceral means paying attention to the senses—

sight, sound, touch, smell and taste—which are a mechanism for visceral arousal.

Drawing on these geographic interventions, a visceral lens enables a deeper understanding of bodies that incorporates both everyday messy, fleshy, and emotional dimensions alongside the discursive, linguistic, and symbolic aspects of social lives. It enables an exploration of spaces inside bodies and how they relate to the external spaces in which bodies are located. Viscerality was first introduced into geography through ideas of food and taste. Hayes-Conroy and Hayes-Conroy (2008) were some of the first to bring visceral experience into feminist geographies by exploring how food feels differently in different bodies. Drawing on the work of Probyn (2000), Hayes-Conroy and Hayes-Conroy (2008) argue that a visceral lens can enhance understandings of the ways people become 'mobilised' or 'moved' by politics. In this sense, visceral geographies can open up understandings of how the sensual and feeling body is shaped by broader socio-political and spatial processes.

Using a visceral lens to explore men and masculinity can reveal how gender is assembled through sensory engagements with bodies and places. Waitt and Stanes (2015) use a visceral lens to explore the strategies men who live in Sydney, Australia, use to avoid feeling disgust and shame at their own sweaty bodies. Anxiety about sweat—a physiological compound that has social meaning—can cause some men to shave their armpits and use deodorant so they do not smell at work. At the same time, men at work would not want to smell 'too good'. Shame and pride would often be used to ensure men did not smell 'too good' at work, which worked to uphold 'intimate bonds of mateship between self-identified "real" men as blokes/mates' (Waitt & Stanes, 2015, p. 36). These tactics highlight the ways men both subvert and reinforce embodied notions of a professional masculinity. They argue that masculinity is assembled through physiological sweat that gains meaning through the spaces in which it appears, the emotional and felt responses to sweat, and the embodied practices used to manage sweat.

I focus on the visceral experience of sound in this chapter—especially the sounds of voices for men when they meet in offline places. I explore how men respond to sounds of voices and how they attempt to negotiate expectations that are formed in online spaces. Therefore, I use a visceral lens to explore how people feel and experience the ways that online/offline spaces can be connected and disconnected. Next, I highlight how sound has come to be understood through ideas of viscerality. Sounds, and their affective capacities, shape how bodies experience spaces, places, and (other) bodies (Smith, 2000). Nancy (2007) has argued that the ways bodies 'listen' is shaped by, and shapes, emotional, corporeal, and psychological experiences. Sounds can make material and discursive spaces meaningful, whilst mobilising bodies in multiple ways (Doughty, Duffy, & Harada, 2016). Exploring the visceral experience of sound can highlight how sounds are entangled in emotions, alongside the way they become culturally comprehensible through discursive and spatial power relations (Duffy et al., 2016; Duffy & Waitt, 2013; Waitt et al., 2014). Duffy and Waitt (2013, p. 468) argue that 'thinking about sound as a mechanism for visceral arousal means thinking about how the sensuous body is embedded in social, cultural and spatial relationships'. Embodied responses are always spatially contingent, subject to the power dynamics that produce places (Longhurst et al., 2009). Therefore, visceral, embodied experiences of sounds can provide insights to how people make sense of place (Duffy et al., 2016; Duffy & Waitt, 2013). As Waitt et al. (2014, p. 287) argue:

> The body's capacity to sense sounds opens up the in-between-ness of sensing and making sense. In this way, bodily judgements of sounds may give rise to moments of heightened intensities that allow people to distinguish between inner and outer selves, individual and group, us and them, here and elsewhere. Sounds may cohere subjectivities, places and a sense of 'togetherness'. At the same time, the same sounds may provoke a sense of alienation because they are felt and understood as disruptive or harmful and so categorised as undesirable or noise.

Sounds, and how we listen to them, are embedded in complex relationships with located bodies. Duffy and Waitt (2013) highlight ways that home can be constituted through how sounds are viscerally felt by people who live in the coastal town of Bermagui, Australia. For example, they argue that the different sounds of waves shape a sense of Bermagui as home. The gut feeling of soothing sounds can connect people to place whilst the gut feeling of rough crashing sounds can disconnect people from places. In this sense, sounds are central to how people make sense of place.

Sounds do not act on their own, but are part of multisensory experiences of places (Rodaway, 1994). The sound that bodies make when they are touched during sex shapes how people makes sense of sexualities and homes. Morrison's (2012) work with 14 women in heterosexual relationships in Hamilton, Aotearoa New Zealand, explores haptic geographies of touch and the home. Her work identifies home as a key site for heterosexual touch, enabling heterosexuality to emerge in different ways. She argues that the importance of touch for heterosexual couples goes beyond the bedroom (Morrison, 2013). For example, sounds of sex can leak into other parts of the home. For people living in shared housing, the risk of housemates hearing bodies touching during sex can prevent couples from engaging in sex. Therefore, sounds, within particular spatial conditions, can shape sexual practices.

I argue that sounds are entangled in the ways we experience touch and a desire to be touched. I explore how sounds reshape the desire to touch other bodies. This is shaped by the performances of gender that are understood as appropriate in public spaces of Newcastle. Multisensory experiences of voices, in and through space, bring sexualised bodies into being in different ways. I explore how the offline meetings of Grindr users are shaped by sensory geographies. Examining this also enables an understanding of the instability of online/offline dualisms. The following section briefly discusses the methodological approaches to this study.

Hearing and Listening to Men Who Use Grindr

The project is shaped by feminist and queer methodologies, which foreground human experiences of gender, sexuality, and embodiment, interrogating how gendered and sexualised power relations organise bodies, lives, and spaces (Browne & Nash, 2010; Di Feliciantonio, Gadelha, & DasGupta, 2017; Knopp, 2007; Tarrant, 2014). I was guided by these intersecting epistemological approaches as they focus attention on the lived experiences of bodies, people, and places (Browne & Nash, 2010; Di Feliciantonio et al., 2017; McDowell & Sharp, 1997). I also wanted to pay attention to the ways bodies feel when they use screens and technologies. Therefore, I chose to interview people in person to unpack the emotional and affective dimensions of their experiences.

I conducted this research between August and December 2015 in Newcastle, interviewing 30 men who use Grindr. The research is part of a wider Economic and Social Research Council (ESRC)-funded project that explores the spatial and embodied experiences of men who use Grindr. The project was granted ethical approval by Newcastle University. I used information sheets to give participants as much detail as possible and had consent forms that were explicit about anonymity, confidentiality, and right to withdraw. All the names used in this chapter are pseudonyms. I asked questions about how men used Grindr, where they used it, what prompted them use it, and about different encounters that they had. All interviews were recorded using a Dictaphone or mobile smart phone and transcribed in full. The interviews were then analysed and coded using Nvivo.

I recruited the participants from Grindr by setting up a profile that stated the research intentions. As Grindr only allows one picture, I used a picture of my face, smiling. I wanted to use my face as a way to make users more comfortable speaking with me than they might with a university logo, for example. Once users started a conversation with me, I would try to move conversations to e-mail and away from Grindr. I would send participants the information and ethics form in advance to make them feel more at ease when meeting me and to attempt to construct some 'boundaries' between myself and the participant (Cuomo & Massaro, 2014). These boundaries were attempts to avoid participants thinking the meeting was sexual or erotic (see Bonner-Thompson, 2017, for discussion of ethical boundary making).

The interviews took place in cafés in Newcastle city centre or in a private room on Newcastle University campus. This method was chosen to protect both myself and the participants from unwanted advances and encounters. I would always provide the participants with the option to choose where the interview would take place. However, some would ask that I choose. I would usually pick somewhere that participants were familiar with so that they felt comfortable discussing intimate details about their Grindr practices. I would often suggest a café that is on the edge of the pink triangle in Newcastle and is 'queer-friendly'. As I discuss in this chapter, voices and sounds shape the ways encounters feel in public spaces (Gallagher, 2016). Discussing intimate sexual practices may cause participants to feel uncomfortable as other people in the café could hear. Choosing queer-friendly places, or places that participants were familiar with, was a way to manage feelings of discomfort that could be felt. Furthermore, in coffee shops, our conversations were often masked by sounds of other people's conversations, orders being made, coffee machines, and doors opening and closing. Therefore, sounds provided increased comfort in these encounters. In the following section, I explore how men who use Grindr experience the sounds of voices in cafés and bars and how this shapes how they understand their desires to touch/be touched.

Sounding Unsexy

As Grindr encounters are first facilitated through a digital medium, new times and spaces are created when bodies meet in the flesh. Participants highlight how voices (sounds) come to matter when Grindr users met for the first time. The pitch, tone, and depth of sounds have effects on bodies, mobilising particular responses. Listening to the sounds of voices can challenge or affirm expectations that are formed online. By engaging with feminist calls to pay attention to the power dynamics that shape emotion and affect (Thien, 2005), I argue that voices can reaffirm bodily boundaries and can render identity categories stable.

The following quote is from Joe, who speaks about meeting up with another Grindr user a couple of days before they were going to go on a date:

Joe: Recently I was speaking to this guy who, I thought he would be geeky, bit reserved, but not that camp, and I met up with him and was totally camp, not gonna lie.

Carl: Why didn't you think he would be? And what made him camp?

Joe: I don't think it was what he was saying over text, I think it was his mannerisms and his voice, it was his total tone of voice and mannerisms, and you can't tell that by text and you can't tell that by photos.
C: How was his tone of voice?
Joe: Camp, it was, I can't explain it … you can't hear someone's tone of voice on instant message. The stuff he was saying wasn't camp at all, it was his tone, like high, and his mannerisms, and you can't tell that by message … I met him and found that out and went 'bye'.
Carl: so you didn't find him attractive?
Joe: no, not at all.
Carl: and you didn't go on a date?
Joe: I was meant to be meeting up with him for a date, but I was around town when he was finishing work, so I met up with him when he finished work, and I kind of cancelled the date … I just walked him to his bus stop and just let him go. (24, White British)

This example highlights how the sound of the voice can (re)shape attractiveness between bodies. Joe was attracted to this person when they communicated across Grindr as the words he used were not 'camp'. By this, he means he did not use words like 'babe', was not overly emotive, and was direct in his responses. Joe highlights that you are unable to 'hear' someone through Grindr. Therefore, voice, sounds, and movements do not always immediately 'matter' when interacting online. Bodies are never fully complete, and are always in processes of becoming (Nast & Pile, 2005). When bodies move between online and offline spaces, they emerge in different ways. Once Joe and the other Grindr user met in public space in Newcastle, voice, movements, and touch came to matter. For Joe, his date became 'de-masculinised'. The 'campness' of this user's voice did not meet Joe's expectations. As he was no longer attracted to this user, Joe cancelled the date.

Other users spoke about going on a date with men who have high-pitched voices, and how they felt during the encounter. The following quote is from Rupert who discusses this:

Rupert: As soon as he spoke, that was quite off putting
Carl: what was off putting?
Rupert: It was the tone of his voice, it was very high pitched, it was almost bordering shrieky, he said petal at the end of every sentence, at one point we were sat at the bar and I was looking around to make sure no one was listening to our conversation, I was embarrassed to be seen with him, which I know is an awful thing to say, cos he was probably a really nice guy, but wasn't the type of guy I would be interested in, that's probably the worst experience I've had … I never saw him again. (37, White British)

Rupert was embarrassed to be seen and *heard* with his date, labelling it the worst Grindr experience he has had. Rupert experiences embarrassment upon listening to the 'shrieky' tone of his dates' voice. As sound travels through and between spaces and bodies, it has the capacity to affect (Gallagher, 2016). Rupert is aware that other people in the bar could hear the 'shrieky-ness' of his date's voice. Therefore, he becomes concerned about the judgements other people may have about his gendered and sexualised body. The embarrassment he experiences, then, is shaped by the presence of other bodies, and their capacities to listen.

In this context, a shrieky, high-pitched, or softly spoken voice is often not considered a 'good' embodiment of masculinity, or of a potential boyfriend or partner. Such voices are constructed relationally with those that are deeper, maybe rougher, and are considered manly (Heasley, 2005). 'Good' forms of masculinity are bound up with what a 'good' boyfriend is. In Rupert's case, his companion's non-masculine voice impelled embarrassment. Probyn (2005) highlights that embarrassment is not necessarily the same emotion as shame, but they are interconnected as they do not enable feelings of pride. For many men in this study, being able to 'pass' as straight was important for constructions of masculinity. Not being visibly, or vocally, 'gay' symbolised 'good' embodied masculinities in public spaces. 'Passing' is also a way for non-heterosexual men and women to avoid homophobic abuse and violence (Leary, 1999). Yet, passing as straight is not always simply about avoiding direct homophobia and violence. Not being read as 'gay' can provide enhanced claims to normative cultural capital—being told 'you don't seem gay' can be used as a compliment in everyday conversations in the West. Issues of passing and masculinity manifest in the lives of non-heterosexual people, shaping how some gay men wish to perform and embody gender (Mark, 2004; Owens, 2017; Payne, 2007). In Newcastle, discourses around working-class white masculinities can dominate public spaces (especially in some pubs and bars). Masculine embodiments that deviate from this might be understood as 'out of place' by some.

The risk of another person listening to conversations between Rupert and his date can, therefore, be understood as a threat to public performances of masculinity in Newcastle. Probyn (2004, p. 345) argues that shame is 'the body saying that it cannot fit in although it desperately wants to', whilst Waitt and Clifton (2013, 2015) argue that men can feel shame if they are unable to embody qualities of hegemonic masculinity. The embarrassment Rupert experiences emerges as he begins to feel 'out of place' with his date—he feels they do not fit in a non-gay pub in Newcastle city centre. The feeling of embarrassment is his body experiencing a desire to 'fit in' and go unnoticed. Rupert himself does not consider his own voice 'less masculine'. However, for others to listen to a conversation between him and his date in a pub would not, in his opinion, enable him to achieve more 'straight' embodiments of masculinities. This leads to feelings of embarrassment. This shapes his desire not to be touched. Therefore, his bodily barriers are re-affirmed, redrawing the boundaries around desirable, embodied masculinities.

Paying attention to the visceral experience of sound has highlighted how Rupert and other participants make sense of public spaces. As men's bodies move away from digital spaces and into public ones, different dimensions of embodiment come to matter. When bodies meet offline, voices become central to understandings of masculinities and desirability. The ability for other bodies to listen to, and be affected by, voices shapes how bodies viscerally experience sound. The sounds of voices produce bodily feelings of shame and embarrassment, as they meet neither the expectations formed through digital exchanges nor the expectations of public embodiments of masculinity that are often celebrated and normalised in pubs in Newcastle. Therefore, for men who use Grindr in Newcastle, public spaces are understood as places where masculinities must be more carefully policed. Forms of gendered embodiment that can be understood as non-manly are more carefully scrutinised. Such policing can performatively render the categories of gay/straight more stable and fixed in public places (Butler, 1990). In this sense, notions of public/private are re-made as certain performances of masculinities are understood to be expressed in public places when men meet through Grindr. This experience of sound reinforces the boundaries between self and other and the gendered performances that are specific to places in Newcastle.

Both Rupert and Joe's experiences of men's voices highlight that non-masculine voices are often constructed as undesirable, unattractive, or unsexy. In these examples, the ways that Grindr users are desired is reshaped through place, as the presence of other bodies in public places in Newcastle shifts how bodies are understood through the senses. When the participants agreed to meet other users in offline places, they usually have established some form of attraction in and through digital environments. However, when voices are heard, this attraction is shifted. For Rupert and Joe, the initial desire that emerged through online conversations is reshaped when the multiple expectations of bodies and masculinities were not met. They did not want to be seen and heard with these men in public spaces. As I have highlighted, there are particular forms of masculinity that are normalised in Newcastle, and these shape how Grindr users can understand the voices of their Grindr dates. Particular gendered and sexualised power dynamics shape how these expectations are felt and experienced. There was a feeling of embarrassment at being 'heard' with these men, as the voices did not 'fit in' with the dominant ways of embodying masculinity in Newcastle. The embarrassment and shame are shaped by heteronormative discourses that can result in stabilising discursive categories (Butler, 1990; Longhurst et al., 2009). The ways discourses emerge between online and offline spaces can (re)produce bodies and places, and thereby reshape desires.

Sounding Sexy

So far, I have highlighted how the sounds of voices produce unsexy and untouchable bodies due to the places in which offline Grindr encounters occur. In this section, I explore two examples where, upon hearing their voices, men from Grindr become more desirable. The following example demonstrates how desire shifts to produce sexy bodies. Jack speaks about a Grindr user he was meeting as a friend:

Jack: There was a guy I was talking to, and like I don't have an issue with feminine people, and we were meeting up as friends, and I would never meet up with someone who I perceived as overly affectionately feminine or even overly masculine for that matter, if it's to the point where they are trying to prove a point that that's just off putting. But he just seemed like a really cool guy, same sense of humour, same sort of outlook kind of thing and I thought we could meet up for a drink and have a chat. He said to me 'oh, I'm not the manliest of people, and I'm not the most feminine either'. When I met him, his voice was a lot deeper than I thought it would have been, and a lot more manly, and it sort of shocked me a little bit, like 'oh, I didn't think you were going to sound like that', and it almost instantaneously made him more attractive. Although we met up as friends it made me look at him in a different way sort of thing, as like 'now that I know you sound like that you've become more appealing on a non-friendship sort of level'.

Carl: What happened?

Jack: Nothing happened, then, but like, you know, something did, later.

Whilst the initial online encounter created feelings of friendship for Jack, actually hearing a deeper, more 'manly' voice enabled feelings of attraction to emerge. Jack was expecting 'not the manliest of people' due to the conversation. For Jack, the manliest person would be 'too muscular', would have a deep voice, and would display arrogance and aggression. Jack had particular expectations about this person through gut feelings produced through digital encounters. Then Jack heard this user in offline space, which challenged his expectations. Although online and offline spaces are not separate or dichotomous, there are some boundaries that mean that particular sensory experiences do not always neatly translate. In this instance, listening enabled sexual and romantic desire to emerge—the deeper tone of voice moved sexual bodies into erotic encounters. The experience of sound, invoking particular understandings of masculinities, produced a desire to be touched.

At the same time, these same binaries do not always produce the same affects. In this example, Russell explains that hearing a 'camper' voice was not necessarily 'off putting', as in other examples.

Russell: There was a gentleman, a mixed raced gentleman, we were kind of speaking on and off, and he just messaged me one time and just asked for my number. So we'd been speaking for a while, built up some level of trust so I gave him my number, we met up a few days later for a drink and yes he was more feminine that I was anticipating. In the photographs he was taking, they were, I would certainly put him in the masc category … his photos, just the way they were taken, I don't know the position, just this whatever, just that kind of look about him and when he turned up. It wasn't as much his mannerisms, as so much his mode of speech and what not, but he talked quite fast and he was little bit … he was more feminine that I was anticipating… We had a really good time, and again that doesn't faze me, it doesn't put me off, it was more. And it wasn't a surprise, it was just not what I was expecting, but it wasn't an unpleasant surprise, is what I'm saying.

Carl: Did that lead to anything more?

Russell: It was obvious that he wanted a full-time relationship with a man, and again I wasn't not looking for anything particular, just not ready to settle down after just one meeting. It got

> very late, he got very drunk, he actually did come to my house, and we did share the same bed.

Russell had a gut instinct about how this person would be in offline settings. However, when these expectations were not met, bodily barriers are not remade. Instead, there are momentary affective forces that disorientated Russell, but it does not stop physical intimacy from occurring. In the conversation, Russell was not concerned about the place that they were in and if other people could hear them on a date. For Russell, traditional associations of what a man should sound like, and the expectations of masculinity in Newcastle, did not alter how he desired this person's body. Therefore, there are moments, times, and places where desire can move beyond fixed ideas of masculinity in particular places. At the same time, Russell speaks about how other aspects of his embodiment still conform to normative understandings of masculinity in Newcastle. Here, gender is made meaningful through contradictory notions of masculinity that emerge as Grindr users become oriented with each other's bodies. In these examples, the experience of voices does not prevent bodies from engaging in other forms of sexual encounters. However, in both examples, there are particular discourses around desirable masculinity that enable bodies to touch—for instance, a deep voice or other 'manly' characteristics. Therefore, even though some bodily boundaries can be disrupted, they are still framed within dominant discourses of what it means to be a man that are specific to Newcastle. Desire can be reconfigured; however, it is through the competing discourses that construct gendered and sexualised categories of man/woman and gay/straight.

Conclusion

In this chapter, I have focused on the ways visceral geographies of sound in public spaces in Newcastle are entangled in Grindr encounters. There are particular expectations, and gut feelings, when people first chat over Grindr. Offline, these expectations can be affirmed or unmet. As I have noted, expectations of masculinity are specific to dominant embodiments of masculinity in Newcastle. As encounters are formed through Grindr, when men move into offline public spaces, places are experienced differently—users have to assess and negotiate the bodies of other men. Therefore, digital technologies are reshaping the ways that bodies engage and experience offline places. Whilst online and offline spaces intertwine, particular sensory dimensions of bodies do not neatly map onto the expectations initially formed through digital encounters. I examined this through the experience of listening to the sounds of other men's voices and how this reshapes how people desire to touch other Grindr users. Waitt et al. (2014) contend that sounds can challenge but also stabilise otherness. In this chapter, I have argued that listening to voices can reaffirm bodily boundaries, but also mobilise bodies into eroticism. The negotiation of self/other in public spaces (bars and streets) emerges through dominant discursive understandings of masculinities that are particular to the context in which people meet. Desire can be reconfigured; however, it is through the spatially specific discourses that construct gendered and sexualised categories of man/woman and gay/straight. The assemblage of bodies, voices, and words in encounters (re)produces spatial experiences of embodiment. Such experiences shape, whilst being shaped by, the discourses that (re)produce normative categories of gender and sexuality.

References

Bitterman, A., & Hess, D. B. (2016). Gay ghettoes growing gray: Transformation of gay urban districts across North America reflects generational change. *The Journal of American Culture, 39*(1), 55–63.

Blackwell, C., Birnholtz, J., & Abbott, C. (2015). Seeing and being seen: Co-situation and impression formation using Grindr, a location-aware gay dating app. *New Media & Society, 17*(7), 1117–1136.

Bonner-Thompson, C. (2017). 'The meat market': Production and regulation of masculinities on the Grindr grid in Newcastle-upon-Tyne, UK. *Gender, Place & Culture, 24*(11), 1611–1625.

Browne, K., & Nash, C. J. (2010). Queer methods and methodologies: An introduction. In K. Browne & C. J. Nash (Eds.), *Queer methods and methodologies intersecting queer theories and social science research* (pp. 1–16). Oxon: Routledge.

Butler, J. (1990). *Gender trouble: Feminism and the subversion of identity.* New York: Routledge.

Caluya, G. (2008). The Rice Steamer': Race, desire and affect in Sydney's gay scene. *Australian Geographer, 39*(3), 283–292.

Crooks, R.N. (2013). The rainbow flag and the green carnation: Grindr in the gay village. *First Monday, 18*(11). Retrieved from http://firstmonday.org/ojs/index.php/fm/article/view/4958/3790

Cuomo, D., & Massaro, V. A. (2014). Boundary-making in feminist research: New methodologies for 'intimate insiders'. *Gender, Place & Culture, 23*(1), 94–106.

Di Feliciantonio, C., Gadelha, K. B., & DasGupta, D. (2017). 'Queer(y)ing methodologies: Doing fieldwork and becoming queer' – guest editorial. *Gender, Place & Culture, 24*(3), 403–412.

Doughty, K., Duffy, M., & Harada, T. (2016). Practices of emotional and affective geographies of sound. *Emotion, Space and Society, 20*, 39–41.

Duffy, M., & Waitt, G. (2013). Home sounds: Experiential practices and performativities of hearing and listening. *Social & Cultural Geography, 14*(4), 466–481.

Duffy, M., Waitt, G., Gorman-Murray, A., & Gibson, C. (2011). Bodily rhythms: Corporeal capacities to engage with festival spaces. *Emotion, Space and Society, 4*(1), 17–24.

Duffy, M., Waitt, G., & Harada, T. (2016). Making sense of sound: Visceral sonic mapping as a research tool. *Emotion, Space and Society, 20*, 49–57.

Gallagher, M. (2016). Sound as affect: Difference, power and spatiality. *Emotion, Space and Society, 20*, 42–48.

Hayes-Conroy, A., & Hayes-Conroy, J. (2008). Taking back taste: Feminism, food and visceral politics. *Gender, Place & Culture, 15*(5), 461–473.

Heasley, R. (2005). Queer masculinities of straight men. *Men and Masculinities, 7*(3), 310–320.

Jaspal, R. (2017). Gay men's construction and management of identity on Grindr. *Sexuality & Culture, 21*(1), 187–204.

Kerr, S.-M., Gibson, C., & Klocker, N. (2018). Parenting and neighbouring in the consolidating city: The emotional geographies of sound in apartments. *Emotion, Space and Society, 26*, 1–8.

Kinsley, S. (2014). The matter of 'virtual' geographies. *Progress in Human Geography, 38*(3), 364–384.

Knopp, L. (2007). On the relationship between queer and feminist geographies. *The Professional Geographer, 59*(1), 47–55.

Landovitz, R. J., Tseng, C. H., Weissman, M., Haymer, M., Mendenhall, B., Rogers, K., et al. (2013). Epidemiology, sexual risk behavior, and HIV prevention practices of men who have sex with men using Grindr in Los Angeles, California. *Journal of Urban Health, 90*(4), 729–739.

Leary, K. (1999). Passing, posing, and "keeping it real". *Constellations, 6*(1), 85–96.

Longhurst, R., Johnston, L., & Ho, E. (2009). A visceral approach: Cooking 'at home' with migrant women in Hamilton, New Zealand. *Transactions of the Institute of British Geographers, 34*(3), 333–345.

Mah, A. (2010). Memory, uncertainty and industrial ruination: Walker Riverside, Newcastle upon Tyne. *International Journal of Urban and Regional Research, 34*(2), 398–413.

Mark, B. N. H. (2004). Digitizing the racialized body or the politics of universal address. *SubStance, 33*(2), 107–133.

McDowell, L. (2003). *Redundant masculinities?: Employment change and white working class youth*. Malden, MA: Blackwell.

McDowell, L., & Sharp, J. P. (1997). *Space, gender, knowledge: Feminist readings*. London: Arnold.

Miles, S. (2017). Sex in the digital city: Location-based dating apps and queer urban life. *Gender, Place & Culture, 24*(11), 1595–1610.

Misgav, C., & Johnston, L. (2014). Dirty dancing: The (non)fluid embodied geographies of a queer nightclub in Tel Aviv. *Social & Cultural Geography, 15*(7), 730–746.

Morrison, C.-A. (2012). Heterosexuality and home: Intimacies of space and spaces of touch. *Emotion, Space and Society, 5*(1), 10–18.

Morrison, C.-A. (2013). Homemaking in New Zealand: Thinking through the mutually constitutive relationship between domestic material objects, heterosexuality and home. *Gender, Place & Culture, 20*(4), 413–431.

Nancy, J. L. (2007). *Listening*. New York: Fordham University Press.

Nast, H., & Pile, S. (2005). Introduction: MakingPlaceBodies. In H. Nast & S. Pile (Eds.), *Places through the body* (pp. 1–19). London: Taylor & Francis.

Nayak, A. (2003). Last of the 'real Geordies'? White masculinities and the subcultural response to deindustrialisation. *Environment and Planning D: Society and Space, 21*(1), 7–25.

Nayak, A. (2006). Displaced masculinities: Chavs, youth and class in the post-industrial city. *Sociology, 40*(5), 813–831.

Obrador-Pons, P. (2007). A haptic geography of the beach: Naked bodies, vision and touch. *Social & Cultural Geography, 8*(1), 123–141.

Owens, Z. D. (2017). Is it Facebook official? Coming out and passing strategies of young adult gay men on social media. *Journal of Homosexuality, 64*(4), 431–449.

Payne, R. (2007). Str8acting. *Social Semiotics, 17*(4), 525–538.

Pink, S. (2012). Visual ethnography and the internet: Visuality, virtuality and the spatial turn. In S. Pink (Ed.), *Advances in visual methodology* (pp. 113–130). London: SAGE Publications.

Probyn, E. (2000). *Carnal appetites: Foodsexidentities*. London: Routledge.

Probyn, E. (2004). Everyday shame. *Cultural Studies, 18*(2–3), 328–349.

Probyn, E. (2005). *Blush: Faces of shame*. Sydney: University of New South Wales Press.

Raj, S. (2013). How Grindr has transformed users' experience of intimacy. *The Guardian*. Retrieved from http://www.theguardian.com/commentisfree/2013/aug/02/grindr-sex-relationship-intimacy

Rendina, H. J., Jimenez, R. H., Grov, C., Ventuneac, A., & Parsons, J. T. (2014). Patterns of lifetime and recent HIV testing among men who have sex with men in New York City who use *Grindr. AIDS and Behavior, 18*(1), 41–49.

Rice, E., Holloway, I., Winetrobe, H., Rhoades, H., Barman-Adhikari, A., Gibbs, J., et al. (2012). Sex risk among young men who have sex with men who use Grindr, a smartphone geosocial networking application. *Journal of AIDS and Clinical Research, 3*(4), 1–8.

Rodaway, P. (1994). *Sensuous geographies: Body, sense, place*. London: Routledge.

Smith, S. J. (2000). Performing the (sound)world. *Environment and Planning D: Society and Space, 18*(5), 615–637.

Stempfhuber, M., & Liegl, M. (2016). Intimacy mobilized: Hook-up practices in the location-based social network Grindr. *Österreichische Zeitschrift für Soziologie, 41*(1), 51–70.

Tarrant, A. (2014). Men, masculinities and methodologies. *Gender, Place & Culture, 21*(9), 1193–1194.

Thien, D. (2005). After or beyond feeling? A consideration of affect and emotion in geography. *Area, 37*(4), 450–456.

Waitt, G., & Clifton, D. (2013). 'Stand out, not up': Bodyboarders, gendered hierarchies and negotiating the dynamics of pride/shame. *Leisure Studies, 32*(5), 487–506.

Waitt, G., & Clifton, D. (2015). Winning and losing: The dynamics of pride and shame in the narratives of men who play competitive country football. *Leisure Studies, 34*(3), 259–281.

Waitt, G., Ryan, E., & Farbotko, C. (2014). A visceral politics of sound. *Antipode, 46*(1), 283–300.
Waitt, G., & Stanes, E. (2015). Sweating bodies: Men, masculinities, affect, emotion. *Geoforum, 59*, 30–38.
Willis, P. E. (1977). *Learning to labour: How working class kids get working class jobs*. Farnborough: Saxon House.

Part III

Activism, Politics and Communities

10

Disrupting Sexism and Sexualities Online? Gender, Activism and Digital Spaces

Jessica McLean and Sophia Maalsen

Introduction

Feminism is "having a moment" (Gill, 2016). This moment is largely facilitated by the increase of online social media campaigns variously focusing on feminist issues. For some, the current heightened visibility of feminism is due to the disruptive powers of digital spaces—its ability to reconfigure spatio-temporal relationships and enable a rapid coalescence and action around campaigns. But this increased feminist energy is a double-edged sword, enabling the same opportunities for anti-feminist and misogynist attitudes. Digital spaces are comprised of contingent spaces where political, emotional and affectual aspects of the everyday play out, and as such is a productive site for geographical analysis.

J. McLean (✉)
Macquarie University, Sydney, NSW, Australia
e-mail: jessica.mclean@mq.edu.au

S. Maalsen
University of Sydney, Sydney, NSW, Australia
e-mail: sophia.maalsen@sydney.edu.au

C. Nash, A. Gorman-Murray (eds.), *The Geographies of Digital Sexuality*,
https://doi.org/10.1007/978-981-13-6876-9_10

While we agree that feminism is having a moment, or moments, it is also important to note that it has always, by definition and in terms of theory and practice, been disruptive. Since Mary Wollstonecraft's (1978 [1792]) "A Vindication on the Rights of Women" argued for a critical gaze on the institution of marriage as a form of servitude for women, feminists have focused on changing the status quo with respect to gendered opportunity. The focus of gendered disruption has changed with the attainment of particular rights; now, the proliferation of digital feminist action invites examination of how gendered geographies of disruption work. Specifically, we are interested in the ways that disruptive play and performativity co-produce powerful feminisms.

By now, an argument can be made that the early hopes for a cyberspace utopia enabled by the reconfiguring of sex and gender in digital spaces (e.g., see Haraway, 1991; Wajcman, 2007) have not emerged as some hoped. This is not to say that digital technologies have not enabled feminist action but that, for all of the digital transgressions that have emerged, the same politics and structural constraints experienced in other spaces still persist. As Johnston (2017) notes, while feminist actions generated by activism, in online and offline spaces, can transform, such interventions can also reproduce normative and constrictive modes of interaction. For every tweet and Facebook comment espousing feminist and gendered action, there is the possibility of trolling, slut-shaming and harassment (Turley & Fisher, 2018). The reproduction of sexism online is unsurprising as digital spaces are complex socio-technical systems comprised of the technologies supported by the internet, software and hardware but also importantly the aesthetic, ontological and discursive elements that circulate through and within the technologies and networks to enable digitality (Ash, Kitchin, & Leszczynski, 2018). For us, then, digital spaces are more than computer code—it is inclusive of technologies, methods, performances, communication tools and practices that enable digital spaces. Thus, the digital is far from neutral—it retains the ideologies, politics and practices that comprise its constitutive parts, yet likewise it can be appropriated to resist, disrupt and parody, and play a part in feminist activism and intervention.

In this chapter, we argue that embracing the digital turn currently underway in geography requires us to ask questions of the roles of gender, emotions and affect within those spaces, and what opportunities and constraints online activities offer for disrupting politics and practices relating to sexism, gender and sexualities. We use a discourse analysis of the social media activist group, Destroy the Joint (DTJ), focusing on their online activity relating to the Australian Marriage Law Postal Survey (here on referred to as AMLPS or the Survey) in 2017, to interrogate the affordances and barriers such a space offers for effective digital action. As this chapter will show, digital and non-digital spaces are co-producing: we emphasise that these are not discrete spaces but are actually deeply entangled (Kinsley, 2013). However, DTJ emerged as a digital space that encourages and facilitates actions in digital and non-digital spaces, existing in a paradoxical space that works across and in social media and face-to-face contexts (McLean & Maalsen, 2013).

In this chapter we first contextualise the potential of action in digital spaces to disrupt sexism and misogyny in debates on gender, sexualities, technology and geography. Second, we illustrate an example of online activism drawing upon DTJ and their discussion of the AMLPS as a case study. The connections between DTJ, AMLPS and global activism will be explored, including the way that disruptive performativity and play brings together activisms. Third, we ask what this means for a digital turn in geography, and observe that recent developments in digital disruption are changing society, culture and spaces in sometimes surprising ways.

By way of context, DTJ works as an online social movement that has grown from a hashtag and diffuse conversation to become a targeted, curated space. This chapter will not explore the origins of DTJ in detail as this has occurred elsewhere (McLean & Maalsen, 2013), but a brief overview shall set the scene for how DTJ began and has continued. Initially, the DTJ hashtag was an online space, or meeting point, for people reflecting on the absurdity of claims that women in political life were destructive forces because of their gender, but grew to encompass critiques of gender inequality and lampooning sexist and misogynistic acts (Gleeson, 2016; McLean & Maalsen, 2013). The emergence of DTJ was made possible partly by the political climate in Australia at the time, and a current of wider discontent with gender inequality. Australia's first female Prime Minister, Julia Gillard, experienced frequent sexism while performing her work, including from the general public, political commentators and politicians alike (Sawer, 2013). McLean and Maalsen (2013) describe how DTJ began as a humorous hashtag, lampooning a sexist comment from Alan Jones, a conservative radio personality based in Sydney, who said that "Women are destroying the joint – Cynthia Nixon in Melbourne, Clover Moore here. Honestly" (Farr, 2012, no page numbers). People started to tweet the diverse ways in which women are apparently destroying the joint with the hashtags #jointdestroyer and #destroythejoint. Soon after, Jenna Price, a journalist and media academic, helped set up Destroy the Joint as a social media movement on Facebook and Twitter (McLean & Maalsen, 2013). As of 2018, it has over 91,000 Facebook followers and 22,000 Twitter followers. It is moderated by a team of people who are anonymous volunteers, and driven by their passions to do something about sexism and misogyny (Gleeson, 2016).

What Can the Digital Offer for Disrupting Sexism and Homophobia?

The disruptions that digital technologies are facilitating have been lauded by technology optimists, such as Schmidt and Cohen (2010), and discursively critiqued by those keen to point out its possibilities and limitations, such as Selwyn (2013). Disruption is defined by the Macquarie Dictionary (2017, online) in three ways: "as forcible separation or division into parts; a disrupted condition, or; in business, an upheaval in a market caused by a technological innovation which renders a product or technology outmoded." In the context of activism, the first and second definitions speak to the possibilities of changing societal or cultural norms. Feminist disruptions can forcibly separate or break down hegemonic structures that are oppressive and/or persistent, and the history of feminist action attests to this (Freedman, 2007).

Defining disruption as an upheaval in a market due to technological innovations rendering previous technologies redundant connects to the emerging disruption literature. For the purposes of this chapter, the usefulness of this definition stems from the connections between upheavals and technologies that underpin disruptions. We can read digital action as taking advantage of social media spaces as an example of disruption in "traditional" feminist or queer activism. Digital media have facilitated new ways of doing activism, within the context of feminisms, and some have argued that this is producing a Fourth Wave. However, we are less interested in categorising waves of feminist thought and practice and prefer to explore how the continuities and changes in feminisms are contained within, and are growing from, digital spaces.

Things are "disrupted" by the digital, which is frequently perceived as immaterial, making it an easy thing to variously celebrate or blame. On a broader scale, the immateriality of digital media is frequently described as a move from material objects to digital equivalents (Dourish, 2017, p. 2). Dourish eloquently notes that "technology pundits applaud this 'substitution of bits for atoms' associated with digital technologies and suggest that the 'future' will be fuelled by some vague and ideal sense of digitality" (2017, p. 3). Such applause is characteristic of "rupture-talk" (Dourish, 2017; Hecht, 2002), the notion that the emerging climate represents a radical break from the past—from atoms to bits (Dourish, 2017, p. 3). But the ruptures are never so clear and bits of the past permeate the ruptured present. Digital spaces are disrupted by the physical world—broken cables, failed servers and the limitations of existing skills, process and materials (Dourish, 2017, p. 3).

How then would this disruption—the digital disruption of the material and the mirroring disruption of the digital by material events—work in the context of gender, sexualities and sexism? Here we draw on the use of "play" and feminist game theory to ask if exploring the intersection between gender, sexualities and technology helps us understand how knowledge can be transformed in to action?

Disruptive Protest and Play in Digital Spaces

Play has the capacity to create alternative worlds. The potential of play lies in the ability to identify what is play and what is not, something that is socially conditioned, and therefore allows the exploration of possibilities not yet materialised in the present space. Johnson's (2017) work on Twitter parody as play illustrates how such an approach allows users to work within and around platforms. Drawing upon Bateson (1972), she describes play as paradoxical in that it is contextually dependent and real and not real: "Play thus allows us to move between different possible worlds and lives" (Bakhtin, 1968[1965]; Johnson, 2017, p. 26).

The heightened mobility that play offers, and its ability to move in and around structural limitations, offers much to digital activists. For instance, Bianca Batti, who hosts the excellent feminist gaming website "Not Your Mama's Gamer," writes that:

> Postmodern feminism, like play, works within the rules of the dominant ideology but also challenges and subverts these rules through critique, and this paradox is both playful and disruptive through the way it represents our social structures and constructions of self in more complex ways. Thus, the disruption enacted by postmodern feminism might be said to be playful because of the manner in which it situates itself in location to such rules and through the manner in which it does ultimately seek change—it seeks to disrupt these norms. (Batti, 2015, no page numbers)

So we could read digital disruptions that emerge from an activist frame as working within the rules of the dominant ideology—drawing on branding, networking and popularist tropes—but also playing with these, and disrupting them in the process.

Ultimately, disruption in this context can be read as building prefigurative politics that aim to challenge norms that marginalise difference. By prefigurative politics, we are referring to the way that social movements can contain, or produce, the change that they want to see in the world (van de Sande, 2013). The mirroring of means and ends is crucial here: "a political action, practice, movement, moment or development in which certain political ideals are experimentally actualised in the 'here and now', rather than hoped to be realised in a distant future" (van de Sande, 2013, p. 230). The process, then, is as important as the outcome achieved. Here, the performative elements of play within online activism come to light for the subversive aspects of disruptive play are simpatico with the goals of equality that underpin feminist and diversity activism.

Central to our analysis of disruptive play in digital activism is Butler's (1999) conceptualisation of performativity: "Whether gender or sex is fixed or free is a function of a discourse which … seeks to set certain limits to analysis or safeguard certain tenets of humanism as presuppositional to any analysis of gender" (Butler, 1999, p. 13). We can see that troubling the boundaries of identity, as digital activism is wont to do, confronts such discourses and renders particular demarcations of valid ways of being as limited. Jenson and de Castell (2008, p. 24) note how gender, and we could expand their argument to sexualities, "is and has been for some time a contested site: it is 'at play' and 'in play' in radically different ways, given different contexts, actors and tools/technologies." Again, we can see productive ground for discussing disruptive play with respect to activism that is reshaping opportunities for gender and sexualities, where prefigurative politics are produced from what is *at* play and *in* play. Overall, then, there are at least two types of disruption at work in this case: disruption of ways that activists communicate with the increase in social media usage, and the critique of activism tropes because of this.

Online Feminist Play and Disrupting Heteronormativity

Online feminism has multiple foci, and different agendas compete for attention at particular times. Here, we discuss how the AMLPS in 2017 was addressed in DTJ spaces to interrogate the affordances and barriers that such a digital space offers for effective digital action. Social media allow for "issue publics"—publics situated as emergent socio-political assemblages that coalesce around an issue of shared concern and which can be multisided (Burgess & Matamoros-Fernández, 2016, p. 80)—to emerge that can facilitate debates between numerous people who may not otherwise have the opportunity to engage with such issues (Segerberg & Bennett, 2011). Similar to what Browne, Nash, and Gorman-Murray (2018) found in their study of the Irish same-sex marriage campaign, the AMLPS reveals important aspects of the sexuality–gender–nation–state nexus. Both processes in Ireland and Australia capture often hidden values of sexuality-and-gender-related norms as governance regimes are challenged or upheld through public discourse. During the AMLPS, people who identified as gay and lesbian were concerned about how the campaigning during the survey period would affect them. For example,

Mazel (2018, p. 7) wrote about how she felt during the survey period: "For me personally, the process of the postal survey feels invasive and a little dangerous. I am concerned about the impact the debate will have on my family and the queer community, and the risk that is being taken for the sake of marriage."

The Australian government asked the Australian Bureau of Statistics (ABS) to run the AMLPS, which invited Australians over the age of 18 to respond to the question: "Should the law be changed to allow same-sex couples to marry?" (ABS, 2017). Following a protracted survey period from 12 September to 7 November 2017, which returned a majority yes response (61.6%), the Australian government passed laws that legalised same-sex marriage. Generally heralded as a mark of Australia's progressive politics, it has also received critique as normalising heterosexual institutions that have traditionally maintained women's subservience to men. Feminists and queer activists have a complex relationship with marriage. For feminists, marriage has long been an institution of critique with claims that it is both sexist *and* privileges heteronormativity; as Chambers (2017) notes, marriage is a practical and symbolic undermining of women's equality. Marriage has variously been critiqued as a site of oppression, guaranteeing few independent rights for women and equating them with property, as well as a site of unequal division of domestic and unpaid labour (Chambers, 2017). For some queer activists, same-sex marriage is problematic in its requirement for cultural assimilation. Inclusion within the institution of marriage de-essentialises lesbian and gay identities and relationships—they become normalised—and such normalisation can limit the effectiveness of activism post-marriage equality (Bernstein & Taylor, 2013). Further, same-sex marriage is limiting in other ways: by sanctioning marriage, it delegitimises other forms of relationships and critiques (Dreher, 2017).

Normalising same-sex marriage—an institution that is characteristic of and reproduces heteronormativity—lessens the critique of the nuclear family and its associated gender norms (Dreher, 2017; Duggan, 2002; Walters, 2012). Duggan (2002, p. 179) refers to this as "homonormativity," which depoliticises gay culture and upholds the dominant heteronormative institutions and assumptions and therefore does nothing to destabilise these. Thus, same-sex marriage can be seen as homonormative and complicit in the reflection and reproduction of hierarchies of privilege

(Dreher, 2017, p. 185; Seuffert, 2009, p. 139 quoted in Dreher, p. 185). As Walters (2012) observes with respect to gay representations in popular media, the acceptance of same-sex marriage is based on its reproduction of heteronormative values and is preferable to feminist critiques of marriage and family: "The mainstream visibility of the unthinkable possibility (gay marriage) hinges on mainstream invisibility of a more unthinkable possibility (feminist, queer families), and helps to bolster the liberal, assimilationist models of 'acceptance' and tolerance of queers" (Walters, 2012, p. 191).

Yet within human geography, the way homonormativity has been uncritically engaged with—as closely associated with neoliberal agendas—has been critiqued. For instance, Brown (2009) stated that there is a certain violence enacted by queer scholars who collapse all gay life as homonormative and driven by neoliberal ideals. To essentialise gay life as only one mode of being reduces inherent diversities within this broad category. As Gorman-Murray (2017, p. 149) puts forward in "Que(e)rying homonormativity," we seek a "less monolithic application of homonormativity."

Differences exist between gay rights activists, feminists and trans activists (Josephson, Einarsdóttir, & Sigurðardóttir, 2017), and there is no guarantee of support from gay rights activists for feminist causes, and vice versa. Further, gay and lesbian activism does not necessarily aspire to the same goals, as Auchmuty, Jeffreys, and Miller (1992) note, the gay male writing of history does not always challenge the patriarchy. "The challenge," as Dreher (2017) notes, is "to allow competing and contested meanings around marriage, mindful that the success of same-sex marriage claims might threaten both the availability to critique marriage and to explore options beyond" (2017, p. 183).

These tensions are played out in the DTJ commentary on the AMLPS. Members variously mention their support for same-sex marriage as part of being a feminist, while others claim it is not a feminist issue but that they support it from a humanist viewpoint. Some comment how intersectional factors influence their decision and experience of marriage equality, while others warn that support does not guarantee support of gay communities in return. Below, we draw upon discussions around DTJ postings on the AMLPS, and in these discussions, we see evidence of "the messiness of the digital mediation of everyday lives"

(Elwood & Leszczynski, 2018, p. 631). We use text boxes to capture sustained dialogue from DTJ pages.

So did DTJ members think that the Survey was a feminist issue? One respondent contests the claim that marriage equality is a feminist issue because of intersectionality, and instead comments that it is a feminist issue because it is an issue of gender equality:

> Reply conversation 4: *It's not just a feminist issue because of intersectionality in general, but because it's an issue of gender equality. Heteronormativity and homophobia are closely linked to the enforcing of strict gender roles, and feminism and struggles for LGBTI rights are closely linked because they both challenge that. (19 likes) 6 replies*

For this feminist, feminism and LGBTI rights are seen as linked because they challenge gender norms and it is this challenge to heteronormativity, rather than intersectional feminism per se, that positions marriage equality as a feminist issue. Postings from other members illustrate the complexity of feminists' relationship with marriage. The discussion below (Fig. 10.1) highlights the tension between wanting equal rights for the LGBTI community and perceptions of women's oppression in marriage.

But how can I as a feminist argue for equal access to a social mechanism 'marriage ' that oppressed women and would oppress others who want to access it? (4 replies)

> Reply 1: Marriage as a religious construct is separate from marriage as a civil contract, which has existed for much longer (3 likes)
>
> Reply 2: In the sense that gay women have the right to have the same societal rights as hetero women there is some leeway for intersectional feminism. If they're daft enough to want to get married it's not my place to deny them that right. But you cannot argue as a feminist that marriage is a positive thing for women, that's for sure. I voted Yes because I am a decent human being who believes in human rights, not because I am a feminist.(4 likes)
>
> R3: Making it less gendered is a good step whether you think it should ultimately exist or not.(3 likes)
>
> R4: The status quo is worse. More sexist, more oppressive..(1 like)

Fig. 10.1 Discussion from DTJ on access to marriage

Here, marriage equality is again positioned as not an inherently feminist issue but one that is a human rights issue. This is also iterated by another member replying to DTJ's post: *Marriage hasn't been that good for Women. The institution of marriage has been very sexist in its origins. In saying that, I am a Feminist, and while I don't personally like marriage, or agree with it in its current form, I DO agree in equal rights, and so I fully support Marriage Equality 100%. (9 likes, 3 replies).*

Later in the conversation, a DTJ participant used humour to express their personal stance against marriage and to stress this does not stop them from supporting others who want the choice: *I agree with any kind of marriage that doesn't involve ME. (8 likes) 1 reply*. Invoking humour, this is a playful critique of marriage, playing with the possibility that marriage can be for anyone regardless of sexuality, while maintaining that marriage is not for everyone. And yet another conversation debates marriage and equal access to it. Again, marriage is positioned predominantly as an oppressive institution, but feminists feel they cannot prevent another marginalised group's fight for equality: Respondent 9 in the replies generated by Reply Conversation 13 (see Fig. 10.2) makes several points that reflect this. The second point in particular encapsulates the prevailing sentiment that arises from feminist perspectives on the debate: that even though, for feminists, marriage can be oppressive, feminists do not have the right to deny that choice to the LGBTI community, even if they are "as radical, OR LESS RADICAL" than feminists think they are. The statement from this participant includes deliberate use of all caps, conveying a wry tone with this exaggerated mode of communication.

Humour and play circulate through this contentious online discussion on DTJ—the dark side of oppression that marriage can invoke is brought up against support for others to pursue different sorts of marriage. Thus, humour is enacted to mediate the seriousness of the debates. This debate over marriage equality as a feminist or humanist issue is perhaps more broadly reflective of the tensions inherent in the popularisation of feminism. Dreher (2017) refers to Fraser's "uncanny double" (2009), which describes the shadowy version of feminism (its uncanny double) and its increasing ambiguity as it becomes co-opted by neoliberalism. For Fraser, feminisms' dance from state-organised capitalism to neoliberalism means that we need to become more "historically self-aware as we operate on a terrain that is also populated by our

Reply Conversation 13.

I'm still confused. I remember feminist marches in the 70's decrying marriage, when ma rriage itself was seen as compromising women's rights (10 replies)

R1: And why did they want it abolished? And does removing the gender requirement in it make it more or less sexist and patriarchal? And regardless of that is it fair to exclude people from it whether you like it or not? (2 likes)

R2 Well no one is asking these questions and no one seems to be answering them. Should I advocate for same-sex relationships to access a status I might find inherently oppressive for the sake of equal access? Because I acknowledge the group wanting it is marginalised like women are and just because of that???? That to me is absurd

R9: GBLTI people deserve our solidarity. At this juncture, supporting them transcends in importance the issue of whether marriage is a socially conservative institution or not, because:

1. Marriage will still be there regardless. A no vote in the postal survey and in parliament will not weaken marriage one iota. And a yes vote will leave marriage much the same. It will become broader, not more entrenched. It's already very entrenched.

2. Even if we agree that marriage is a socially conservative institution, LGBTI people deserve the civil right to make their own choices in life equal with everyone else. Or put another way, they deserve the right to be as radical, OR LESS RADICAL than we think we are. Anything else is paternalism.

3. Every loss for the homophobic, patriarchal shitheads like Tony Abbott, Cory Bernadi, Lyle Shelton, John Howard, Cardinal George Pell, George Christensen and Concetta Fierravanti-Wells is a victory for us and for progressive politics. (2 likes)

Fig. 10.2 DTJ participants discussing solidarity between feminists and LGBTI activists seeking access to marriage

uncanny double" (2009, p. 114). Post-neoliberal feminism is positioned as an opportunity for feminists, who have observed and critiqued neoliberal instrumentalisation of feminist ideas and goals and can now possibly reclaim those (Fraser, 2009). The DTJ discussions are potentially reflecting this reclaiming of feminism—and disrupting gender relations in the process.

To return to the challenge identified by Dreher (2017, p. 183) earlier, that is to ensure that marriage can still be critiqued and contested in the wake of same-sex marriage success, the DTJ discussion offers a place to enact just that. Through exchanges that are sometimes playful and humorous, while at other times combative or considered, the DTJ pages offer space for members to assert feminism and its critique of marriage while understanding that, through their own marginality, they cannot deny others the choice. In this way, the group disrupts gender, and boundaries for expressing sexualities, via online spaces.

Disrupting Normative Sexualities and Gendered Norms Online

Tensions between different forms of activism are nothing new, and neither are tensions within activist groups. Multiple viewpoints and positionings co-exist to produce a lively conversation that contributes to disruption of social and legal norms, as this sampling of debate, dialogue, humour and reflection surrounding the AMLPS within a feminist space illustrates. At the same time, dissent and resistance to (re)producing oppressive structures flows through the discussion—homonormativity is repudiated in this intersectional space—and playful engagements with politics are glimpsed.

There is no singular narrative of how AMLPS was positioned within DTJ—having over 90,000 participants engage with this feminist space accounts for some of this multiplicity. Common to feminist activism more broadly, the situation surrounding feminist efforts in DTJ is too complicated for narrow explanations. As Gill (2016, p. 613) writes "for every uplifting account of feminist activism, there is another of misogyny; for every feminist 'win', an outpouring of hate, ranging from sexual harassment to death threats against those involved; for every instance of feminist solidarity, another of vicious trolling." Gay rights activism shares similar dilemmas of progressive and regressive steps in everyday efforts to strip back homophobic policies and practices.

Underpinning this activism is the need for digital labour that is unpaid and fraught. DTJ is a moderated space, which volunteers manage, and the intimacies that it demands, akin to other digital workspaces (Richardson, 2016), are emotionally draining and relentless (Gleeson, 2016; Turley & Fisher, 2018, p. 129). For Schuster (2013), social media can connect people beyond their locality, and involve those who may not be able to connect face to face, and this is certainly a strength of digital spaces. Academic literature is increasingly focused on the national, transnational and global connections between feminism and social media, and much of the literature is transdisciplinary (see, e.g., Baer, 2016; Gill, 2016; Hutton, Griffin, Lyons, Niland, & McCreanor, 2016). This literature does not shy away from the fact that digital feminisms work within corporate institutions that are limited and problematic.

A growing number of academics and activists see the digital as a space of potential for generative change, while others see it as recreating oppressive spaces. Of the former, Jons (2013, online) declares that "Feminism has left the Academy and spilled into the world wide web" in an article for *Blue Stocking*, an online feminist publication. The enthusiasm in her claim is clear, but it tends to render shifts in feminist practice as disconnected to those that have come before. An ahistorical perspective does not help situate current movements in relation to those that have come before. Clark (2015) analyses the strengths and weaknesses of a range of digital movements to ascertain strategic opportunities for future feminist digital movements. She argues that:

> Digital feminist activism is a new iteration of feminist activism, offering new tools and tactics for feminists to utilize to spread awareness, disseminate information, and mobilize constituents. (Clark, 2015, iv)

The tools and tactics afforded by digital feminist activism are largely facilitated by corporate entities, that are generally unregulated, and this unfettered capitalist context may affect the capacities of those seeking transformative change. Further, the "play" that underpins engagement with some digital spaces, such as social media, is co-opted by capitalist hegemonies. There are conflicting and contradictory forces at play in digital spaces. For example, Sicart (2017) observes that games like Pokémon GO augment public space as a commercial entity, but such tools can also be used to occupy spaces, and perhaps even reclaim them, as augmentation of reality is far from a new process.

There are glimpses of productive possibilities, where digital disruptions are emerging from a range of activist spaces. Digital feminist activism frequently emerges from reporting of personal narratives that capture experiences of feminism and sexism. Hashtags are begun on Twitter and Facebook, and people share stories of similar experiences to amass a moment of anger, outrage, playfulness and sadness. The contradictory possibilities of the "more-than-real" (McLean, Maalsen, & Grech, 2016) are present at a global scale with the expansion of access to these spaces, and the deepening reach of the digital in everyday life. Drawing on more-than-human thinking, the "more-than-real" is an idea that explains the paradoxical ways that digital spaces amplify and collapse geographies, reworking spatial connections and disconnections. Feminist digital spaces have arisen as countervailing forces to entrenched sexism and misogyny, in the digital and elsewhere, and some are calling this growth the Fourth Wave of feminism (Munro, 2013). Diversity is at the core of feminisms today, but a common underlying feature is frequent use of, and sometimes reliance on, digital technologies (Munro, 2013). The "call out" culture (Munro, 2013) that is facilitated by digital spaces—and specifically social media where users have some control over their profiles and can curate their feeds—is a key component of this global Fourth Wave. Continuing the micropolitics focus of the Third Wave, this form of feminist action enables individuals to post experiences of sexism and misogyny online and to give voice to their grievances. Sometimes, as in the case of the #MeToo moment that has become a movement (Rodino-Colocino, 2018), the coalescing of multiple individual stories can drive efforts that affect social and cultural change.

Politics, Play and Intersectional Approaches

To conclude this chapter, we ask what possibilities do debate, multiplicity and play offer as resistance techniques, and perhaps also as prefigurative political strategies, as explored in DTJ and digital spaces for disrupting the politics and practices relating to sexism, gender and sexualities; and more broadly what does this mean for geography? In this chapter, we have explored a case study of how multiple discourses pertaining to sexism and same-sex marriage intersect, collide and are challenged within an online digital feminist space. It is apt to return to Dreher's (2017, p. 183) observation about the importance of not letting the success of same-sex marriage constrain the critique of marriage and the imagining of other possibilities. While there is much to be celebrated in achieving marriage equality, the DTJ discussions around the AMLPS show that this is experienced contextually and that the work of equality is not done. Engaging in sometimes playful and humorous exchanges, participants are acknowledging competing experience of, and claims to, marriage, in ways that accommodate multiple viewpoints. This offers a space to variously support and contest same-sex marriage through feminist and humanist lens. Thus while predominantly supporting same-sex marriage as a human right, the digital allowed members to also express their concern around marriage as an oppressive system. In doing so, they establish the importance of possibilities beyond marriage. The online becomes a place to curate critiques and imagine alternatives.

Second, what does this mean for the digital turn in geography? To date, digital geographies have focused on the geographies by, of and through digital media (Ash et al., 2018). There is room however to further investigate the affective responses and political economies generated by digital media (Ash et al., 2018; Schwanen, 2015). Here we add another way in which to start thinking about how geography may engage with digital spaces: conceptualising ways to imagine and occupy future alternatives where heteronormativity and homonormativity are not necessarily dominant. While much has been made of the #MeToo movement across media and academia, little has looked at the future making and reconfiguration of space that this affective labour engenders. The discussions that play out, and are at play, on the DTJ page similarly enable members to occupy space in diverse ways. It is in these dramas of critique and imaginaries that alternative future possibilities are preliminarily mapped out and their disruptive potential established. It is here that we urge geographers look to understand not only what the digital is both maintaining and disrupting, but at the future imaginaries and alternative possibilities being envisioned.

References

Ash, J., Kitchin, R., & Leszczynski, A. (2018). Digital turn, digital geographies. *Progress in Human Geography, 42*(1), 25–43.

Auchmuty, R., Jeffreys, S., & Miller, E. (1992). Lesbian history and gay studies: Keeping a feminist perspective. *Women's History Review, 1*(1), 89–108.

Australian Bureau of Statistics. (2017). *Australian Marriage Law Postal Survey, 2017*, Thursday, 5 July. Retrieved from http://www.abs.gov.au/ausstats/abs@.nsf/mf/1800.0

Baer, H. (2016). Redoing feminism: Digital activism, body politics, and neoliberalism. *Feminist Media Studies, 16*(1), 17–34. https://doi.org/10.1080/14680777.2015.1093070

Bakhtin, M. (1968 [1965]). *Rabelais and his world.* Translated by Helene Iswolsky. Cambridge, MA: MIT Press.

Bateson, G. (1972). *Steps to an ecology of mind.* New York: Ballantine Books.

Batti, B. (2015). Feminism and play: Toward a methodology of disruption. *Not your mama's gamer.* 30 December 2015. Retrieved from http://www.nymgamer.com/?p=12504

Bernstein, M., & Taylor, V. (2013). *The marrying kind: Debating same-sex marriage within the lesbian and gay movement.* University of Minnesota Press. Retrieved November 4, 2018, from https://www.jstor.org/stable/10.5749/j.ctt32bcxt

Brown, G. (2009). Thinking beyond homonormativity: Performative explorations of diverse gay economies. *Environment and Planning A, 41*(6), 1496–1510.

Browne, K., Nash, C. J., & Gorman-Murray, A. (2018). Geographies of heteroactivism: Resisting sexual rights in the reconstitution of Irish nationhood. *Transactions of the Institute of British Geographers.* https://doi.org/10.1111/tran.12255

Burgess, J., & Matamoros-Fernández, A. (2016). Mapping sociocultural controversies across digital media platforms: One week of #gamergate on Twitter, YouTube and Tumblr. *Communication Research and Practice, 2*(1), 79–96.

Butler, J. (1999). *Gender trouble: Feminism and the subversion of identity.* New York: Routledge.

Chambers, C. (2017). *Against marriage: An egalitarian defense of the marriage-free state.* Oxford Scholarship Online. Retrieved from https://doi.org/10.1093/oso/9780198744009.001.0001

Clark, C. (2015). *#TrendingFeminism: The impact of digital feminist activism.* Masters Research Thesis, The Faculty of The Columbian College of Arts and

Sciences of The George Washington University. Retrieved from https://pqdtopen.proquest.com/doc/1691802140.html?FMT=ABS
Dourish, P. (2017). *The stuff of bits*. Cambridge, MA: MIT Press.
Dreher, T. (2017). The 'uncanny doubles' of queer politics: Sexual citizenship in the era of same-sex marriage victories. *Sexualities, 20*(1–2), 176–195.
Duggan, L. (2002). The new homonormativity: The sexual politics of neoliberalism. In R. Castronovo & D. D. Nelson (Eds.), *Materialising democracy: Toward a revitalised cultural politics* (pp. 175–194). Durham, NC: Duke University Press.
Elwood, S., & Leszczynski, A. (2018). Feminist digital geographies. *Gender, Place & Culture, 25*(5), 629–644. https://doi.org/10.1080/0966369X.2018.1465396
Farr, M. (2012). Alan Jones: Women are destroying the joint. *The Herald Sun*. Retrieved from https://www.heraldsun.com.au/news/alan-jones-women-are-destroying-the-joint/news-story/402a32a90a61275ac789a6cbfb45c31d
Fraser, N. (2009). Feminism, capitalism and the cunning of history. *New Left Review, 56*(March–April), 97–117.
Freedman, E. (2007). *No turning back: The history of feminism and the future of women*. New York: Ballantine Books.
Gill, R. (2016). Post-postfeminism?: New feminist visibilities in postfeminist times. *Feminist Media Studies, 16*(4), 610–630.
Gleeson, J. (2016). (Not) working 9–5: The consequences of contemporary Australian-based online feminist campaigns as digital labour. *Media International Australia, 161*(1), 77–85.
Gorman-Murray, A. (2017). Que(e)rying homonormativity: The everyday politics of lesbian and gay homemaking. In *Sexuality and gender at home: Experience, politics, transgression* (pp. 149–162). London: Bloomsbury.
Haraway, D. (1991). *Simians, cyborgs and women: The reinvention of women*. New York: Routledge.
Hecht, G. (2002). Rupture-talk in the nuclear age: Conjugating colonial power in Africa. *Social Studies of Science, 32*(5–6), 691–727.
Hutton, F., Griffin, C., Lyons, A., Niland, P., & McCreanor, T. (2016). "Tragic girls" and "crack whores": Alcohol, femininity and Facebook. *Feminism & Psychology, 26*(1), 73–93.
Jenson, J., & de Castell, S. (2008). Theorizing gender and digital gameplay: Oversights, accidents and surprises. *Eludamos: Journal for Computer Game Culture, 2*(1), 15–25.
Johnson, A. (2017). *Twitter and the body parodic: Global acts of re-creation and recreation*. PhD Thesis, MIT.

Johnston, L. (2017). Gender and sexuality II: Activism. *Progress in Human Geography, 41*(5), 648–656.
Jons, R. R. (2013). Is the "4th Wave" digital? *Bluestockings Magazine.* 5 December 2019. Retrieved from http://bluestockingsmag.com/2013/08/19/is-the-4th-wave-of-feminism-digital/
Josephson, J., Einarsdóttir, Þ., & Sigurðardóttir, S. A. (2017). Queering the trans: Gender and sexuality binaries in Icelandic trans, queer, and feminist communities. *European Journal of Women's Studies, 24*(1), 70–84. https://doi.org/10.1177/1350506815625694
Kinsley, S. (2013). The matter of 'virtual' geographies. *Progress in Human Geography, 38*(3), 364–384. https://doi.org/10.1177/0309132513506270
Macquarie Dictionary. (2017). *Disruption.* Retrieved from https://www-macquariedictionary-com-au.simsrad.net.ocs.mq.edu.au/features/word/search/?word=disruption&search_word_type=Dictionary
Mazel, O. (2018). The politics of difference: Posting my 'vote' on marriage equality. *Alternative Law Journal, 43*(1), 4–9. https://doi.org/10.1177/1037969x17753164
McLean, J., & Maalsen, S. (2013). Destroying the joint and dying of shame? A Geography of revitalised feminism in social media and beyond. *Geographical Research, 51*(3), 243–256.
McLean, J., Maalsen, S., & Grech, A. (2016). Learning about feminism in digital spaces: Online methodologies and participatory mapping. *Australian Geographer, 47*(2), 157–177.
Munro, E. (2013). Feminism: A fourth wave? *Political Insight.* https://doi.org/10.1111/2041-9066.12021
Richardson, L. (2016). Feminist geographies of digital work. *Progress in Human Geography, 42*(2), 244–263. https://doi.org/10.1177/0309132516677177.
Rodino-Colocino, M. (2018). Me too, #MeToo: Countering cruelty with empathy. *Communication and Critical/Cultural Studies, 15*(1), 96–100.
Sawer, M. (2013). Misogyny and misrepresentation: Women in Australian parliaments. *Political Science, 65*(1), 105–117. https://doi.org/10.1177/0032318713488316
Schmidt, E., & Cohen, J. (2010). The digital disruption-connectivity and the diffusion of power. *Foreign Affairs, 89*(6), 75–85.
Schuster, J. (2013). Invisible feminists? Social media and young women's political participation. *Political Science, 65*(1), 8–24.
Schwanen, T. (2015). Beyond the instrument: Smartphone app and sustainable mobility. *European Journal of Transport & Infrastructure Research, 15*(4), 675–690.

Segerberg, A., & Bennett, W. L. (2011). Social media and the organization of collective action: Using Twitter to explore the ecologies of two climate change protests. *The Communication Review, 14*(3), 197–215.

Selwyn, N. (2013). *Discourses of digital 'disruption' in education: A critical analysis.* Fifth International Roundtable on Discourse Analysis, City University, Hong Kong, pp. 23–25.

Seuffert, N. (2009). Same-sex immigration: Domestication and homonormativity. In A. Bottomley & S. Wong (Eds.), *Changing contours of domestic life, family and law: Caring and sharing* (pp. 131–149). Oxford: Hart Publishing.

Sicart, M. (2017). Reality has always been augmented: Play and the promises of Pokémon GO. *Mobile Media & Communication, 5*(1), 30–33.

Turley, E., & Fisher, J. (2018). Tweeting back while shouting back: Social media and feminist activism. *Feminism and Psychology, 28*(1), 128–132.

van de Sande, M. (2013). The prefigurative politics of Tahrir Square—An alternative perspective on the 2011 revolutions. *Res Publica, 19*(3), 223–239.

Wajcman, J. (2007). From women and technology to gendered technoscience. *Information, Communication and Society, 10*(2), 87–298.

Walters, S. (2012). The kids are all right but the lesbians aren't: Queer kinship in US culture. *Sexualities, 15*(8), 917–933.

Wollstonecraft, M. (1978 [1792]). *Vindication of the rights of woman* (Vol. 29). London: Broadview Press.

11

"I want my story to be heard…": Examining the Production of Digital Stories by Queer Youth in East and South-East Asia

Benjamin Hanckel

Introduction

In August 2013 a call to action[1] was broadcast online calling on "Independent Filmmakers" across East and South-East Asia[2] to share the stories of "young people who are comfortable and happy with who they are regardless of their sexual orientation or gender identity". Organised and funded by a regional-based community development organisation, the call-to-action sought to fund "stories told by the [young] people themselves" about diverse sexuality and gender identity, which could be shared across video-sharing platforms, such as YouTube. By November

[1] This included a video (1:05 minutes long and included both a male and a female voiceover that read different coloured English text on the video), and an accompanying website in English.

[2] This sought stories from Bangkok, Beijing, Hanoi, Jakarta, Kuala Lumpur, Manila, Phnom Penh and Singapore.

B. Hanckel (✉)
King's College London, London, UK

University of Tasmania, Hobart, TAS, Australia
e-mail: benjamin.hanckel@kcl.ac.uk

C. Nash, A. Gorman-Murray (eds.), *The Geographies of Digital Sexuality*,
https://doi.org/10.1007/978-981-13-6876-9_11

2013, seven filmmakers were successful and were awarded US$2000 to produce their films. This chapter examines how the filmmakers and storytellers told and constructed these stories.

Regionally across Asia, queer/LGBTIQ+[3] young people continue to face ongoing experiences of stigma and marginalisation. Discrimination remains embedded in legislation (Carroll & Mendos, 2017), evident, for instance, in Singapore, Bhutan, Brunei, Malaysia, India and Aceh in Indonesia. In addition, in some countries, such as Indonesia (see Ridwan & Wu, 2018, for more), there is also evidence of increasing intolerance towards LGBT people. Such forms of exclusion can work to prevent access to local supportive resources, decrease the health and well-being of those who experience this marginality, as well as contribute to forms of economic exclusion (see, e.g., Badgett, Park, & Flores, 2018; Dyson et al., 2003; Manalastas, 2013; Manalastas et al., 2017; Thoreson, 2011).

In such contexts, digital technologies have been shown to be important for LGBTIQ+ people, and particularly young people, who are exploring and coming to terms with diverse genders and sexualities. As recent work has shown, online spaces afford LGBTIQ+ people with social connection to similar others, as well as access to important (sub)cultural knowledge and information, which is often not available in the everyday spaces they live within (see, e.g., Austria Jr, 2004; Castañeda, 2015; Fox & Ralston, 2016; Gray, 2009; Hanckel & Morris, 2014; Hillier & Harrison, 2007; Paradis, 2016). Research has also shown how young people utilise existing technologies and platforms to document and present their experiences of living with diverse genders and sexualities (Alexander & Losh, 2010; Horak, 2014; O'Neill, 2014; Pullen, 2014; Vivienne, 2016; Wuest, 2014), where often such representations are absent. Utilising new technologies, such as YouTube, young people have (at least the potential) to create diverse representations of LGBT/queer lives, and in so doing, contribute to "offer[ing] alternative ways of understanding sex, sexuality and gender" (Alexander & Losh, 2010, p. 24).

[3] The terms queer, LGBT and LGBTIQ+ are used interchangeably in this chapter. They are used as inclusive terms for individuals who identify with a same-sex identity and/or desire and also include those who identify with or may be questioning a gender identity other than their assigned sex and/or assigned gender. These terms also include those who may have same-sex attractions and/or are gender-questioning but do not identify with a specific same-sex identity and/or gender identity.

In this chapter, I am interested in the use of networked platforms by LGBT youth to circulate content, and how these platforms structure the content that is produced. In particular, the videos discussed in this chapter are made for the video-sharing networked platform YouTube. Social media sites, like YouTube, boyd (2011) argues, are a genre of "networked publics". They restructure publics, and as such "are simultaneously (1) the space constructed through networked technologies and (2) the imagined collective that emerges as a result of the intersection of people, technology, and practice" (boyd, 2011, p. 39). I am interested in how these networked publics are used to present LGBT identity, and in particular how LGBT filmmakers and storytellers use them to present representations of LGBT life.

In total, of the ten filmmakers and storytellers, nine participated in in-depth interviews. Of the seven films, four films discussed the filmmakers' own stories, and three films told the stories of others, the "storytellers" (see Table 11.1 for an overview of these films). I conducted eight interviews with the filmmakers/storytellers via Skype, and one was conducted as an email interview. Two interviews included translation during the interview. The interviewees all held "activist" identities prior to participating in the production of their films. These identities, and their personal political projects, were, as I discuss below, extended through participation in this film project. Eight interviewees identified with diverse genders and sexualities, and one person identified as heterosexual. Interviews were conducted following the development of the films and prior to their release, in early 2014. The filmmakers and storytellers came from Indonesia, Singapore, Thailand, Cambodia, the Philippines, China and Nepal. Six of the seven[4] filmmakers had formal education in film/communication studies and two of the filmmakers had setup their own film production company, allowing them to produce the films with their existing cultural capital and knowledge of filmmaking.

The videos that are "in-production" in this chapter can be conceptualised as "digital stories", which

[4] The one other individual had experience working on films for an NGO and prior experience creating and uploading videos to YouTube.

Table 11.1 Filmmakers and synopsis of films

Name	Country of residence	Age	Story	Film URL
Imam Wahyudi	Indonesia	30	This story documents Imam's life as both a Muslim and a gay identifying man	https://www.youtube.com/watch?v=_TvfAUp6r2E
Darius Zee	Singapore	26	Tells the story of Darius, a gay Singaporean who lives at home with his family who do not know about his sexuality	https://www.youtube.com/watch?v=xn6rLGSHCI4
Isari Lawang	Thailand	19	Tells the story of Sophon, a gay identifying man with a dis/ability in Thailand	https://www.youtube.com/watch?v=PNriNRIloQc
Pivoine Beang	Cambodia	33	This film tells the story of Menghourng's (age 28) experiences living as a gender diverse person in Cambodia	https://www.youtube.com/watch?v=xn6Wlc3cOw4
Cha Roque	Philippines	28	This film tells the story of Cha, a lesbian with a female partner and a child	https://www.youtube.com/watch?v=ltWLJiq2g8c
Fan Popo	China	28	This film tells the story of Iron (age 29), an activist who identifies as bisexual from Beijing	https://www.youtube.com/watch?v=UhhjHS79VOM
Nilu Doma Sherpa	Nepal	31	This film tells the story of Nilu, a lesbian who asks what love means to people in Nepal	https://www.youtube.com/watch?v=ncdCYL2jO14

> are short (3–5 min) rich media autobiographical videos, combining personal photographs and/or artworks, narration and music ... 'Digital' refers to the digital tools used by storytellers' for production (computers, digital cameras, editing software, etc.) and in some cases the digital distribution mediums. (Vivienne, 2016, p. 3)

We might think about digital stories as a form of contemporary documentary filmmaking. The digital story draws on the narrative traditions and storytelling conventions that have come to define documentary filmmaking to present "portraits of real life" (Aufderheide, 2007, p. 3). As is evident throughout this chapter, these stories serve a similar function to the documentary, to display an argument and/or raise awareness about an issue from a particular perspective (Grierson, 1932; Zoellner, 2009). I examine the construction of these seven digital stories, the "digital tools" the filmmakers have access to, *as well as* their "digital distribution" and how the internet functions as a structuring "distribution medium" for the creation of these digital stories. My focus is on the development of films for YouTube, a networked public and the "imagined collective" whom the filmmakers/storytellers seek to engage as part of a broader project of "queer world-making" or what Yue (2016) terms queer "life-making". As I show throughout this chapter, this work aims to present alternative versions of reality across local, national and transnational space/s, where YouTube becomes a "valuable performative and discursive space" (O'Neill, 2014, p. 36) for this work.

To explore these concerns, I draw on Bourdieu's (1977, 1986, 1989, 1991) concepts of habitus, field and symbolic power. My work here considers how the habitus, the acquired "systems of durable, transposable dispositions" (Bourdieu, 1977, p. 72), which give an individual a point of view, or position, in the world, is both a structuring mechanism for the production of the videos and also something that is sought to be disrupted within the sexual field that privileges heteronormativity. I argue that the production of the filmmakers' and storytellers' digital stories is an investment in shifting the habitus of others, and it also works to extend their own political projects.

Networked Publics and the Habitus: A Conceptual Framework

Networked Publics: Online Video-Sharing in the Contemporary World

New information and communication technologies (ICTs) were understood as "a critical component" in the development plans of nations across East and South-East Asia in the 1990s, forming diverse investment in "the informationalisation of their societies" (Ho, Kluver, & Yang, 2003, p. 2). The internet became an important feature of this development. It required limited resources to put in place and offered the potential to enhance economic outcomes. Whilst not uniformly distributed throughout each country in Asia (Baskaran & Muchie, 2006; Kluver & Banerjee, 2005), the internet is now increasingly accessible due, in part, to the decreasing costs of internet plans, and that it can now be accessed through smartphone technology (Doshi & Narwold, 2014).

An increasing trend evident across this region, and globally, has been engagement with online video, and online video-sharing platforms, and in particular YouTube[5] (We Are Social and HootSuite, 2018a, 2018b). YouTube, similar to other video-sharing platforms, is branded as "a convenient and useable platform for online video sharing" (Burgess & Green, 2009, p. 4). Similar to other platforms YouTube positions itself as a crucial distribution channel for video (Lange, 2007). In doing so these platforms afford the sharing of content amongst "networked individuals" (Rainie & Wellman, 2012) across "networked publics" (boyd, 2008, 2011). The ways these new platforms are structured "introduces distinct affordances that shape how people engage with these environments. The properties of bits—as distinct from atoms—introduce new possibilities for interaction" (boyd, 2011, p. 39). These distribution technologies reshape who might come into contact with a digital story (expanding a potential audience), and in so doing, have the potential to (re)shape the practices of those who produce content.

[5] Whilst YouTube remains banned in China, a similar trend towards video-sharing platforms in China (e.g. Youku) is also evident.

Heteronormativity and the Habitus

Pierre Bourdieu, interested in practices, argued that individuals make sense of their place in the world through their *habitus* (Bourdieu, 1977). The habitus, Bourdieu (1977, p. 72) argues, is the acquired "systems of durable, transposable dispositions", which give an individual a point of view, or position, in the world. They are more than just attitudes *but* also include "a spectrum of cognitive and affective factors: thinking *and* feeling" (Jenkins, 2002, p. 76) which "naturally generate practices adjusted to the situation" (Bourdieu, 1990, p. 108). These "durable and transposable systems of schemata of perception, appreciation, and action ... result from the institution of the social in the body (or in biological individuals)" (Bourdieu & Wacquant, 1992, pp. 126–127), and in so doing represent a "socialised subjectivity" (Bourdieu & Wacquant, 1992, p. 126) through "the internalisation of the structures of that world" (Bourdieu, 1989, p. 18). Importantly, it acts as a "structuring mechanism" operating from within agents (Wacquant, 1992, p. 18), and thus influencing the way the world is understood, and how bodies move through the world. Whilst durable, it is not eternal, but "most people are statistically bound to encounter circumstances that tend to agree with those that originally fashioned their habitus" (Bourdieu & Wacquant, 1992, p. 133). An example of this is heteronormativity, which Bourdieu (1991) considers as part of the habitus. Heteronormativity produces an "everydayness of compulsory heterosexuality" (Ahmed, 2004, p. 147), which normalises heteronormative activities in the world, and makes activities associated with these norms feel "natural" in the world.

An important part of the habitus is that it is a historically situated embodiment of what Bourdieu (1986) calls *capital*. He discusses three generic types of capital, economic, cultural and social, which he argues are important as their distribution plays a crucial role in the organisation of social life. An individual's habitus contributes to how individual choices are made, based on tacit calculations that take into account their capital, as well as the past experiences of the individual within the opportunities and constraints of their structured environments (Swartz, 2013, p. 48). Importantly, this takes place within what Bourdieu refers to as *fields*. There are many overlapping fields in everyday life (e.g. political field, religious field, sexual field). They are "a kind of arena in which people play a game which has certain rules" (Bourdieu, 1991, p. 215), and access to certain types of capital within the field, dependent on the field, "commands access to the specific profits that are at stake in the field" (Bourdieu & Wacquant, 1992, p. 97). In this chapter I focus on the sexual field, the place of contestation for the filmmakers and storytellers in this study.

In addition to the three generic types of capital, Bourdieu also discusses a fourth type of capital—symbolic capital. It is a dimension of the other capitals, and can be considered a metacapital (Swartz, 2013), which is associated with accumulated legitimacy, authority, prestige and honour. Symbolic capital is important to the extent that those with it, within certain fields, have the capacity to impose and legitimise symbolic meaning (symbolic power). In this sense, symbolic capital structures what is viewed as valid and rational:

> [T]he categories of perception, the systems of classification, that is, essentially, the words, the names which construct social reality as much as they express it, are the crucial stakes of political struggle, which is a struggle to impose the legitimate principal of vision and division. (Bourdieu, 1990, p. 134 cited in Swartz, 2013, p. 87)

The focus on imposing a legitimate vision of the world for Bourdieu is important symbolic work and is crucial in his framework to both developing and maintaining power. What is at stake here for the filmmakers and storytellers is what is legitimatised and normalised in the sexual field.

Producing Films in Contentious Spaces: Rachel's Story

I begin with a vignette[6] of one of the filmmakers' stories, which shares common threads with the other filmmakers'/storytellers' experiences. Rachel's story locates the making of an intimate digital story within the

[6] The vignette is anonymised and de-identified. All other interviewees' quotes have also been anonymised and de-identified to protect their identities.

local context and her own activist work. Similar to the other interviewees she discusses how the film is situated locally but made to communicate to an "imagined collective" across local, national and transnational contexts, with the intent to disrupt and shift internalised perceptions of the world.

At the time of the interview Rachel lived with her female partner in the capital city of her country. Her identity as a lesbian is a contentious issue in her country, where she indicates that "people are … more open about these things now than before but I guess there's still a big majority that still doesn't understand". She and her partner, at the time of the interview, owned a "production house" that she began after finishing a communication/arts degree in college. They primarily work on marketing and campaign videos for "corporate clients … non-government organisations and also other government organisations". Her access to film equipment and knowledge about video making, important cultural capital, is entangled with the way she generates an income, which is similar to that of many of the other interviewees.

In parallel with this work, Rachel is involved with/in queer activist spaces in her local area. She describes how she participates as a committee member of an organisation that undertakes "social change through the form of art … through creative ways, like … film screenings or by exhibits". She has participated in public events held by the organisation around LGBT issues. She recalled a particularly important event that took place on the International Day Against Homophobia (IDAHO). At this event, she participated as a speaker in the "Coming Out Monologues", which she explained were "kind of like the vagina monologues but with … coming out as the main topic". This was, as she articulated, an important experience:

> I am a very open person in terms of my sexuality but it was just during the time of ummm the Coming Out Monologues that I mentioned that I actually shared my story so before uh I tried to write literature or make films about LGBTs but not really my story. So after the 'Coming Out Monologues' it was a … very empowering experience for me and after that it made it easier for me to share my story so when I found out about it, about the [filmmaking project] I was really excited to do it because [its] in the medium … that I really like to make it … uhh film so there.

This quote captures the importance of sharing her story in a public space. For her, she indicates this was an "empowering experience" and an important point in her activist journey. Indeed, as she articulates, it played a crucial role in giving her the confidence ("made it easier") for her to share her story for this film project. As in the case of the other interviewees, the video project was important to the extent that it provided the economic capital, a grant of US$2000, to access equipment, travel to the destinations they needed to and, most importantly, use the time they had available to them to develop the films to share their stories through a creative "medium" they prefer presenting in.

Her story, similar to the other stories, included individuals within her immediate network—friends, family and colleagues. These individuals spoke in her film about their experiences of knowing her, an LGBT person. In producing the digital story, she discussed how she had to confront the stigma that her family members experienced because of her sexuality: "[I]t was just during that time when we were shooting that I saw her [family member] actually cry about it [being bullied by others due to Rachel's sexuality]." Evident here is the persistence of narratives of "compulsory heterosexuality" within the sexual field that the participants and their families and friends are subject to. Important to note here is the reach of stigma and the negative symbolic capital (Bourdieu et al., 1999, p. 185 cited in Swartz, 2013, p. 106) that not only becomes marked on individuals' bodies, but also extends to the family of the filmmakers/storytellers. In doing so, it has the potential to add an extra burden onto those with non-heterosexual bodies. For Rachel, whilst she indicated that the stigma was negative, she explained how it gave her and her family members the space to reflect on these concerns together and discuss the role stigma played in their lives. She discusses this as a positive development:

> [I]t's one … one of the positive things cause umm I think for a while, I thought … that it's just a story we talk about and that … she's in a way over it already. After I just found out that during filming that it still hits her … we had the talk after that and … it was relieving [for me].

Filming opened up the space for her to reflect on how stigma affects her family. Following a family member's request, she deleted the first video of her family member discussing the impact of Rachel's sexuality on the family, and then subsequently reshot the scene. Stigma had an impact on the other filmmakers films as well—family members refused to participate on camera, and, in one case a film subject no longer wanted to be involved, as one male filmmaker indicated, because it was "complicated to join with me and then uh he scared about maybe somebody will know him about sexuality like that". This inevitably had an impact on what the filmmakers included in their films and on what was absent, as they created their "portraits of reality" for a networked public.

The inclusion of family members here is important, Rachel argues, as it creates a relatable story, as she discusses below:

> It will be like a parent umm appealing to other parents to be open about their children's identities. So it's more striking I think if my mum actually said those words than if I did ... Then it would be more easier for other parents to connect with her since she's the mother and not just me speaking.

As Rachel indicates, she is developing a relatable story so "other parents" can understand. What is interesting here is that Rachel imagines one audience of this film as parents of LGBT young people. However, it is not just parents of LGBT young people who make up this audience, but rather it is a complex multi-layered audience that Rachel seeks to communicate with, as the following quotes indicate:

> [U]mm gay families so I wanted to share my experience with them, to inspire them about coming out and umm having your family accept you for that.
>
> I want my story to be heard ... by the LGBT community here [in my country] and also in Asia but also I think ... the bigger audience should be those who doesn't ahh know much yet about LGBTs uhh the straight people ... cause we interact with them all the time.

Like all the other interviewees, Rachel emphasises the need to speak to multiple audiences. This includes "gay families" and the "LGBT community", as well as "the bigger audience"—"the straight people" across geographic space/s. In doing so she wants to tell her story, which she argues is "not really usual"—a portrayal of a lesbian family, with the intent to "open the minds of the viewers that such families exist and that we're no different from them and that we also deserve acceptance". Put another way, Rachel and the filmmakers/storytellers desire to shift the symbolic meaning of sexuality and thus disrupt the habitus of the imagined viewer/s through using the (potential) reach of the networked public. For Rachel and the filmmakers/storytellers the goal is for acceptance, with the intent to shift the existing discourses that frame and classify sexuality, and, as Rachel argues,

> to spark discussions and to make people ask questions … even if their reactions are negative … the mere fact that it will be open for discussion and that people may be interested in knowing more about it umm I think that's … a big umm step already.

Constructing Narratives for Multiple Imagined Audiences

Across all the films, the filmmakers and storytellers linked their participation in the project to broader political and activist goals, as well as participation in forms of "LGBT community". Activism and participation in LGBT community is important here, for what it is allowing the filmmakers/storytellers to do. As Ridwan and Wu (2018, p. 124) explain, participation in the LGBT community "enables activists to do collective work with people who share the same identity, and allies in wider partnerships. It also enables international activism and builds transnational solidarity." In this sense, it gets used as a way of joining a broader collective, which, as I describe below, is important for their digital stories.

Across all digital stories, there was an emphasis on constructing videos for multiple audiences, with the intent to shift the habitus of the imagined viewer/s. The targets of their films included those with queer/LGBTIQ+ identities and desires *as well as* those with heterosexual identities/desires ("straight people") including the families of LGBT people, and for one male filmmaker, his own family, oppositional targets ("fundamentalists" and "conservatives"), and decision-makers ("governments"). Consider, for instance, the following quote:

> [M]y audience is a general people and … like gay or lesbian … and also like family that have children who are gay or lesbian and also organisation or the government. (Female filmmaker)

This filmmaker discusses her imagined audience: the multi-layered publics whom she anticipates coming into contact with in her film. These imagined publics are, additionally, located across local, national and transnational levels. The expectation here that the films will be seen by spatially diverse audiences is important and talks to the potential anticipated networked audience who might come into contact with the videos through a global platform for distribution of content, a networked public: *YouTube.*

In connecting to these audiences, the filmmakers and storytellers discuss the presentation of their messages in three ways: to inspire the LGBT community, to present alternative narratives of LGBT identity and to normalise identity and present versions of sameness.

To Inspire the "LGBT Community"

The films work on one level as a supportive device, to educate—"to inspire and lift up people" as one filmmaker put it. The filmmakers and storytellers seek to speak to other LGBT people, and particularly young people who are coming to terms with diverse sexuality and/or gender identity/desires. As one male filmmaker put it, he hopes his film "will find a place in … LGBTs who sort of have issues coming out". Their aim here is to present narratives that emphasise that there is nothing individually wrong with being LGBT and presenting digital stories, from a particular perspective, of what it is like living with non-heterosexual identities and desires within the contexts in which they live (e.g. national laws, and ongoing stigmas). The filmmakers/storytellers seek to emphasise and normalise non-heterosexual identities and, as one filmmaker indicated, show that there is "nothing weird about being yourself".

In some ways, the emphasis here on providing messages of "hope" and "inspiration" is similar to the *It Gets Better Project (IGBP)* developed in the US by *The Trevor Foundation*. Pullen (2014, p. 80), in responding to this work, argues for a greater focus on peer narratives, rather than adult-based narratives, to connect LGBT youth who "are looking for communion and co-presence". I argue that, in part, the videos do this. They provide peer-based perspectives on a networked public that documents issues faced regionally and culturally within Asia, by young people in the LGBT community. The filmmakers/storytellers aim to provide a sense of "communion and co-presence" with other young people, and explain that their sexuality and gender identities are not "weird" or unusual. Coming from particular intersectional positions they highlight the structural issues that persist within their own contexts that frame their sexuality/gender as "negative" or "problematic". In doing so they respond to a field that privileges heterosexuality by offering alternative narratives, representations of sexuality and gender diversity, that situate non-heterosexual sexuality as not an individual's problem, but society's.[7] Thus they seek to confront persistent narratives within the sexual field, which are embedded in the habitus, and in so doing attempt to bring heterosexuality as "normal" into question for young people coming to terms with diverse genders and sexualities.

Aims to Present Alternative Narratives and Discourses to Mainstream Representations

The filmmakers and storytellers also discussed how they sought to contribute to the existing representations of LGBT people within the region. They sought to present stories where "the story is not really usual" or common in the media. Such narratives and representations include topics of bisexuality, same-sex parenting and the presentation of intersectional lives of those living with diverse sexualities, dis/ability and religious beliefs. For many of the filmmakers, they indicated that these topics rarely get discussed, and when they are discussed, the representations/narratives are quite negative. Their contribution here was framed as both local *and* regional with the aim to showcase broader representations and discussion about LGBT identities within the region. They discussed this

[7] A point I have made about the affordances of online spaces for queer youth elsewhere (Hanckel & Morris, 2014).

as contributing to how the "LGBT community" and "mainstream" audiences understand and classify sexuality. This is arguably an intervention into what is legitimated and normalised in the sexual field. Using their cultural capital (filmmaking skills) as well as their economic capital (the grant from the organisation) they seek to intervene in the symbolic meaning of sexuality, and the existing boundaries that establish what is "normal". Their digital stories aim to add to the representations of sexuality/gender that circulate across contemporary networked space/s. In Ahmed's work she discusses how presentations of non-normative scripts, or not following these scripts in everyday life, can makes things queer or "oblique":

> [Q]ueer lives are about the potentiality of not following certain conventional scripts of family, inheritance, and child rearing, whereby "not following" involves disorientation; it makes things oblique, which in turn opens up another way to inhabit those forms. (Ahmed, 2006, p. 569)

I argue here that the films, presented for a networked public, seek to make things *more* "oblique". Moving away from "conventional scripts", they seek to present liveable lives that do not coincide with the well-travelled scripts of heterosexuality, and, for many, they are seeking to widen the scripts associated with queerness/LGBT identities within East and South-East Asia that are "not really usual". In doing so they aim to disrupt the symbolic meaning of sexuality, to contribute to shifting the habitus of the imagined viewer/s, and thus contribute to a broader understanding of what it means to be LGBT within the region.

Appealing to Sameness: Constructing Stories that Are "Like Other People"

The filmmakers and storytellers also placed an emphasis on framing their narratives in ways that normalised being LGBT, and, in so doing, appealed to sameness. This was evident in the vignette above and was a recurring theme throughout the interviews. As the following quotes by two of the filmmakers indicate:

> I just hope that where ever it is shown people will like it and it will make them think of our community [as] one with society and not treat it as an alien entity. (Female filmmaker)

> The reason I decide to select him [the storyteller is] because I think he has got talent and he try[s] to … show his friend and family that he … even though he is gay … he can still do everything like other people. (Female filmmaker)

The aim of the filmmakers is to present a narrative of LGBT people being "just like any other people". The digital stories work in this way to reposition the LGBT community—moving away from its current position as an "alien entity" and rather focusing efforts on finding points of connection with others, emphasising LGBT people as being capable of doing "everything like other people". As Rachel said, "I want to share my story for them to know that we are like you too". In doing so, the filmmakers incorporate elements into their stories that they argue appeal to sameness, with broader goals of acceptance and reduced discrimination. The appeal to sameness is part of a broader struggle for contesting the meaning of sexuality, and a way to shift and disrupt the habitus of those who are antagonistic towards and position non-heteronormative sexualities and desires as problematic and not "normal".

Taken together the goals of creating alternative discourses and appealing to sameness might seem almost contradictory. However, this presentation of the alternative and the same, arguably, works together to strengthen the "oblique" path that is created by those who come into contact with it.

Concluding Comments

> [S]ubversion exploits the possibility of changing the social world by changing the representation of this world which contributes to its reality … It contributes practically to the reality of what it announces by the fact of uttering it, of predicting it and making it predicted, of making it conceivable and above all credible and thus creating the collective representation and will which contribute to its production. (Bourdieu, 1991, p. 128)

The filmmakers' and storytellers' production of digital stories is, as I have argued throughout this chapter, part of a "political struggle" to impose a legitimate (alternative) vision of the world, within the sexual field in which they are participating. The filmmakers present "conceivable" and "credible" narratives in "oblique" ways to (attempt) to change the representation of those with diverse sexualities and gender identities locally, nationally and transnationally. Bringing together the personal and political, they seek to contribute to collective identity-making, as well as support, educate and present complex narratives of sameness and alternative discourses of sexuality and gender identity for multiple audiences located across diverse spaces.

Ahmed contends "that queer unfolds from specific points, from the lifeworld of those who do not or cannot inhabit the contours of heterosexual space" (Ahmed, 2006, p. 566). I argue that networked publics present new opportunities for this "unfold[ing]" to occur. New technologies, in this case video-making technologies and distribution platforms, present new socio-political resources for addressing social issues for those who are marginalised by mainstream society (Antony & Thomas, 2010; Kim, 2011; Soriano, 2015). The filmmakers, as I have shown, utilise their existing levels of social capital and cultural capital, and filmmaking knowledge, as well as take advantage of the economic capital—the grant from the organisation—to undertake this work. They utilise these resources to address their marginalisation and put forward new representations of sexuality and gender diversity, as part of an ongoing "political struggle" within the sexual field they are participating within. The potential for disruption and queering the field becomes further possible because of the networked nature of the platform. This extends an individual's political project, as it has the potential to be seen and shared across diverse publics. In this sense, the networked capacity of the platform for the filmmakers' and storytellers' life projects opens up further opportunities to shift the possibilities of the sexual field, disrupting what is perceived as "normal".

References

Ahmed, S. (2004). *The cultural politics of emotion*. Edinburgh: Edinburgh University Press.

Ahmed, S. (2006). *Queer phenomenology: Orientations, objects, others*. Durham: Duke University Press Books.

Alexander, J., & Losh, E. (2010). Chapter Two: "A YouTube of One's Own?" "Coming Out" videos as rhetorical action. In C. Pullen & M. Cooper (Eds.), *LGBT identity and online new media* (pp. 37–50). New York, NY: Routledge.

Antony, M. G., & Thomas, R. J. (2010). 'This is Citizen Journalism at its Finest': YouTube and the public sphere in the Oscar grant shooting incident. *New Media & Society, 12*(8), 1280–1296. https://doi.org/10.1177/1461444810362492

Aufderheide, P. (2007). *Documentary film: A very short introduction*. New York: Oxford University Press.

Austria Jr., F. (2004). JUDING_GERZI ONLINE: Insights into the potentials of virtual communities on Yahoo! Groups in addressing the challenges of being gay in the Philippines. *Plaridel, 1*(2), 21–48.

Badgett, L., Park, A., & Flores, A. (2018). *Links between economic development and new measures of LGBT inclusion*. Los Angeles, CA: Williams Institute, University of California, Los Angeles School of Law. Retrieved from https://williamsinstitute.law.ucla.edu/wp-content/uploads/GDP-and-LGBT-Inclusion-April-2018.pdf

Baskaran, A., & Muchie, M. (2006). *Bridging the digital divide: Innovation systems for ICT in Brazil, China, India, Thailand and Southern Africa*. London: Adonis & Abbey Publishers Ltd.

Bourdieu, P. (1977). *Outline of a theory of practice* (1st ed.). Cambridge: Cambridge University Press.

Bourdieu, P. (1986). The forms of capital. In J. G. Richardson (Ed.), *Handbook of theory and research for the sociology of education*. New York: Greenwood Press.

Bourdieu, P. (1989). Social space and symbolic power. *Sociological Theory, 7*(1), 14–25.

Bourdieu, P. (1990). *In other words: Essays toward a reflexive sociology*. Stanford, CA: Stanford University Press.

Bourdieu, P. (1991). *Language and symbolic power*. Cambridge: Harvard University Press.

Bourdieu, P., & Wacquant, L. (1992). *An invitation to reflexive sociology*. Chicago: University of Chicago Press.

boyd, D. (2008). Why youth (heart) social network sites: The role of networked publics in teenage social life. In D. Buckingham (Ed.), *Youth, identity, and digital media* (pp. 119–142). Cambridge, MA: MIT Press.

boyd, D. (2011). Social network sites as networked publics: Affordances, dynamics, and implications. In Z. Papacharissi (Ed.), *Networked self: Identity, community, and culture on social network sites* (pp. 39–58). New York: Routledge.

Burgess, J., & Green, J. (2009). *YouTube: Online video and participatory culture.* Cambridge: Polity Press.

Carroll, A., & Mendos, L. R. (2017). *State sponsored homophobia 2017: A world survey of sexual orientation laws: Criminalisation, protection and recognition* (12th ed.). Geneva: ILGA.

Castañeda, J. G. M. (2015). Grindring the self: Young Filipino gay men's exploration of sexual identity through a geo-social networking application. *Philippine Journal of Psychology, 48*(1), 29–58.

Doshi, K. P., & Narwold, A. (2014). Determinants of mobile phone penetration rates in Asia and Africa: A panel data analysis. In *Proceedings of 9th international business and social science research conference,* Novotel World Trade Centre, Dubai, UAE.

Dyson, S., Mitchell, A., Smith, A., Dowsett, G., Pitts, M., & Hillier, L. (2003). Don't ask, don't tell. In *Hidden in the crowd: The need for documenting links between sexuality and suicidal behaviours among young people.* Melbourne: La Trobe University, Australian Research Centre in Sex, Health and Society.

Fox, J., & Ralston, R. (2016). Queer identity online: Informal learning and teaching experiences of LGBTQ individuals on social media. *Computers in Human Behavior, 65,* 635–642.

Gray, M. L. (2009). *Out in the country: Youth, media, and queer visibility in rural America.* New York: NYU Press.

Grierson, J. (1932). The documentary producer. *Cinema Quarterly, 2*(1).

Hanckel, B., & Morris, A. (2014). Finding community and contesting heteronormativity: Queer young people's engagement in an Australian online community. *Journal of Youth Studies, 17*(7), 872–886.

Hillier, L., & Harrison, L. (2007). Building realities less limited than their own: Young people practising same-sex attraction on the internet. *Sexualities, 10*(1), 82–100.

Ho, K. C., Kluver, R., & Yang, C. C. (2003). *Asia.com: Asia encounters the internet.* London & New York: Routledge.

Horak, L. (2014). Trans on YouTube: Intimacy, visibility, temporality. *TSQ: Transgender Studies Quarterly, 1*(4), 572–585.

Jenkins, R. (2002). *Pierre Bourdieu* (2nd ed.). London & New York: Routledge.

Kim, G. (2011). Online videos, everyday pedagogy, and female political agency: "Learning from YouTube". *Global Media Journal, 11*(18), 1–16.
Kluver, R., & Banerjee, I. (2005). The internet in nine Asian nations. *Information, Communication & Society, 8*(1), 30–46.
Lange, P. G. (2007). Publicly private and privately public: Social networking on YouTube. *Journal of Computer-Mediated Communication, 13*(1), 361–380.
Manalastas, E. J. (2013). Sexual orientation and suicide risk in the Philippines: Evidence from a nationally representative sample of young Filipino men. *Philippine Journal of Psychology, 46*(1), 1–13.
Manalastas, E. J., Ojanen, T. T., Torre, B. A., Ratanashevorn, R., Choong Chee Hong, B., Kumaresan, V., et al. (2017). Homonegativity in Southeast Asia: Attitudes toward Lesbians and gay men in Indonesia, Malaysia, the Philippines, Singapore, Thailand, and Vietnam. *Asia-Pacific Social Science Review, 17*(1), 25–33.
O'Neill, M. (2014). Transgender youth and YouTube videos: Self-representation and five identifiable trans youth narratives. In C. Pullen (Ed.), *Queer youth and media cultures* (pp. 34–45). New York: Palgrave Macmillan.
Paradis, E. (2016). Searching for self and society: Sexual and gender minority youth online. In A. Wilson & V. Bloomfield (Eds.), *LGBTQ voices in education: Changing the culture of schooling* (pp. 87–101). New York: Paradigm Publishers.
Pullen, C. (2014). Media responses to queer youth suicide: Trauma, therapeutic discourse and co-presence. In C. Pullen (Ed.), *Queer youth and media cultures* (pp. 63–80). New York: Palgrave Macmillan.
Rainie, L., & Wellman, B. (2012). *Networked: The new social operating system.* Cambridge: The MIT Press.
Ridwan, R., & Wu, J. (2018). 'Being young and LGBT, what could be worse?' Analysis of youth LGBT activism in Indonesia: Challenges and ways forward. *Gender & Development, 26*(1), 121–138.
Soriano, C. R. (2015). Strategic activism for democratization and social change. In D. Holtzhausen & A. Zerfass (Eds.), *The Routledge handbook of strategic communication* (pp. 424–438). London & New York: Routledge.
Swartz, D. L. (2013). *Symbolic power, politics, and intellectuals: The political sociology of Pierre Bourdieu.* Chicago: University of Chicago Press.
Thoreson, R. (2011). Capably queer: Exploring the intersections of queerness and poverty in the Urban Philippines. *Journal of Human Development and Capabilities, 12*(4), 493–510.

Vivienne, S. (2016). *Digital identity and everyday activism: Sharing private stories with networked publics*. New York: Palgrave Macmillan.
Wacquant, L. (1992). Toward a social praxeology: The structure and logic of Bourdieu's sociology. In P. Bourdieu & L. Wacquant (Eds.), *An invitation to reflexive sociology* (pp. 1–59). Chicago: University of Chicago Press.
We Are Social and Hootsuite. (2018a). *Digital in 2018 in SouthEast Asia*. Retrieved from https://wearesocial.com/blog/2018/01/global-digital-report-2018
We Are Social and Hootsuite. (2018b). *Digital in 2018 in Eastern Asia*. Retrieved from https://wearesocial.com/blog/2018/01/global-digital-report-2018
Wuest, B. (2014). Stories like mine: Coming out videos and queer identities on YouTube. In C. Pullen (Ed.), *Queer youth and media cultures* (pp. 18–30). New York & London: Palgrave Macmillan.
Yue, A. (2016). Queer youthscapes in Asia: Embodied modernities and trans-embodiments. In J. Coffey, S. Budgeon, & H. Cahill (Eds.), *Learning bodies:* (pp. 23–38). Singapore: Springer.
Zoellner, A. (2009). Professional ideology and program conventions: Documentary development in independent British television production. *Mass Communication and Society, 12*(4), 503–536.

12

'Does Your Mother Know? Digital Versus Material Spaces of Queer Encounter in Singapore'

Jason Luger

Introduction: *Does Your Mother Know?*

Anonymous: 'Shake it shake it'
Anonymous 2: 'Does your mother know????' (From DYMK [public] Facebook page, retrieved 30 January 2018)

On a steamy Friday night in Singapore, dozens of men gather in the long, narrow space of 'DYMK', a bar on Neil Road in the Tanjong-Pagar district. On one particular evening in January 2014, several men are bare-chested, revealing fastidiously honed pectoral muscles. Others are more conservatively dressed, in attire ranging from shorts and T-shirts to business-casual. The din of conversation and laughter rises as the pop music becomes louder. Floating around the bar is a man giving out free condoms and pamphlets about free HIV testing. The crowd assembled is

J. Luger (✉)
University of California, Berkeley, CA, USA
e-mail: jdluger@berkeley.edu

C. Nash, A. Gorman-Murray (eds.), *The Geographies of Digital Sexuality*,
https://doi.org/10.1007/978-981-13-6876-9_12

perhaps 75 per cent Chinese-Singaporean and Malay, with a smaller but visible contingent of Westerners. There are maybe five or six women scattered around, in mixed groups. On the back wall, the meaning of the bar's acronym is displayed: *Does Your Mother Know?* What, exactly, is it that your mother might know is left open for interpretation, but it was explained to me by the friend across the table from me that the name implies one question: does your mother know (*that you are queer?*). The bar's name implies this without telling directly; the 'DYMK' acronym found on the bar's façade and social media pages provide a further cloak of cheeky ambiguity.

Herein emerges the complex urban spatiality of the queer encounter in Singapore, a soft-authoritarian City-State where open discussion of, and representation of, LGBTQ themes often occurs cloaked in ambiguity, symbols, and codes. This spatiality is also paradoxical, in terms of how liberal attitudes towards the LGBTQ community (the allowance of bars, nightlife) can coexist, somewhat uneasily, with 'illiberal' repression and containment of LGBTQ public discourse and the occupation of urban space (what Singaporean feminist scholar Audrey Yue calls 'illiberal pragmatism', 2007; Yue & Zubillaga-Pow, 2012). In Yue's (2007) framing, illiberalism, in terms of state-society relations, extends into a variety of areas/themes, including sexual orientation. The 'pragmatism' Yue describes is the way that the authoritarian state tolerates or even encourages LGBTQ life as a necessary by-product of economic development and Singapore's positioning as a global city. However, 'illiberalism' is still pervasive in the way state authorities placate so-called 'heartland' conservatives by relegating LGBTQ representation, civil rights, and open expression to the margins. In other words, LGBTQ tolerance is superficial (at best) and (more cynically) an economic tool aimed at placating cosmopolitans without a genuine attempt to provide real support, recognition, and full social/civil rights to LGBTQ persons. Thus, 'illiberal pragmatism' with regard to LGBTQ life in the City-State is a sort of window dressing, or, to use a regional idiom, 'wayang' (a Javanese word meaning 'shadow' but referring to the shadow puppetry that is often cloaked in hidden meaning and symbol).

The row of LGBTQ bars in Tanjong-Pagar pulse and thrive with vibrancy, yet bar-goers step out of the front doors into a world of acronyms, subtleties, taboos, and Victorian sociocultural mores (fittingly, another nearby popular gay bar is called 'Taboo'). As of this writing, the controversial law 377a of Singapore's penal code—implemented under British colonial rule in the early twentieth century—remains on the books: the law forbids 'sodomy' (even between consenting individuals). Penal Code 377a has survived several court challenges as well as scrutiny from international institutions with branches in Singapore that are wary of the awkward divergences from company/corporate inclusivity policies: 377a was one of the sticking points when US-based faculty critically questioned the opening of the Yale/NUS Liberal Arts College in Singapore (Sleeper, 2012), for example.[1]

Outdoor manifestations of LGBTQ rights, identity, and activism are likewise cloaked in representation and subtlety. The most notable example of this is the annual 'Pink Dot' gathering, held each June in Hong Lim Park, which is Singapore's designated 'Speakers' Corner'. 'Pink Dot' involves the coming together of thousands of members of the local LGBTQ community along with friends and allies for a day of speeches, music, performances, and other events. The denouement of the gathering is the aerial photo taken of the park, with thousands of pink 'dots' held in the air, coalescing into a giant, illuminated pink 'dot' in the evening. After this, the crowd disperses. 'Pink Dot', though it corresponds (in terms of its calendar date) with global 'Gay Pride' celebrations, is not *officially* an LGBTQ rights event; furthermore, the event comes with restrictions (see Luger, 2016). One of these, which has been controversial, is that non-Singaporeans are prevented from attending, and multinational companies are forbidden from being sponsors. This has, once again, caused some awkward contradictions for multinational companies (such as Google or Visa) who have substantial operations in Singapore, the Southeast Asian business hub. Pink Dot's transformational power, however, is twofold: it is the largest pro-LGBTQ gathering in Singapore's history, and the only one to regularly occupy public space. Secondly, and perhaps more notably, it has generated tremendous digital publicity, and digital images of the pink 'dots' have been viewed by millions of people

[1] Yale/NUS Liberal Arts College is a stand-alone joint venture between Yale University (USA) and faculty from the National University of Singapore, located adjacent to the National University of Singapore. It opened its doors to students in 2012.

inside and outside of the City-State. Facebook groups both in support of and against Pink Dot have thousands of followers.

Thus, this chapter argues for the importance of the interstitial spaces between material urban space and cyberspace for the queer encounter in Singapore, which is a highly temporal, liminal grey area of clues, cues, and negotiations. In this in-between space, identity is performed in ways reliant on fixed urban sites (such as bars, or other LGBTQ meeting sites) and cyber-relations on dating apps and social media. These liminal relations, however, struggle to extend into more visible, permanent forms, thereby failing to achieve the *right to the city* that Lefebvre (1968) argues requires access to centrality. Authors such as Merrifield (2013) have proposed an urban centrality that is not fixed and can exist in both digital and material forms: however, LGBTQ life in Singapore is so quickly shifting between digital networks and material encounters that establishing any sort of societal centrality, at the moment, remains impossible. Within the interstices of the authoritarian City-State's urban fabric, LGBTQ life consists of small openings followed by closures, whispers rather than shouts, and subtle performances rather than proud expressions.

This chapter therefore aims to use Singapore's case, specifically by contrasting bars and urban sites like 'DYMK' and 'Pink Dot' with cyberspaces, groups, and forums such as 'People Like Us' and WeArePinkDot.sg, to illustrate the complex negotiation and performance of social relations across scale and place. Through the following examples, I argue that Singapore's 'illiberal pragmatic' approach to the LGBTQ community has created a socio-spatial ecosystem where both the cyber and the material encounter are necessary for the realisation of sexual identity, and LGBTQ access to the urban 'centre' in the City-State, and neither can exist without the other. However, authoritarian and illiberal restrictions prevent either spatial form—the material or the cyber—from pushing forward dramatic sociocultural transformation that might result in full LGBTQ liberation. I will start with a brief critical survey of some recent literature on the queer cyber-encounter, on LGBTQ life and activism in Singapore, and on Singapore's authoritarian/illiberal production of space. Following this will be the introduction of selected examples of the tensions and socio-spatial relations of material and cyber-queer encounters drawn from both fieldwork conducted in Singapore (2012–2014) and ongoing digital ethnography. This will lead to some concluding thoughts about the implications of Singapore's example for further discussions on geo-spatial relations, the queer encounter, and the diversity of variegated global queer social terrains.

Reckoning with the Cyber-Queer Encounter

Cyberspace and cyber-encounter have reconfigured and rescaled the queer encounter in dramatic ways in a short amount of time, and emerging studies have attempted to chart the ways in which the queer encounter is stretched and condensed between (and across) digital and material forms (see Miles, 2017 and this volume). However, much of this new queer cartography has been constructed with a Western lens and with a consideration of Western-liberal contexts: the way, for example, dating apps like 'Grindr' have reconfigured queer socio-spatial relations in a setting such as London, which is the focus of Miles's, 2017 study. Other studies have focused on other hegemonic global queer capitals such as the San Francisco Bay Area, Los Angeles, and New York (e.g. Cockayne and Richardson, 2017b). Explorations of the way that cyberspace has transformed the queer encounter—and the way that space is produced and negotiated between material and digital sites—are largely absent from contexts where authoritarian and illiberal restrictions exist on the LGBTQ use and occupation of the built environment. Studies of these illiberal contexts are crucial in order to understand both the emancipatory power and the limitations of the digital queer encounter.

The *digital turn* surrounding the advent of internet technologies since the 1980s has changed the speed, scale, and texture of social encounters dramatically. Older concepts in urban theory, such as that of 'mimesis' (see Hanssen, 2004's interpretation of W. Benjamin), have been redeployed for the cyber-urban age. Gandy (2005) explored the meeting point of human and non-human in his idea of the 'cyborg-city': the networked urbanity of digital media and other communication infrastructures becoming an everyday exoskeleton for the human body (building, digitally, upon the idea of 'mimesis'). Emerging geographical work on digitally networked, fluid social spaces has attempted to broaden understandings of the relationships between technology, space, and social systems in diverse global urban landscapes (Goriunova, 2012). Digital media allow new productions, circulations, and velocities of rhythm, time, more-than-human being, and, following Amin and Thrift's (2002) musings, an overall re-imagination of the urban condition.

The links between digital technology and the queer social encounter, and the way that such cyber-material links have complicated queer production of space, form a nascent body of research within urban geography, the digital humanities, media studies, and queer studies. Mobile phone social apps such as 'Grindr' and 'Tinder' have formed an important element in many of these studies, which are also emerging in disciplines such as public health and epidemiology that explore questions such as how dating apps have influenced the spread of sexually transmitted diseases such as HIV (e.g. Race, 2015).

Within urban geography, studies have emerged focusing on the complex concepts like public versus private space and the ways that behaviour and the occupation of space vary from cyber-encounters to material encounters. Miles (2017) explored these questions from the vantage point of London, concluding that even as cyber-encounters shrink and speed up the scale and scope of queer sociality, awkward disconnections exist between digital and material encounters. Miles concludes that while the formation of queer social relations often occurs via cyber-conversations, these cyber-meetings do not necessarily translate into coherent physical encounters and indeed are 'uneasily embodied' in everyday practice. Similarly, Cockayne and Richardson (2017a) build on Kitchin and Dodge's (2011) concept of 'code/space' to explore the ways that social codes are formed in and across hybrid digital and material spaces, and the way that these codes regulate and transform the socio-spatial experience. Roth (2016), Bonner-Thompson (2017), and Blackwell, Birnholtz, and Abbott (2015) (among others) have likewise highlighted the implications for queer connectedness, identity, and socio-spatial behaviour. What links many (if not the vast majority) of these studies together is their Anglo-American focus, based normatively from hegemonic queer communities such as London, New York, the San Francisco Bay Area, and Los Angeles.

While there are undoubtedly practical reasons for this (language barriers; the size and diversity of these queer communities; the relatively liberal sociocultural context that has allowed these queer communities to flourish), there remains a large gap in studies looking at digital queer socio-spatial relations in less typical contexts. These understudied terrains include areas where queer identity comes with more hazards and restrictions, but also contexts where the use and proliferation of smartphone dating apps has not been as widespread (or occurs via different apps and in different corners of cyberspace). Many of these studies focus primarily on gay-male communities (the spaces of lesbian cyber-encounters are notably understudied, with Murray & Ankerson, 2016, a notable exception), and, predominantly white gay men. It is also worth remembering that large segments of the world and also arguably of the global queer community are not digitally connected (or, at least, not in the same way). For all these reasons, it is useful to consider emerging literature that is now beginning to broaden the conversation to less typical contexts and cases from the illiberal/authoritarian world and the non-white, non-West.

Illiberal/Authoritarian Terrains and the Queer Encounter

Belatedly, studies are emerging that bring to light the diversity of queer encounters, the proliferation of new and culturally specific types of social web apps, and the huge range of site-specific, socio-political views of homosexuality. These studies look more closely at prevalent (Western-developed) apps such as Grindr and Facebook to see the way that atypical contexts see these apps being used quite differently—in some cases, Grindr (and similar apps) take on greater power to stimulate meeting and conversation when open expression of homosexuality is frowned upon or even legally banned; in other cases (such as in China), many Western-developed apps are not available, but queer encounters have been stimulated by other apps and by creative/subversive ways of negotiating around/across China's 'great [digital] firewall'.

Arora (2015) looked at how Facebook becomes a digitally mediated site of romance across context and national borders in the Global South, tracking the way that 'courtship' is performed within the interstices of the internet's varying degrees of regulation, censorship, and sociocultural mores. This study joins studies like Brown (2008), Browne and Brown (2016), and Visser (2016) which have outlined a more global scope/scale of queer socio-spatiality. Still, these global surveys do not fully engage with questions of authoritarian/illiberal contextual specificities; the variations of religious and cultural understandings/approaches to homosexual themes; and the full range of the way urban space is produced, occupied, and deployed according to social/cultural/political temporalities, language, and racial/ethnic specificities.

However, site-based studies from contexts such as India (arguably the world's most populous nation and one of the most digitally connected) are enriching this conversation. Arora and Scheiber (2017) delve into what they term 'Slumdog Romance'—the Facebook-enabled love geographies of/in (poor) Indian cities and the layers of religious, ethnic, and class-related factors in the formation of cyber-romance among groups including the LGBTQ community. Subtle Indian contexts such as caste form interesting hybridities vis-à-vis digital social encounters. Lodder (2014) and Mohamed (2015) explore the way that global social/dating apps (LGBTQ-specific such as Grindr, and a more general communication app WhatsApp) stretch and redefine social encounters across borders in the Arab World, where open queer expression is difficult or even impossible. African cases are less frequent, perhaps due to the difficulty of doing LGBTQ-themed research in many parts of Africa where homosexuality is taboo (and may even come with severe punishments). However, there are recent studies, notably emerging from South Africa, where LGBTQ rights are protected in the national Constitution, and cities like Cape Town have large and (racially) diverse LGBTQ communities. Henderson (2017) discusses the codes and identity signifiers in the male gay population in Cape Town and the way that digital encounters help to shape these sexual communications.

Studies on the digital networks of queer sociality are now emerging from East and Southeast Asian contexts featuring varying shades of authoritarian state-society structures. Szulc (2014) offers a useful review of some of the literature on this topic emerging from cases such as Japan, South Korea, and Taiwan. China has been a focal point for other authors, who have charted the rise of Grindr and other social apps within China's brand of authoritarian state managerialism, where there are a number of

China-specific competitor apps such as WeChat and 'Blued' (some Western apps and websites are not accessible within China or are accessed only via Virtual Private Networks (VPNs)). Many of these studies are found in health-related journals (e.g. Tang et al., 2016) and focus on the link between dating apps and the rise and spread of sexually transmitted diseases. Missing from a Chinese context—and, more broadly, from East Asian and Southeast Asian contexts—are explorations of the production of space and the reconfiguration of socio-spatial relations in the interstitial flows between cyberspace and the urban environment (specifically, authoritarian and quasi-authoritarian urban environments). It is this gap where my chapter sits, using Singapore's soft-authoritarian, socio-political context; Southeast Asian geography; and the City-State scale as rationale for probing how politics, place, and context are so crucial for charting the contours of urban queer social relations.

'Saints' and Sinners: Building Singapore's Illiberal Society

LGBTQ life in Singapore is complicated, as it is everywhere. But Singapore's unique state-society context and hybrid sociocultural textures (often envisioned as a meeting point of authoritarian 'East' and liberal 'West') further complicate LGBTQ relations. This is due to Singapore's 'soft-authoritarian' (Ooi, 2009) or 'illiberal pragmatic' (Yue, 2007) governance structure—in which public discourse is censored and certain topics/themes deemed controversial are restricted—as well as the simple reality of Singapore's small physical size. Adding a further layer of complexity is the structure of land and building ownership in the City-State: most land is state-owned (a legacy of the large-scale transfer of land from the British to the nascent Singapore post-colonial government in the 1960s).

Singapore's racial, ethnic, religious, and cultural potpourri is also complex in the way it relates to, and signifies, LGBTQ identity and the temporalities of the socio-sexual encounter. The City-State is of about 75 per cent Chinese ethnicity; 11–12 per cent Malay (who are primarily Muslim); 9–10 per cent Indian (who are Hindu, Muslim, Sikh, Jain, and others); and then 3–4 per cent 'other', a category that includes Eurasian expatriates (Europeans, North Americans, Australians) and small numbers of other migrants. This racial/ethnic dynamic, a result of British colonial settlement patterns, is carefully maintained and curated in what is known locally as 'CMIO'—*Chinese, Malay, Indian, and Other*. The harmonic coexistence of these groups has been a key feature—and necessity—in many of the government's post-1965 policies. One example of this is how these ratios (above) are mandated in state HDB (Housing and Development Board) estates, where most Singaporeans live. There are also careful rules—both written and unwritten—about the representation of these groups in various spectra of society and governance, so as not to offend or over-/underrepresent. As Singaporean cultural scholars like Ooi (2009) and Yue (2007) suggest, the approach to governance—one of economic pragmatism combined with social conservatism—has generated a rather contradictory history of liberal/progressive approaches to cosmopolitanism combined with illiberal/authoritarian restrictions and repression of those cosmopolitanisms deemed unstable to Singapore's sociocultural fabric. The People's Action Party's (PAP) hesitance to offend is justified, at least in official state rhetoric, by the spectre of race and religious riots: tensions erupted into riots in the 1960s between Malay and Chinese communities, and again as recently as 2013, when riots erupted in 'Little India' when a Chinese bus driver hit and killed an ethnic Indian pedestrian.

Also, factors in Singapore's socially conservative culture have been the lasting residue of British-era Victorian punitive attitudes towards vice and morality, some of which remain in Singaporean law. One example of this is Penal Code 377a, which forbids—at least on paper—consensual sex between men. This law has survived several recent legal challenges. British Victorian-era laws such as this have formed locally constituted hybrids with the socially conservative and traditional beliefs of Chinese Confucianism, but also the Malay-Muslim and (culturally traditional) Indian communities. Finally, the finishing ingredient in Singapore's unique sociocultural stew is the recent rise of Western-style evangelical/charismatic protestant Christianity in the City-State, especially popular in the Chinese-ethnic community. 'Mega churches', with sermons held in massive auditoriums with thousands of seats, have become popular in Singapore's middle and upper middle class heartland

(Economist, 2018). These sermons have generally been critical of LGBTQ rights, and prominent pastors have emerged as leading voices against LGBTQ rights in the City-State. The delineation of Singaporean society into 'cosmopolitan' and 'heartland' factions has been a common sociological approach to theorising the City-State, and to explaining the rationale for government approaches to cultural and social policy (e.g. Luger, 2016; Tan, 2008). This is similar to the way American sociologist Elijah Anderson (2011) frames 'cosmos' (those with worldly, liberal, tolerant beliefs) and 'ethnos' (more reactionary, intolerant, and traditional beliefs). In a Singaporean framing, the quasi-authoritarian government is both 'cosmo' and 'ethno', making policy, place, and space for discourses for cosmopolitan and heartland aims and factions. Caught with this dialectic is Singapore's LGBTQ community, subject to cycles of opening and closure, progressive gestures, and reactionary swings. Also caught within the push-pull of liberal and illiberal are the spaces of the built and digital environment for queer encounters and assembly, likewise dynamic, opening, closing, and reopening.

Singapore's early days were somewhat less orderly and disciplined than would be the case as the City-State modernised and became wealthier: 1960s/1970s Singapore was a less wealthy, less developed, and, less buttoned up place when it came to things like nightlife and sex. The legacy of being a military base and port city with a liberal-trade economy actually meant that Singapore had a rather seedy reputation in its initial years; this may seem hard to believe, but is captured in Paul Theroux's (1973) *Saint Jack*—the 1979 film version of which was banned in the City-State until 2006. In the book, the American pimp Jack Flowers navigates Singapore's underbelly and red-light districts of brothel and sex workers, neon, transvestites and transsexuals, and the tension between this side of the city and the emerging authoritarian moralism forms a central theme. The film's ban in 1980 reflected the increasing social conservativism of Singapore's ruling party as the City-State became wealthier, more developed, and more connected to the global economy as a key business hub.

The 1980s was a fraught time for LGBTQ life, and civil society more generally in Singapore. Several crises occurred in which state authorities went after civil society groups, the most dramatic of which was 'operation spectrum' in 1987. It was an example of the way that Singapore's *Internal*

Security Act (ISA) can be applied—22 people were arrested and detained without trial, accused to being part of a 'Marxist conspiracy'. Those arrested included social workers and human rights activists, Catholic priests, theatre practitioners, and overseas-educated public intellectuals. Though the LGBTQ community was not specifically targeted, the operation certainly sent shivers through Singapore's grass roots.

Another, more recent incident, however, which has become known as the 'AWARE' saga, was more directly related to Singapore's LGBTQ community and civil society groups (see Chong, 2011). AWARE, or the Association of Women for Action and Research, is a civil society group advocating for gender equality, the empowerment of women, and support for female victims of sexual assault (among other things). At the organisation's annual general meeting on 28 March 2009, there was a dramatic takeover of the executive board by a new group of members, backed by anti-LGBTQ supporters including an openly anti-LGBTQ mega church. This was notable because AWARE was not, ostensibly, an LGBTQ advocacy group, but also, because much of the LGBTQ discourse in Singapore surrounds gay men and not lesbian women. The AWARE coup d'état was later reversed after public outcry, and many original board members won back their seats, but the episode remains an uneasy marker in Singapore's conflicted moral terrain.

This moral terrain is constantly shifting, and LGBTQ civil society groups have had mixed success in pushing through openings in the authoritarian fabric by utilising different methods and tactics. Chua (2012), in her exploration of the legal tactics used to challenge anti-LGBTQ laws like 377A, illustrates a landscape of 'pragmatic resistance', where small legal victories, despite setbacks, culminate in steps forward. Yue (2007), Yue & Zubillaga-Pow, 2012, and Oswin (2010) likewise paint a picture of an everyday queer lived experience containing constant mediation and negotiation of illiberal state structures and institutions, from Singapore's state housing apparatus (in which married couples and those with children receive preference) to the way the queer body relates to the city's public spaces. The overarching theme within the portrayal of the queer everyday is a carefully deliberated, pragmatic, and highly self-conscious set of daily decisions, micro-interactions, and subtle subversions. Cyberspace and the digital encounters it enables is crucial to this lived experience.

Finding 'People Like Us': *The Interstitial Spaces of Singapore's Queer Encounter*

The ISA—another remnant of British colonial rule (the law had been used to detain presumed anti-colonial agitators)—has also been invoked to arrest gay men for violating Penal Code 377a, sometimes as part of covert sting operations. This occurred several times in the 1980s and 1990s, and though arrests of gay men in Singapore have been a less frequent occurrence over the past 20 years, the state retains the ability (at least on paper) to do so. This threat, even if rarely (or never) applied given Singapore's more recent repositioning as a cosmopolitan global city, complicates the relationship of the LGBTQ community to space.

Further complicating this relationship are other Singaporean-authoritarian laws and regulations relating to public assembly and the use of the built environment. The 'Societies Act', another relic of colonialism that has been incorporated into authoritarian rule, places strict limitations on the scale, theme, and form that public gatherings can take (see Luger, 2016; Rodan, 2003). This law applies not only to protests, but also to any gathering in the City-State that is public in nature and surpasses a certain size. These gatherings must gain permission from authorities after a review period and must not cross certain 'out of bounds' lines in terms of topic or themes. Herein it becomes more complicated, because, as Lee (2002) discusses, the 'out of bounds' (locally known as 'ob') is a dynamic and highly subjective grey area, dependent on the discretion of certain policy officials in different bureaucratic departments and agencies. Topics/themes involving race, religion, and opposition politics are especially sensitive: direct attacks on public officials and government members are generally forbidden. LGBTQ-themed events, discussions, and activities are sometimes approved, sometimes not, though the general stance is that while events can 'celebrate' LGBTQ life, they cannot actively 'promote' an 'LGBTQ agenda' (Chong, 2017).

A prime example of the ambiguity surrounding the application of the 'Societies Act' is the aforementioned annual 'Pink Dot' gathering/celebration, which is held each June at Speakers' Corner in Hong Lim Park (pictured in Fig. 12.1). Though corresponding on the calendar with

Fig. 12.1 Hong Lim Park/Speakers' Corner, site of 'Pink Dot'. Photo courtesy of author, 2013

global 'Gay Pride' events held in many cities, 'Pink Dot' is unable to market itself as and identify with 'Gay Pride', but that would be seen to cross the line between acknowledging LGBTQ rights and *actively promoting them*. State authorities are fully aware that 'Pink Dot' is a pro-LGBTQ rights event; the talks, events, and other activities do not hide their message and feature many openly LGBTQ local figures (such as Samantha Lo, the street artist, who identifies openly as a lesbian). Yet the event is contained (thematically) by its inability to take on a more political agenda; it is contained physically by its designated location, the 0.94-hectare Hong Lim Park; and it is further contained by the restrictions on non-Singaporean permanent-resident attendance or corporate sponsorships. In cyberspace, however, none of these restrictions exist: anyone is free to 'attend' Pink Dot's Facebook page, or digitally participate (and thus co-create and co-mediate) in the event. Online, of course, 'Pink Dot' also exists beyond the City-State, in a space of flows far bigger (indeed infinitely bigger) than 0.94 hectares. The physical site cannot gain transformative power without the website, and vice versa. The question of how Singapore's laws, restrictions, and 'out of bounds' markers apply and extend to digital space—and the degree to which digital space extends, transforms, or enables the queer encounter—is an ongoing debate at the heart of this chapter's discussion.

'People Like Us' was an early LGBTQ social and support group in the 1990s, which faced the dilemma of finding a physical space to meet and hold its meetings. Unable to find a permanent home, 'People Like Us' (or PLU) met in rehearsal space in the Substation Theatre, which is a progressive community theatre space in central Singapore. The Substation, which is partly autonomous (receiving some state money but many private donations), has been at the forefront of utilising physical space for groups, events, and topics that may not be allowed in other places. Still, PLU was unable to open their meetings up to the public: The *Societies Act* required that the meetings remain 'private', 'closed-door', and not publicly advertised (according to research interview with PLU member, Singapore, 2012). Otherwise, the group would have needed to officially register as a 'Society', which, as an LGBTQ-themed group, was impossible. Repeated attempts to register were denied. The 1990s corresponded to the rise of cyberspace as a social meeting place, and by the mid-1990s, PLU realised the potential of the web as a 'place' to supplement its private, informal meetings at the Substation. Where fliers or advertisements on city walls were not permitted, the web allowed announcements, organisation, and networking. Most importantly, cyberspace allowed 'People Like Us' to find other people—to grow and include members across and even beyond Singapore who could not meet in the 'closed' meetings, either because of restrictions of numbers or because of the lasting stigma of being openly gay in Singapore and preferring a more discrete or even anonymous digital encounter. By the early 2000s, the rise of new forms of social media and gay dating websites, combined with Singapore's relative loosening on restrictions on LGBTQ groups, rendered PLU less and less necessary, and the group disbanded. The case demonstrates though the uneasy yet crucial relationship between 'real' space and digital space in order to provide the group legitimacy and the ability to achieve its mission of networking, support, and advocacy for the queer community. Despite the lingering social conservatism and the inability to erase all anti-LGBTQ laws, events like 'Pink Dot' indicate that the rescaling of PLU's small, private meetings into Singapore's largest annual public gathering has been in some ways a phenomenal transformation. The restrictions on 'Pink Dot' itself, and the continued necessity for social media to supplement public assembly, indicate that this transformation is by no means complete, and liberation remains deferred.

The past decade has introduced 'Web2.0', the tech-industry's slang for the digital revolution enabled by smartphones and digital app innovations. The rise of LGBTQ socio-sexual GPS location-based apps such as Grindr (and others) has once again rescaled and reconfigured the socio-spatial nature of the queer encounter, and once again complicated the relationship between material and digital space within relational queer flows. Yet, Singapore's geography and lasting illiberal climate mean that Grindr has not had the same impact it has had in many cities. Though the raid and arrests of gay men are somewhat of a memory, the state retains the legal ability to do this. Safe queer encounters, therefore, are relegated to the home, or to a designated (and permitted) LGBTQ space like a bar or club.

Another factor is Singapore's housing structure, the aforementioned HDB estates where the vast majority of Singaporeans live. HDB estates feature many eyes on the street—the surveillance that comes with a public housing estate of thousands of units, but also Singapore's natural climate of authoritarian surveillance. Needless to say, the Singaporean home is not conducive to sexual encounters in the same way that a private flat in London or even Tokyo might be. This is further complicated by the fact that it is difficult (to near impossible) for unmarried, single, or same-sex couples to gain HDB housing, which usually has a lengthy waitlist. Therefore, a significant number of Singapore's LGBTQ community members live with family or a collection of roommates. Those who choose private-market housing may have more options, but since these units are typically expensive, many are likewise forced to live with roommates and there are other rules that govern visitors and guests in these complexes.

For all these reasons, the physical spaces of queer socio-spatial encounters are limited. So, Singapore's 'Grindr' geographies still require physical meeting places such as 'Does Your Mother Know?', and the LGBTQ-safe bar, club, or meeting space is both necessary and thriving in Singapore at the same time these spaces are declining in many other parts of the world (see Miles, 2017). While the social encounter may begin on an app such as Grindr or Facebook, it likely culminates in one of the City-State's designated (and restricted) built spaces, to assure that *your mother doesn't know*. Metaphorically, the paternal authoritarian state is wink-winking and nod-nodding its tacit approval for queerness while refusing to publicly discuss it—these 'illiberal pragmatic' gestures (as Yue, 2007 describes) to placate the LGBTQ community without ruffling the Singaporean heartland's feathers.

The rationale for this gestural and superficial treatment of the LGBTQ community warrants a separate discussion, but the discourse on the presumed needs of the (Western)-liberal business community and Singapore's recent repositioning as a cosmopolitan global city and tourist destination is worth considering. Singapore's official rhetoric towards and about the LGBTQ community has often walked a fine line between recognising that global cities have a vibrant nightlife and that LGBTQ nightlife is included in that vibrancy. I refer to Prime Minister Lee Hsien Loong's comments that 'bungee jumping' and 'tabletop dancing' should be allowed in the 'new' Singapore (see Tan, 2007). External Western entities—from the Yale/NUS Liberal Arts College to major multinational companies that use the City-State as their Asian hub—are actively recruited and indeed central to Singapore's repositioning; the government recognises that a draconian and punitive approach to LGBTQ rights may scare off these entities and the investment and prestige they bring. At the same time, should Singapore develop a reputation as a fully inclusive, tolerant LGBTQ mecca it would inflame conservative groups and potentially raise tensions with Malaysia and Indonesia, Singapore's large, Muslim neighbours, and both countries in which conservative Muslim factions have been gaining influence. In summary, LGBTQ Singapore is caught in something of a stalemate, allowed to bloom, but not too brightly; to use space, but not too loudly; and free to gather and perform identity, but as long as *mother doesn't know*.

Conclusion

The examples of 'People Like Us', a former LGBTQ social group, as well as the bar 'DYMK' paint a picture of a queer landscape that moves quickly between and across digital and material space, relying on both spatial forms for any sense of permanence or emancipatory possibility. However, the simple necessity of cyberspace as a supplement and/or complement to the ephemerality of material spaces of encounter limits the ability for queer life in Singapore to take root in the urban environment in a way where subtlety, disguise, caution, and double entendre are no longer necessary. Tactical and cautious performances of queerness remain necessary given Singapore's high level of state control, limited physical size, and sociocultural conservativism: both online and offline, there remains a general reluctance to embrace the expression of a 'self' that may be loudly and even arrogantly queer. An alternate reading, however, and one that is more hopeful, is that queerness in Singapore is embodying the potential micro-resistances at the same time it internalises repressive power.

In a less restrictive environment free of the degrees of self-censorship and self-regulation inherent to a soft-authoritarian, illiberal pragmatic cityscape, it would not matter if your mother knew that you were queer: one would be free to wear a queer identity inside, outside, online, or offline, and not relegated to the perpetual Singaporean closet. That said, the deliberately subversive word play, and the vibrancy of Singapore's LGBTQ ecosystem *despite* the site-specific limits on queer life, displays flashes of emancipatory potential. The online/offline interfaces between places like DYMK, 'People Like Us', 'Pink Dot', and the socio-spatial corners of the internet display uniquely Singaporean aspects of resilience and tactical reconfiguration. The (slow) forward progress of queer liberation in the City-State—through small openings allowed in the legal and political infrastructure as well as the built environment—points to the possibility that queer Singapore may be planting more permanent seeds capable of generating firmer roots.

References

Amin, A., & Thrift, N. (2002). *Cities: Reimagining the urban*. London: Polity Press.

Anderson, E. (2011) *The Cosmopolitan Canopy: Race and Civility in Everday Life*. New York: Norton.

Arora, P. (2015). Facebook and the digital romance economy: Courtship, scams, and internet regulation in the global South. *Impact of Social Sciences Blog*. Retrieved February 4, 2017, from http://blogs.lse.ac.uk/impactofsocialsciences/

Arora, P., & Scheiber, L. (2017). Slumdog romance: Facebook love and digital privacy at the margins. *Media, Culture & Society, 39*(3), 408–422.

Blackwell, C., Birnholtz, J., & Abbott, C. (2015). Seeing and being seen: Co-situation and impression formation using Grindr, a location-aware gay dating app. *New Media & Society, 17*(7), 1117–1136.

Bonner-Thompson, C. (2017). 'The meat market': Production and regulation of masculinities on the Grindr grid in Newcastle-upon-Tyne, UK. *Gender, Place & Culture, 24*(11), 1–15.

Brown, G. (2008). Urban (homo) sexualities: Ordinary cities and ordinary sexualities. *Geography Compass, 2*(4), 1215–1231.

Browne, K., & Brown, G. (2016). An introduction to the geographies of sex and sexualities. In *The Routledge research companion to geographies of sex and sexualities* (pp. 1–12). Oxon: Routledge.

Chong, J. (2017). Ch. 8, LGBTQ activism in Singapore. In *A history of human rights society in Singapore: 1965–2015* (p. 150). London: Taylor and Francis.

Chong, T. (Ed.). (2011). *The AWARE Saga: Civil society and public morality in Singapore*. Singapore: NUS Press.

Chua, L. (2012). Pragmatic resistance, law, and social movements in authoritarian states: The case of gay collective action in Singapore. *Law & Society Review, 46*(4), 713–748.

Cockayne, D. G., & Richardson, L. (2017a). A queer theory of software studies: Software theories, queer studies. *Gender, Place & Culture, 24*(11), 1587–1594.

Cockayne, D. G., & Richardson, L. (2017b). Queering code/space: The co-production of socio-sexual codes and digital technologies. *Gender, Place & Culture, 24*(11), 1–17.

Gandy, M. (2005). Cyborg urbanization: Complexity and monstrosity in the contemporary city. *International Journal of Urban and Regional Research, 29*, 26–49.

Goriunova, O. (2012). New media idiocy. *Convergence: The International Journal of Research into New Media Technologies, 19*, 223–235.

Hanssen, B. (2004). Language and mimesis in Walter Benjamin's work. In D. Ferris (Ed.), *The Cambridge companion to Walter Benjamin* (pp. 54–72). Cambridge: Cambridge University Press.

Henderson, N. J. (2017). 'Top, bottom, versatile': Narratives of sexual practices in gay relationships in the Cape Metropole, South Africa. *Culture, Health & Sexuality, 20*(5), 1–12.

Kitchin, R., & Dodge, M. (2011). *Code/space: Software and everyday life*. Cambridge: MIT Press.

Lee, T. (2002). The politics of civil society in Singapore. *Asian Studies Review, 26*(1), 97–117.

Lefebvre, H. (1968). *Le droit à la ville* [The right to the city]. Paris: Anthropos.
Lodder, A. R. (2014). When 'there' can be everywhere: On the cross-border use of WhatsApp, Pandora, and Grindr. *European Journal of Law and Technology, 5*(2). Retrieved from http://ejlt.org/article/view/364/454
Luger, J. (2016). Singaporean 'spaces of hope?' Activist geographies in the city-state. *City, 20*(2), 186–203.
Merrifield, A. (2013). *The politics of the encounter: Urban theory and protest under planetary urbanization* (Vol. 19). Athens: University of Georgia Press.
Miles, S. (2017). Sex in the digital city: Location-based dating apps and queer urban life. *Gender, Place & Culture, 24*(11), 1–16.
Mohamed, M. S. (2015). *Sexuality, development and non-conforming desire in the Arab world: The case of Lebanon and Egypt* (No. IDS Evidence Report; 158). IDS.
Murray, S., & Ankerson, M. (2016). Lez takes time: Designing lesbian contact in geosocial networking apps. *Critical Studies in Media Communication, 33*(1), 53–69.
Ooi, C.-S. (2009). Government and creativity: 'Arts City' Singapore. *Creative Industries, 3*, 44–47.
Oswin, N. (2010). The modern model family at home in Singapore: A queer geography. *Transactions of the Institute of British Geographers, 35*(2), 256–268.
Race, K. (2015). 'Party and play': Online hook-up devices and the emergence of PNP practices among gay men. *Sexualities, 18*(3), 253–275.
Rodan, G. (2003). Embracing electronic media but suppressing civil society: Authoritarian consolidation in Singapore. *The Pacific Review, 16*(4), 503–524.
Roth, Y. (2016). Zero feet away: The digital geography of gay social media. *Journal of Homosexuality, 63*(3), 437–442.
Sleeper, J. (2012, May 4). Yale has gone to Singapore, but can it come back? *The Huffington Post*. Retrieved from https://www.huffingtonpost.com/jim-sleeper/yale-has-gone-to-singapor_b_1476532.html
Szulc, L. (2014). The geography of LGBTQ internet studies. *International Journal of Communication, 8*, 5.
Tan, K. P. (Ed.). (2007). *Renaissance Singapore? Economy, culture, and politics*. Singapore: NUS Press.
Tan, K. P. (2008). Meritocracy and elitism in a global city: Ideological shifts in Singapore. *International Political Science Review, 29*(1), 7–27.
Tang, W., Best, J., Zhang, Y., Liu, F. Y., Tso, L. S., Huang, S., & Tucker, J. D. (2016). Gay mobile apps and the evolving virtual risk environment: A cross-

sectional online survey among men who have sex with men in China. *Sexually Transmitted Infections*, sextrans-2015.
The Economist. (2018). Escalators to heaven: Evangelicalism is spreading among the Chinese of Southeast Asia, January 4.
Theroux, P. (1973). *Saint Jack*. London: Houghton Mifflin.
Visser, G. (2016). Sexualities and urban life. *The Routledge research companion to geographies of sex and sexualities* (p. 55). London: Routledge.
Yue, A. (2007). Hawking in the creative city: Rice rhapsody, sexuality and the cultural politics of 'New Asia' in Singapore. *Feminist Media Studies, 7*(4), 365–380.
Yue, A., & Zubillaga-Pow, J. (Eds.). (2012). *Queer Singapore: Illiberal citizenship and mediated cultures* (Vol. 1). Hong Kong: Hong Kong University Press.

13

Queerying Public Art in Digitally Networked Space: The Rise and Fall of an Inflatable Butt Plug

Martin Zebracki

Rationale

This chapter analyses the under-examined topic of social engagement with public artwork in digitally networked space. Conventionally taken as artworks commissioned and designed for freely accessible public material sites (Miles, 1997), digital technologies have provided new tools and reconfigured spaces for engagement with public artwork (Freeman & Sheller, 2015). The "digitisation of our existence" (Bishop, 2012, p. 436) requires public art to be understood through the dialectic between the physical and the virtual. Rose (2015) argued that geographers should further embark on the role of digital mediation of culture/arts in everyday life. The digital dimensions of public-art engagement, where online users curate, exchange and co-create content on Web 2.0 (i.e., the digitally networked spaces of social media), have remained a particularly under-charted terrain.

M. Zebracki (✉)
University of Leeds, Leeds, UK
e-mail: m.m.zebracki@leeds.ac.uk

C. Nash, A. Gorman-Murray (eds.), *The Geographies of Digital Sexuality*,
https://doi.org/10.1007/978-981-13-6876-9_13

Hence, this study expands scholarship on the roles and uses of public art in physical contexts (e.g., Cartiere & Zebracki, 2016) and attends to how digital engagement with material public art rearranges spaces of experience as much as experiences of space in digital culture. I provide an in-depth, virtual ethnographic case study on *Tree*, created by the leading American contemporary artist Paul McCarthy. This 24-metre inflatable in Paris' historically prominent Place Vendôme was meant as temporary installation as part of 2014 FIAC, the International Fair of Contemporary Art. But its material existence was very short-lived, as it was demolished just two days after its unveiling on 16 October 2014. Building on his oeuvre, McCarthy acknowledged that his work was partially inspired by an anal sex toy (*Le Monde* [Jardonnet], 2014).

Tree was a different, odd, "queer" public artwork. It was deemed, by many, as abnormal, inappropriate, indecent, and so on, while others appreciated its playful and radical elements. Triggered by the artwork's ambiguous, sexuality-related framing, I have adopted the word play and tenet "queerying" to question, to "query", the opacities and ambivalences of *Tree*'s digitally networked space in juxtaposition with how public art has been primarily studied "offline".

This chapter, first, explains the research context and method, followed by a conceptual framing of what queer studying of digitally mediated public art entails. I then discuss the data collection that feeds into the critical analysis of the artwork's digitally networked modus operandi. I conclude with a discussion of how critical geographers can take this study further.

Context and Queer Method

The inflammatory debate about *Tree* navigated between serious dialogue and foremostly phatic and whimsical communications driven by a so-called network sociality: the maintenance of a network of often cursory digital social connections/"friendships" (see Miller, 2008). Interactions on the leading social networking site Facebook, the key microblogging site Twitter, and the photo- and video-sharing platform Instagram dominated the online discussion about the artwork (Figs. 13.1 and 13.2).

Fig. 13.1 (top) and Fig. 13.2 (bottom) Impressions of playful threads on Instagram. The photos show *Tree*'s relation to surrounding edifices, most notably the 44-metre-tall Vendôme Column (1871). At the time, the Column was under restoration and pictured on the construction box

Dissatisfaction was also expressed on-site. A local resident slapped McCarthy's face upon *Tree*'s unveiling and yelled out that he is "not French and the work has no place on the square" (*Le Monde* [Jardonnet], 2014, translated in *London Evening Standard* [Rucki], 2014). The inflatable's guide wires were vandalised just two days after. Both events resulted in viral media coverage.

Tree's digitally networked space was filled with ambiguous meanings and fractured social engagements. McCarthy's work renders the Christmas tree, a butt plug in disguise, an indictment of the wrongdoings and perverse pleasures of capitalism. By a compelling academic analogy, Sedgwick (1993) employed the term "Christmas effect" in reference to what Gibson-Graham (1999, p. 80), in their seminal work *Queer(y)ing Capitalism*, described as "the 'depressing' set of [capitalist] circumstances". Detamore (2010a, p. 60) defined this effect as one that "brings the multiple voices such as the Church, State, markets, media, and so on into a monolithic voice aiming toward the expectation of a similar predictable outcome (in this case Christmas)". *Tree*'s scale, as an aesthetic strategy, I argue, set forth such monolithic voice. The "light" temporary structure, made of air, was queerly at odds with the tradition of "heavy" permanent bronze sculptures. Spectators did not necessarily see the intimate/sexualised, and perhaps frivolous, theme as appropriate for such a central public space as Place Vendôme, known for its historically important, "serious", classical genius loci.

Queer studies have offered a myriad of ways to destabilise (dominant) knowledges, in particular around sexual identity politics (Browne & Nash, 2010), including the tenacity of the emic homosexual/heterosexual dichotomy (Sedgwick, 1993), as challenged by *Tree*. Queerying as situated qualitative methodology verbally speaks out a transformative disposition: "a chance for movement, a means to transform the static of a noun—*queer*—into the action of a verb—*queer[y]ing* … moving theory into methodological activism" (Jones & Adams, 2010, p. 203). As put by Cohen (2013, p. 151), "as a verb, as an action, queer holds limitless possibilities for unanticipated conjugations". I queerly inscribed myself into the research field and assembled and reiteratively problematised (tacit) knowledges of the digitally mediated human-art-space nexus. Here, queerying implies a synergy of method and knowledge, unsettling the binary between techne (craft or practical knowledge) and the study outcome: episteme (knowledge as such) (Boellstorff, 2010, p. 229).

Queerying, or queer studying, implies a situated approach, "grounded in the physicality of specific human bodies and their artefacts" (Barnes, 2000, p. 743). The ensuing situated knowledges divulge "partial perspectives" and compel an acknowledgement of positionality (Haraway, 1991). In my case: a white middle-class queer geographer with a deep interest in public art, with sexuality-inflected content, and its role in negotiating online and offline spaces, as virtual/actual "surfing binarisms" (Boellstorff, 2010).

Queerying Public Art Online

Dodge and Kitchin (2001) sparked an extensive debate about the socio-spatial implications of interacting through global computers and internet networks. For those "connected", where we should remain wary of digital divides due to e-inaccessibility and digital/technological illiteracy, it is hard to imagine contemporary culture without the digital (Rose, 2015). Rather than a "second action space" (Kellerman, 2014), I argue that digitally networked space acts as a "holistic action space": the mutuality of the virtual and actual breaks conventional divides between body/inorganic, present/absent, close/far, individual/environment, representations/non-representation, and so on (see Crang, 2015; de Souza e Silva, 2004).

For everyday online users and researchers, too, digital technologies have far-reaching implications (see digital geohumanities; Crang, 2015). They can be used as tools to explore new experiences of space, but also to alter and "query" those experiences and "co-create" visual culture (Rose, 2015). Informed by multidisciplinary geographical, cultural, and media studies literature, I have identified user agency and spatial connectivity as conceptual lenses for queerying digitally mediated public art, respectively, as discussed below.

User Agency

In public-art practice, the digital has increasingly provided possibilities for user agency: capacities/choices for participation and co-creation. The digital has "socially networked" objects of art, which has enhanced user imaginaries of these objects and associated physical locales, if any (see Zebracki, 2017a). There are many thinkable forms of digitally mediated or networked public artworks, for example, packaged as or accompanied by QR codes, augmented-reality applications, and interpretative websites (see Geroimenko, 2014; Rhodes, 2015). The analysis of *Tree* focuses on *mediated* discourse rather than *direct* experience, where social media have a strong part to play. Three queerying particularities of user agency are relevant in this context.

First, contrary to public-art engagement offline, digital engagement is not necessarily inscribed around specific material sites (if there are any at all). Moving beyond Habermasian conceptions of the (material) public sphere, this expands both the socio-spatial and aesthetic strategies of public art. Digital public-art engagement, thus, sheds new light on the site specificity of the artwork (Kwon, 2004) and on the audiences/engagers of public art as dispersed publics, who can simultaneously hold multiple social media accounts and multiple "squared" screen realities (Freeman & Sheller, 2015; Gauthier, 2015). Depending on the media's affordances and people's technological literacies, the digital empowers co-creation, sharing, and so on, which is, hence, queerying artist/audience, expert/amateur, and authenticity/quality divides (Kidd, 2014).

Second, the digital may globally distribute public art beyond its local material reference, if any, and may, thus, enable that it "outlives" in a digital capacity (see Zebracki, forthcoming). This not only reconfigures but also extends socio-spatial and temporal possibilities for engagement. Following Mitchell (2005), it is now the digital image that is pivotal to the reception and reproduction of public art, while, in a (saturated) digital image culture too, images might be disregarded or forgotten (Rhodes, 2015).

Third, much social internet activity overshadows informational and dialogical purports, as understood under network sociality. Malinowski (1994) conceptualised this as part and parcel of a "phatic communion".

According to Miller (2008), the latter has gained the upper hand on social media, considering inconsiderate, facile, ludic, and so forth interactions (see Zebracki & Luger, 2018), especially where sexual(ity) issues are concerned (see, e.g., Alexander, 2014). As Margolis (2014) pointed out, a deep online interplay between cultural objects and information processing is more often the exception than the rule. Limited engagement might be related to the limitations of the platform (e.g., former 140-character limit to tweets) (see Kidd, 2014). Also, the possibilities for (co-)creation and reuse of data might be (inappropriately) controlled and limited by top-level state authorities and digital monitors. Despite rich potentials for inclusive participation and empowerment in the digital society (Lichty, 2015), such control and limitations, therefore, are queerying grander matters of surveillance, censorship, authorship, and so on, in the digital age (see Goriunova, 2012; Lodi, 2014).

Spatial Connectivity

Hybrid space, introduced by de Souza e Silva (2004), is a useful notion for grasping the condition of connecting or being connected, that is, spatial connectivity, through multi-user environments, involving various desktop and mobile screen spaces (see Verhoeff, 2012). This condition translates into ambiguous experiences of the binarisms of presence/absence and here/there in a "space of in-betweenness". In this context, Bishop (2012) made a plea for a post-digital "return" to the object/physicality (see affective turn in Thrift, 2008), as materiality remains primordial, or becomes even more intensified, in today's digital lifeworld. Technological devices, as portals to the digital, produce new senses of publicness that may be geographically distant from, but experientially related to, the material object of art. As Freeman and Sheller (2015) argued: "digital mediation layered onto public space" (p. 4), or the "manner in which the virtual actually appears" (p. 16) (see also Deleuze, 1994), "brings with it an embodied re-thinking of materiality" (p. 4).

Thus, object art and digital art are co-emerging and activated at once (Rhodes, 2015). Digitally mediated interactions with public art, potentially in real time, might relay in situ experiences. As such, they may provide vicariously close connections with both the material public artwork and other users, including those who have not encountered the artwork in "real life". Indeed, as Freeman and Sheller (2015, p. 2) conveyed, "the digital, ironically, returns us to the world's potentialities, and re-animates its material, spatial, corporeal aliveness". Here, not only the material but also the digital should be queeried in understanding spatial connectivity, which should move beyond the "false divide" (Lichty, 2015) between analogue/ digital worlds (see convergence culture in Jenkins, 2008) as much as between old/new media (see polymedia in Madianou & Miller, 2013). Digital life worlds are geographically connected/constructed through code (Kitchin & Dodge, 2011), where code/space not only questions conventional dyads of human/object and software/hardware but also reshapes and heightens experiences of the hybrid space (de Souza e Silva, 2004).

Hybrid space, then, further queeries the specificity of public artworks. Kwon (2004) critiqued the "commodification and serialisation of [sterile] places" (Kwon, 2004, p. 55) through public art (or, rather, so-called plop art). However, its social and aesthetic strategies and implications for (authentic) user engagement and (re)producing uniform aesthetics, experiences, and expectations in digitally networked space have remained under-addressed. As the analysis will reveal, despite the deemed lack of local specificity, or disconnection from the material locale, *Tree* was given a specific locus for engagement over social networks.

Data Collection and Analysis

I conducted a case study on patterns of digitally mediated engagement with *Tree* just after its removal in 2014; the resulting analysis dates from 2014–15 (originally published in Zebracki, 2017b). I conducted virtual ethnography (see Hine, 2000) on online users' uses and experiences of the artwork and their meanings in online cultural settings—thus indicating some kind of digital praxiography (after Mol, 2002). The conceptual lenses of user agency and spatial connectivity steered the analysis of publicly available social media content and news data (see Batrinca & Treleaven, 2015) until I reached an unprompted data saturation point (Bryman, 2008).

I employed the search engines of Facebook, Twitter, and Instagram, where engagement with *Tree* trended after its vandalisation. I used keywords and hashtags in relation to the artwork, artist, and locality and applied snowball data sampling to gather about 200 distinct posts (exclusive of identical crosspostings such as retweets/shares and comments within posts), which covered textual, audio, and/or video content. In playful reference to the 1974 Watergate scandal, #pluggate appeared to be a particularly popular hashtag, culminating in a "social media mania" and a "mourning Twitterverse" (*The Huffington Post* [Brooks], 2014b).

The analysis of social media data in combination with a comparative examination of about 60 news items[1] allowed me to identify two overarching, ambiguous discursive themes: remembering/forgetting and materiality/digitality, which structure the findings section. These analyses allowed me to triangulate findings, based on a collection of user-created content by "private" persons and content produced by formal, "public" newsagents. Although Kidd (2014) argued that the former might critically intervene in elitist journalism, I ask for queerying the expert/layman and private/public binaries by looking into how formal and informal content informed each other.

Adopting Driscoll and Gregg's (2010) ethical advice, I pursued research on publicly accessible sites and content only. This study involved covert observations without direct interactions with online users to not influence/disturb the authenticity of communication and user-created content. As per Zimmer (2010), data, including online user identity details, have been fully anonymised in this analysis. Nevertheless, I remain wary of queer criticism of how research might reproduce the hegemonic hierarchy of the named researcher/author and the unnamed informant/researched (see Detamore, 2010b).

Lastly, following partial/situated knowledges (Haraway, 1991), I refrain from making any claims on full representation and external validity. Nonetheless, the presented impressionistic insights, taken as "opportunities to learn" (Stake, 2000), resonate with the overarching themes and might be transferable to commensurable contexts.

[1] The majority of these news reports were in English, many of which covered French key papers, such as *Le Monde*.

A Digitally Networked Story of Public Art and Its (Dis)Contents

The (social) media quarrel about *Tree* indicated its design and placement as "offensive" and "indecent": it would not chime with Place Vendôme, the city of Paris, and even French culture at large. *Tree* clearly fitted McCarthy's grander oeuvre that for decades has been serving a meta-critique, a ludic anti-symbol, or up-yours if it may be, regarding capitalist consumer society (Curtis, 2014; Zebracki, 2012). On *Tree*, the artist argued:

> It all started with a joke. Originally, I thought that a butt plug had a shape similar to the sculptures of Constantin Brâncuşi. Afterwards, I realised that it looked like a Christmas tree … People can be offended if they want to think of it as a plug, but for me it is more of an abstraction. (Paul McCarthy, cited in *Le Monde* [Jardonnet], 2014, translated in *The Independent* [Saul], 2014)

McCarthy, with *Tree*, was the lead artist of the 2014 cohort of FIAC's ongoing *Hors les murs* (Beyond the Walls) programme. The commissioner, who did not issue any formal statement, gave McCarthy carte blanche. Although *Tree* bequeathed substantial publicity to McCarthy's butt plug series, members of the public were not necessarily aware of the associated, deeper art historical codes and societal critiques. Rather, *Tree* met with strong opposition and was often described in the media as an "art scandal" (*Time* [Lacayo], 2014). As mentioned before, this scandal was fuelled by the facts that McCarthy was punched in his face and that his artwork was ultimately vandalised. Obviously, these radical incidents signalled that, at least for some, both *Tree* and its creator did not belong to the site.

The following analysis delves further into the nuances of digitally mediated engagement with this artwork. It queeries the overarching ambiguous discursive themes of remembering/forgetting and materiality/digitality. I interrogate how engagements negotiated (i.e., mediated) and augmented each other in both online and offline spaces, which in turn are queerying the conceptions of user agency and spatial connectivity.

Queerying Remembering/Forgetting

Social media and news coverage about *Tree* reached its culmination when it was vandalised. France's then president François Hollande issued an "auspicious" statement that backed up the artwork's raison d'être (*AFP*, 2014):

> France will always stand beside artists, as I stand beside Paul McCarthy, whose work was marred, regardless of what one's opinion of the work was ... We must always respect the work of artists. France is always ready to welcome artists and designers from all over the world. France is not herself [sic] when she is curled up, plagued by ignorance and intolerance. (Translated in *The Huffington Post* [Brooks], 2014b)

Hollande's view was supported by the French Ministry of Culture and the mayor of Paris (*BBC*, 2014). Such authoritative voices upheld the democratic freedom of expression. Perhaps this could be seen as an implicit response to rising state and populist controls of the web (see Zebracki & Luger, 2018), including social media platforms and user-created content, as is notoriously the case in China and Turkey, for example. However, considering the largely deterritorialised dimensions of the web, such top-down control is tricky or impossible in some cases (Ibrahim, 2015).

Public resistance amongst some radical collectives, including Catholic conservatives and right-wing identity activists, suggested that *Tree*, perceived as deviant and obscene, was pushing freedom of expression "too far". For instance, the right-wing pressure group Printemps Français (*Le Monde* [Jardonnet], 2014) tweeted: "a giant 24-metre high butt plug has just been set up at Place Vendôme! Place Vendôme disfigured! Paris humiliated!" (translated in *RT*, 2014).

Disconcerted and negative reactions uncovered a compelling field of tension between artistic freedom vis-à-vis social norms around identity expression in public space. Some associated the figure of the butt plug with pornography, excused under the veil of "art" (*Apollo* [Holmboe], 2014), which therefore should not have a place in public. *Tree*, also, became a plaything to question online borders of normality. Some policing digital publics, or "digilantes" (Jane, 2016), politicised online spaces in an effort to forget the artwork, or ban it altogether. Interestingly, this indicated censorship from below and counter-voiced liberal state and art-world values.

Despite negative investments, some well-disposed digilantes created fan pages, including the *Tree*-dedicated Twitter account "Parisian Buttplug" (@Pbuttplug), with rhyming bio: "ceci n'est pas un Christmas Tree". Its first post read "Bonjour, Paris! Je suis in you!" Many trivial responses represented *Tree* as a humorous and whimsical intervention, accompanied by engagements that Hartley (2012) would phrase as acts of "silly citizenship". Popular hashtags, such as #buttplug, #paulmccarthy, #plugvendome, and #pluganal, created a digital index for sketchy navigations of user-created content across social media platforms. Deep mnemonic engagement did not quite happen.

However, some online users playfully negotiated conventions and norms. Some took the anal sex toy, especially associated with gay male culture, as rejection of heteropatriarchy, that is the hegemony of heteronormativity and patriarchy. This queeried the borders of free expression in digitally networked space, too. For example, the photoshopped image in Fig. 13.3 shows an act of silly citizenship: balls/testicles in the image and the "plastic aesthetic" of *Tree* have been added to the Column's base. This humorous post was soon retweeted over more than 150 times and became memorialised as a meme (trending, oft-mimicking concept or content), which was indicative of network sociality (Miller, 2008). In one of the many more *Tree* memes, the butt plug figure replaced the black monolith in a scene of *2001: A Space Odyssey* (1968). *Tree* has become "immortalised" online: "Paul McCarthy's 'tree' sculpture may be gone, but it lives on in memes" (*Los Angeles Times* [Miranda], 2014).

Gauthier (2015) argued that *Tree* became an outward rejection of public artwork in the digital age. But the networked story of *Tree* was ambiguous. Some embraced the subversion of aesthetic and sexual norms. Others disdained the object as morally abject, a travesty of postmodern art that was out of place and out of touch with local people, which therefore should be disremembered and "invisibilised" online, too.

Although news and user-created content about *Tree* still circulated as of writing, the "hotness" of the topic had somewhat subsided. Online content seemed to serve as a kind of digital archive of the artwork's

Fig. 13.3 A ludic photomontage of *Tree* on Twitter. Translation: "#PlugGate: McCarthy 'understands reactions to his work' and is already planning a 'less ambiguous' installation"

ephemeral material appearance. For example, an online user operated as curator of *Tree*'s ordeal in a public YouTube video, accessible at https://www.youtube.com/watch?v=ttJ7CmDvJVM. This user-created content provides a meta-analysis of *Tree*'s provenance along with positive and negative sentiments as they were mediated in print and digital media. The video collage is an example of Web 2.0's bottom-up 'remix' culture (Kidd, 2014), where we can find "the convergence of sound, image, videos and semantic words" (Ibrahim, 2015, p. 10). This example demonstrates how ordinary users can widely broadcast their unsolicited views and act as journalists and researchers, but not as we traditionally know these roles.

Judging by the comments on this video (viewed more than 20,000 times as of writing), it appealed to somewhat self-selected publics, who were apparently acquainted with some esoteric art-world codes. The comments thread draws a compelling analogy with disrupting the status quo through graffiti, seen as an unauthorised creative intervention. Some comments took the vandalisation of *Tree* as legitimate public response; for instance, "I would venture to say that, vandalism or not, the reactions to this 'work' … are an integral part of it, regardless of the artistic media used". I echo this point; the YouTube video with comments operates as a digital interpretative panel, a form of virtual graffiti, which allows everyday online users to "rewrite", and thereby republicise, the artwork.

This video might be dug up and engaged further by future user audiences, who wish to learn about the digitally distributed support, or rejection, of this sexuality-related type of contested artwork. But there remains a paradox. Digital content, such as this video, might contain a valuable space of engagement for those who want to remember *Tree*. However, it is simultaneously challenging for those who wish to forget, or invisibilise, this artwork.

Queerying Materiality/Digitality

Digital user-created content was not a premeditated component of the artwork as it was initially conceived by the artist. This has lent a meta-reality to the material artwork and, correspondingly, offered new possibilities for engagement. The velocity and "mass" of online mediation engaged global online users far beyond *Tree*'s (former) material locality. Thereby, it might have provided imaginations, immersive experiences, and digital "immediacies" (Bell & Lyall, 2005) in places and at times different from *Tree*'s original exhibition venue. For instance, a tweet read: "woke up to sad news that #pluggate in #Paris has been deflated—good news is I hear it's coming to #Hollywood". The accompanying manipulated image showed the Hollywood sign, of which the two consecutive o's were replaced by depictions of *Tree*. Thus, places might not only become geographically connected. They can also become individually augmented through user-created content, rendered as digital portals to simulacra of real-world contexts.

Tree embodied an "othered" materiality (i.e., plastic inflatable filled with air) and temporality (i.e., short-lived intervention). So, as an anti-monumental and anti-permanent work (see Gauthier, 2015), *Tree* opened a radical dialogue with traditional urban heritage of equestrian statues, "sunken" memorial architecture, and the like. As put by an art critic:

> This tree is like a giant fantasy … In the French tradition it is a fantastical work. It is oversized; it can be analysed from different angles. It needs this kind of ambiguity, too. It is like a big dream that has entered the public space. (Chiara Parisi, cited in *The Huffington Post* [Brooks], 2014a)

Despite the fact that there is no longer a material reification of *Tree*, user-created content about its manifestation continues to convey digital (counter-)stories of "the tradition". For example, the post in Fig. 13.4 tellingly puts *Tree* in the lineup of previous controversial, phallus-shaped structures. Although their right to exist was initially challenged, too, they have become iconic public artworks over time. Notably, the Eiffel Tower was due to be demolished in 20 years after its incarnation, but this edifice soon became a national emblem. This sometimes happens beyond the artist's will. For example, the Buren Columns (erected in 1985–86) at Palais Royal became an "ancient monument to modernity", "beloved by tourists [but] no longer popular with the man who created it", as maintenance came to a standstill (*The Independent* [Lichfield], 2008; see also Heinich, 1998). What is different in the case of *Tree*, being not particularly "beloved" by all, is how its "post-materiality" has adopted a meme-fied iconography, or networked (anti-)memorial status, in digitally networked space (see Gauthier, 2015). The digitally mediated aesthetic strategy of user-created content, hence, sheds new light on site specificity (Kwon, 2004).

The satirical source Easyvoyage fuelled the social media controversy about *Tree* by the below April fool's hoax:

> As the Parisian landmark celebrated its 126th birthday yesterday, the French capital announced plans to deconstruct the Eiffel Tower. The iron structure will be replaced by a giant sculpture designed by Paul McCarthy, widely agreed to be more in keeping with the city's romantic tone. (Easyvoyage ["The Editorial Team", 2015)

As striking precedent, *The Local* (2013) released an April fool's joke arguing that feminist activist collectives have united to campaign for

Fig. 13.4 This photo compilation suggests a historical analogy between *Tree* and the ambiguous trajectories of rejection/acceptance surrounding previous controversial (temporary) artworks that have grown into permanent icons. Has *Tree* become a landmark of digitally networked space today?

replacing the Eiffel Tower, "symbol of France's outdated male-dominated culture", by a "Tour Eiffelle" (ibid.). Both instances indicated that the offline "real world" sets dialectic parameters for the public mediation, and imagination, of public artwork and the negotiation of social norms. The "comeback" of McCarthy's butt plug figure, both offline and online, was particularly magnified and disputed over social media. Following Gauthier (2015), the key incidents, that is the assault on McCarthy and the vandalisation of the inflatable, could be considered an extrapolation of the online dispute to the physical world, while such in situ events were immediately fed back and co-experienced online.

Another salient illustration of *Tree*'s augmentation of online and socio-material spaces was a flashmob held by proponents of *Tree*, both in response to and as reinforcement of the social media commotion (see *Hyperallergic* [Vartanian], 2014). An Instagram post showed protestors holding placards, depicting *Tree*, who campaigned against the unanticipated swift removal of the inflatable, after it was demolished and the "artist agreed that its time in Place Vendôme was over" (*Hyperallergic* [Nechvatal], 2014). So, social interactions overlapped material and digital spaces, contributing to a complex, mixed spatial presence/experience of the public artwork (see hybrid space in de Souza e Silva, 2004).

The ensuing digitally networked debate functioned as an interface with news coverage. The following peculiar (unverified) "outcome" of the *Tree* ordeal was highlighted on social media:

> [A local sex-toy wholesaler] noted that previously customers for anal plugs were almost exclusively male and gay, but in recent weeks [November 2014] heterosexuals—with an equal mix of men and women—had been snapping up the products. (*The Local* [Mulholland], 2014)

This anecdote puts *Tree*'s interpretation as anti-heteronormative message into inverted perspective; now the butt plug was recognised as "guilty pleasure" for all. Beyond some cheeky tweets, such as "I plug Paris! The Great Lobby love pluging [sic] Paris!", there were also some rather inconsiderate appropriations. For instance, a Twitterer published an image of Michelle Obama holding a paper with the script "#BringBackOur[image of a hand holding *Tree*]". Similar to the previously mentioned use of the "-gate" suffix, this was done to recall the #BringBackOurGirls hashtag in outrage over Boko Haram's mass abduction of school children in Nigeria in 2014.

So, as Goriunova (2012) argued, Web 2.0 engagement has arrived at a so-called "new media idiocy": why do people exchange "silly", misplaced, and insensitive content on social media? (see Zebracki & Luger, 2018) Mass image culture drives user agency too in the ever-intensifying socially networked space; in recalling Mitchell (2005, NP): "why do we behave as if pictures were alive, possessing the power to influence us, to persuade us, seduce us, or even lead us astray?"

Conclusion and Discussion

This chapter has presented an in in-depth, virtual ethnographic case study on (social) media engagements with *Tree*. It has provided new critical insights into how the site specificity of public artwork (Kwon, 2004) becomes extended as digital strategy for interacting and co-creating discursive and (audio)visual content. The latter augmented and "memorialised" the artwork in digital public space (far) beyond the original intentions of the artist as well as the original material location and life span of the artwork. As such, this study has filled a specific gap in geographical scholarship on public art, which has remained mostly focused on engagement with permanent and "offline" public artwork.

Considering the ambiguous and sexuality-related ramifications of *Tree*, I pursued social media as queerying action space. I examined how engagement with public art of this calibre (temporary, postmodern, anti-permanent, and "sexualised") operated in digitally networked space, and in so doing queeried knowledges of public-art engagement as it has been conventionally studied. So, this research has showed the value of queerying as mode for the unsettling of knowledges in research fields that are not directly associated with "queer" (Plummer, 2011). Similarly, scholars do not need to be identified as "queer" to undertake queer research (Yekani, Kilian, & Michaelis, 2013). I identified user agency (i.e., the capacities for participation/co-creation) and spatial connectivity as conceptual lenses for challenging online mediated public-art engagement.

Remembering/forgetting and materiality/digitality emerged as two ambiguous themes from the analysis: online mediated engagements appeared to walk a tightrope between encouraging the remembering of *Tree* and adversely forgetting it through overlapping, equivocal dimensions of materiality and digitality. The networked debate revealed a fluid, virtual-actual ecology of *Tree*, where user-created content critically negotiated art conventions and social norms—ranging across critiques of the perceived obscene butt plug figure, the alleged mismatch between *Tree* and the surrounding classical architecture, the dominant tradition of permanent public statuary, hegemonic heteropatriarchy, and the grander capitalist condition.

Global digital publics engaged *Tree* online and (re)collected, or "directed", their own networked story about this artistic manifestation. Despite some profound exceptions, user-created content of *Tree* was prevalently fraught with frivolous responses and played along with it on equally ludic-oriented sites of interaction. There was usually scant attention to either the artwork's socio-physical context or the affordances of digital and online technologies. A more digital site-specific appropriation would, then, require stronger commitment to the functionality, user groups, and readerships/"userships" of social networking sites.

This study informs future research about the digital mediation/(re) negotiation of the roles, (mis)uses, and values of, in particular, controversial temporary, sexuality-related public-art spaces (for another example see Anish Kapoor's *Dirty Corner* in *The Independent* [Jenne], 2015). How are new "permanent" realities and mnemonic immediacies of public art exchanged in digitally networked space in real time or otherwise? How do the material and digital inform/augment each other without being subsidiaries of one another? Furthermore, this research is particularly useful to scholars with interest in queer semiotics (see Zebracki & Milani, 2017), considering the use of both textual and visual language, to question norms and hegemonic social values.

Research in digitally networked space, through dual attention to technological hardware and social software, involves space-time navigations through on-and-offline multi-user environments in an abstract global network of computers and screens (see Zebracki, forthcoming). As this study has shown, digital and online technologies have reconfigured as well as estranged relationships between here/there, presence/absence and the researcher/researched, and so on, as conventionally understood in offline geographical fieldwork. Hence, I encourage further empirical work on fathoming the fluid geographies of online/offline spaces of engagement with public artwork—and queerying the ethics and care involved in collecting and analysing data on how human practice digitally meets the inorganic.

Acknowledgements This chapter reflects a significantly shortened and edited version of the article "Queerying Public Art in Digitally Networked Space", published in *ACME: An International Journal for Critical Geographies, 16*(3): 440–474. I owe a debt of gratitude to the *ACME* Editor Kath Browne and four referees, whose incisive comments have enabled me to strengthen the original manuscript. Moreover, I thank Catherine J. Nash and Andrew Gorman-Murray for further comments that helped to shape the text in its current form. The analysis dates from 2014–15.

References

AFP. (2014). Hollande soutient l'artiste vandalise. October 20. Retrieved from http://next.liberation.fr/arts/2014/10/20/hollande-soutient-l-artiste-vandalise_1126078

Alexander, R. (2014). Sex sculptures in the woods of Can Ginebreda. August 9. Retrieved from http://journeywonders.com/sex-sculptures-in-the-woods-of-can-ginebreda

Apollo [Rye Holmboe]. (2014). Paul McCarthy's obscene art world. November 1. Retrieved from http://www.apollomagazine.com/paul-mccarthys-obscene-art-world

Barnes, T. (2000). Situated knowledge. In D. Gregory, R. Johnston, G. Pratt, M. Watts, & S. Whatmore (Eds.), *The dictionary of human geography* (pp. 742–743). Oxford: Blackwell.

Batrinca, B., & Treleaven, P. (2015). Social media analytics: A survey of techniques, tools and platforms. *AI & Society, 30*(1), 89–116.

BBC. (2014). Paris 'sex toy' sculpture sabotaged at Place Vendome. October 18. Retrieved from http://www.bbc.co.uk/news/world-europe-29675893

Bell, C., & Lyall, J. (2005). "I was here": Pixelated evidence. In D. Crouch, R. Jackson, & F. Thompson (Eds.), *The media and the tourist imagination: Converging cultures* (pp. 135–142). London: Routledge.

Bishop, C. (2012). Digital divide. *Art Forum, 51*(1), 435–441.

Boellstorff, T. (2010). Queer techne: Two theses on methodology and queer studies. In K. Browne & C. Nash (Eds.), *Queer methods and methodologies: Intersecting queer theories and social science research* (pp. 215–230). London: Routledge.

Browne, K., & Nash, C. (Eds.). (2010). *Queer methods and methodologies: Intersecting queer theories and social science research*. London: Routledge.

Bryman, A. (2008). *Social research methods*. Oxford: Oxford University Press.
Cartiere, C., & Zebracki, M. (Eds.). (2016). *The everyday practice of public art: Art, space, and social inclusion*. London: Routledge.
Cohen, J. (2013). Queering the inorganic. In E. Yekani, E. Kilian, & B. Michaelis (Eds.), *Queer futures: Reconsidering ethics, activism, and the political* (pp. 149–164). London: Routledge.
Crang, M. (2015). The promises and perils of a digital geohumanities. *Cultural Geographies, 22*(2), 351–360.
Curtis, H. (2014). *Ketchup and blood: Documents, institutions and effects in the performances of Paul McCarthy 1974–2013*. PhD thesis, Queen Mary, University of London, London.
Deleuze, G. (1994). *Difference and repetition* (P. Patton, Trans.). London: Athlone Press.
Detamore, M. (2010a). *Queer appalachia: Toward geographies of possibility*. PhD thesis, University of Kentucky, Lexington, KY.
Detamore, M. (2010b). Queer(y)ing the ethics of research methods: Toward a politics of intimacy in researcher/researched relations. In K. Browne & C. Nash (Eds.), *Queer methods and methodologies: Intersecting queer theories and social science research* (pp. 167–182). London: Routledge.
de Souza e Silva, A. (2004). Mobile networks and public spaces: Bringing multiuser environments into the physical space. *Convergence: The International Journal of Research into New Media Technologies, 10*(2), 15–25.
Dodge, M., & Kitchin, R. (2001). *Mapping cyberspace*. London: Routledge.
Driscoll, C., & Gregg, M. (2010). My profile: The ethics of virtual ethnography. *Emotion, Space and Society, 3*(1), 15–20.
Easyvoyage ["The Editorial Team"]. (2015). Paris to tear down iconic Eiffel Tower [hoax]. April 1. Retrieved from http://www.easyvoyage.co.uk/travel-headlines/eiffel-tower-to-be-pulled-down-to-make-way-for-paul-mccarthy-sculpture-33167
Freeman, J., & Sheller, M. (2015). Editors' statement: Hybrid space and digital public art. *Public Art Dialogue, 5*(1), 1–8.
Gauthier, D. (2015). Networked monumental: Site, production, and distributed publics – Online, and in everyday life. *Public Art Dialogue, 5*(1), 17–54.
Geroimenko, V. (Ed.). (2014). *Augmented reality art: From an emerging technology to a novel creative medium*. Dordrecht: Springer.
Gibson-Graham, J. K. (1999). Queer(y)ing capitalism in and out of the classroom. *Journal of Geography in Higher Education, 23*(1), 80–85.

Goriunova, O. (2012). New media idiocy. *Convergence: The International Journal of Research into New Media Technologies, 19*(2), 223–235.
Haraway, D. (1991). *Simians, cyborgs, and women: The reinvention of women*. New York, NY: Routledge.
Hartley, J. (2012). *Digital futures for cultural and media studies*. Oxford: Wiley-Blackwell.
Heinich, N. (1998). *L'art contemporain exposé aux rejets: Études de cas*. Nîmes: J. Chambon.
Hine, C. (2000). *Virtual ethnography*. London: Sage.
Hyperallergic [Joseph Nechvatal]. (2014). Solemn protest against public art reactionaries as McCarthy goes chocula in Paris. October 24. Retrieved from http://hyperallergic.com/158221/solemn-protest-against-public-art-reactionaries-as-mccarthy-goes-chocula-in-paris
Hyperallergic [Hrag Vartanian]. (2014). Paul McCarthy's epic Plug de Noël goes flaccid after mounting problems. October 19. Retrieved from http://hyperallergic.com/156735/paul-mccarthys-epic-plug-de-noel-goes-flaccid-after-mounting-problems/
Ibrahim, Y. (2015). Tank Man, media memory and Yellow Duck patrol: Remembering Tiananmen on social media. *Digital Journalism, 4*(5), 582–596.
Jane, E. (2016). Online misogyny and feminist digilantism. *Continuum, 30*(3), 284–297.
Jenkins, H. (2008). *Convergence culture: Where old and new media collide*. New York, NY: New York University Press.
Jones, S., & Adams, T. (2010). Autoethnography is a queer method. In K. Browne & C. Nash (Eds.), *Queer methods and methodologies: Intersecting queer theories and social science research* (pp. 195–214). London: Routledge.
Kellerman, A. (2014). *The internet as second action space*. New York, NY: Routledge.
Kidd, J. (2014). *Museums in the new mediascape: Transmedia, participation, ethics*. Farnham: Ashgate.
Kitchin, R., & Dodge, M. (2011). *Code/space: Software and everyday life*. Cambridge, MA: The MIT Press.
Kwon, M. (2004). *One place after another: Site-specific art and locational identity*. Cambridge, MA: MIT Press.
Le Monde [Emmanuelle Jardonnet]. 2014. McCarthy agressé pour l'érection d'un arbre de Noël ambigu, place Vendôme. October 17. Retrieved from http://www.lemonde.fr/arts/article/2014/10/17/mccarthyagresse-pour-l-erection-d-un-arbre-de-noel-ambigu-place-vendome_4507834_1655012.html

Lichty, P. (2015). The digital: A false division? *Public Art Dialogue, 5*(1), 95–103.

Lodi, S. (2014). Spatial narratives in art. In V. Geroimenko (Ed.), *Augmented reality art: From an emerging technology to a novel creative medium* (pp. 277–294). Dordrecht: Springer.

London Evening Standard [Alexandra Rucki]. (2014). Inflatable Christmas tree in Paris compared to sex toy. October 17. Retrieved from http://www.standard.co.uk/news/world/inflatable-christmas-tree-in-paris-compared-to-sex-toy-9801667.html

Los Angeles Times [Carolina Miranda]. (2014). Paul McCarthy's 'tree' sculpture may be gone, but it lives on in memes. October 19. Retrieved from http://www.latimes.com/entertainment/arts/miranda/la-et-cam-paul-mccarthy-tree-sculpture-paris-vandalized-memes-20141019-column.html

Madianou, M., & Miller, D. (2013). Polymedia: Towards a new theory of digital media in interpersonal communication. *International Journal of Cultural Studies, 16*(2), 169–187.

Malinowski, B. (1994). The problem of meaning in primitive languages. In J. Maybin (Ed.), *Language and literacy in social practice: A reader* (pp. 1–10). Avon: Open University Press.

Margolis, T. (2014). Immersive art in augmented reality. In V. Geroimenko (Ed.), *Augmented reality art: From an emerging technology to a novel creative medium* (pp. 149–159). Dordrecht: Springer.

Miles, M. (1997). *Art, space and the city: Public art and urban futures*. London: Routledge.

Miller, V. (2008). New media, networking and phatic culture. *Convergence: The International Journal of Research into New Media Technologies, 14*(4), 387–340.

Mitchell, W. (2005). *What do pictures want?: The lives and loves of images*. Chicago, IL: The University of Chicago Press.

Mol, A. (2002). *The body multiple: Ontology in medical practice*. Durham, NC: Duke University Press.

Plummer, K. (2011). Critical humanism and queer theory: Living with the tensions. In N. Denzin & Y. Lincoln (Eds.), *The SAGE handbook of qualitative research* (pp. 195–207). Thousand Oaks, CA: Sage.

Rhodes, G. (2015). Future museums now – Augmented reality musings. *Public Art Dialogue, 5*(1), 59–79.

Rose, G. (2015). Rethinking the geographies of cultural 'objects' through digital technologies: Interface, network and friction. *Progress in Human Geography, 40*(3), 334–351.

RT. (2014). Giant sex toy or Christmas tree? Paris baffled and outraged (VIDEO). October 18. Retrieved from http://www.rt.com/news/197064-sex-toy-christmas-tree-paris

Sedgwick, E. (1993). *Tendencies*. Durham, NC: Duke University Press.

Stake, R. (2000). Case studies. In N. Denzin & Y. Lincoln (Eds.), *The handbook of qualitative research* (pp. 435–454). Thousand Oaks, CA: Sage.

The Huffington Post [Katherine Brooks]. (2014a). This 80-foot 'butt plug' in Paris isn't a giant sex toy, it's a Paul McCarthy sculpture. October 17. Retrieved from http://www.huffingtonpost.com/2014/10/17/paul-mccarthy-paris_n_6003192.html

The Huffington Post [Katherine Brooks]. (2014b). French President is definitely okay with that giant 'butt plug' sculpture. October 21. Retrieved from http://www.huffingtonpost.com/2014/10/21/butt-plug-sculpture_n_6023378.html

The Independent [John Lichfield]. (2008). *Les Deux Plateaux*: Monument to the French malaise? January 5. Retrieved from http://www.independent.co.uk/news/world/europe/les-deux-plateaux-monument-to-the-french-malaise-768339.html

The Independent [Heather Saul]. (2014). Paris 'sex toy' Christmas tree sculpture deflated by vandals. October 18. Retrieved from http://www.independent.co.uk/news/world/europe/paris-sex-toy-sculpture-deflated-after-vandals-cut-cables-on-controversial-christmas-tree-9803514.html

The Independent [Amelia Jenne]. (2015). 'Dirty Corner': Anish Kapoor's Versailles sculpture dubbed 'The Queen's Vagina' starts a cultural war after artist refuses to remove graffiti. September 21. Retrieved from http://www.independent.co.uk/arts-entertainment/art/news/dirty-corner-anish-kapoors-versailles-sculpture-dubbed-the-queens-vagina-starts-a-cultural-war-after-10511633.html

The Local. (2013). Feminists want 'phallic' Eiffel Tower torn down. [hoax]. April 1. Retrieved from http://www.thelocal.fr/20130401/eiffel-tower-feminists-torn-down-phallic

The Local [Rory Mulholland]. (2014). Parisians snap up 'butt plugs' after 'Tree' fiasco. December 2. Retrieved from http://www.thelocal.fr/20141202/parisians-butt-plug-sex-toy-paul-mccarthy

Thrift, N. (2008). *Non-representational theory: Space, politics, affect*. New York, NY: Routledge.

Time [Richard Lacayo]. (2014). The Parisian sex toy Christmas Tree is the latest great art scandal. October 20. Retrieved from http://time.com/3525271/parisian-sex-toy-christmas-tree-butt-plug

Verhoeff, N. (2012). *Mobile screens: The visual regime of navigation*. Amsterdam: Amsterdam University Press.

Yekani, E., Kilian, E., & Michaelis, B. (Eds.). (2013). *Queer futures: Reconsidering ethics, activism, and the political*. London: Routledge.

Zebracki, M. (forthcoming). Digital public art: Installations and interventions. In: Z. Krajina & D. Stevenson (Eds.), *The Routledge companion to urban media and communication*. London: Routledge.

Zebracki, M. (2012). Engaging geographies of public art: Indwellers, the 'Butt Plug Gnome' and their locale. *Social & Cultural Geography, 13*(7), 735–758.

Zebracki, M. (2017a). A cybergeography of public art encounter: The case of *Rubber Duck*. *International Journal of Cultural Studies, 20*(5), 526–544.

Zebracki, M. (2017b). Queerying public art in digitally networked space [original publication of this chapter]. *ACME: An International Journal for Critical Geographies, 16*(3), 440–474.

Zebracki, M., & Milani, T. (2017). Critical geographical queer semiotics. *ACME: An International Journal for Critical Geographies, 16*(3), 427–439.

Zebracki, M., & Luger, J. (2018). Digital geographies of public art: New global politics. *Progress in Human Geography*. https://doi.org/10.1177/0309132518791734

Zimmer, M. (2010). "But the data is already public": On the ethics of research in Facebook. *Ethics and Information Technology, 12*(4), 313–325.

Index[1]

[1] Note: Page numbers followed by 'n' refer to notes.

C. Nash, A. Gorman-Murray (eds.), *The Geographies of Digital Sexuality*,
https://doi.org/10.1007/978-981-13-6876-9

FSC
www.fsc.org
MIX
Papier | Fördert gute Waldnutzung
FSC® C083411

Kolibri 360 GmbH
Ferdinand-Jühlke-Straße 7
99095 Erfurt, Deutschland
produktsicherheit@kolibri360.de